WHAT A TIME IT WAS

The Best of W. C. Heinz on Sports

W. C. Heinz

Foreword by David Halberstam
Introduction by Jeff MacGregor

DA CAPO PRESS

Copyright © 2001 by W. C. Heinz

All rights reserved. No part of this publication may be reproduced, stored in a retrieval system, or transmitted, in any form or by any means, electronic, mechanical, photocopying, recording, or otherwise, without the prior written permission of the publisher. Printed in the United States of America.

Cataloging-in-Publication data is available from the Library of Congress.
ISBN 0-306-81043-3

First Da Capo Press Edition 2001

Published by Da Capo Press
A Member of the Perseus Books Group
http://www.perseusbooksgroup.com

Set in 10-point Janson by Jane Raese

1 2 3 4 5 6 7 8 9--05 04 03 02 01

To G. G. and K.

CONTENTS

MASH AND OTHER FICTION

"BEER DRINKER" AND OTHER COLUMNS

FOREWORD

by David Halberstam

Foreword to come

ACKNOWLEDGMENTS

As the owner of a 1932 Remington portable typewriter, but neither printing press nor computer, I'm sincerely grateful to Kevin Hanover and Da Capo Press for preserving these pieces of fact and fiction from another time. To David Halberstam, who started the ball rolling, and Jeff MacGregor, who joined him with his own perceptions and kind words, I shall be forever grateful.

w.c.h.

INTRODUCTION

by Jeff MacGregor

Intro to come

"BROWNSVILLE BUM"
& OTHER PROFILES

Brownsville Bum

from *True*

It's a funny thing about people. People will hate a guy all his life for what he is, but the minute he dies for it they make him out a hero and they go around saying that maybe he wasn't such a bad guy after all because he sure was willing to go the distance for whatever he believed or whatever he was.

That's the way it was with Bummy Davis. The night Bummy fought Fritzie Zivic in the Garden and Zivic started giving him the business and Bummy hit Zivic low maybe 30 times and kicked the referee, they wanted to hang him for it. The night those four guys came into Dudy's bar and tried the same thing, only with rods, Bummy went nuts again. He flattened the first one and then they shot him, and when everybody read about it, and how Bummy fought guns with only his left hook and died lying in the rain in front of the place, they all said he was really something and you sure had to give him credit at that.

"So you're Al Davis?" one of the hoods said. "Why you punch-drunk bum."

What did they expect Bummy to do? What did they expect him to do the night Zivic gave him the thumbs and the laces and walked around the referee and belted Bummy? Bummy could hook too good ever to learn how to hold himself in, if you want the truth of it.

That was really the trouble with Bummy. Bummy blew school too early, and he didn't know enough words. A lot of guys who fought Zivic used to take it or maybe beef to the referee, but Bummy didn't know how to do that. A lot of guys looking at four guns would have taken the talk and been thinking about getting the number off the car when it pulled away, but all Bummy ever had was his hook.

Bummy came out of Brownsville. In the sports pages they are always refer-
ring to Brownsville as the fistic incubator of Brooklyn, because they probably
mean that a lot of fighters come out of there. Murder, Inc., came out of there,
too, and if you don't believe it ask Bill O'Dwyer. If it wasn't for Brownsville
maybe Bill O'Dwyer wouldn't have become the mayor of New York.

The peculiar thing about Brownsville is that it doesn't look so tough.
There are trees around there and some vacant lots, and the houses don't look
as bad as they do over on Second Avenue or Ninth Avenue or up in Harlem.
Don't tell Charley Beecher, though, that you don't think it's so tough.

"What's the matter you sold the place?" Froike said to Charley the other
day. "It ain't the same, now you sold it."

Charley Beecher used to run the poolroom with the gym behind it on the
corner of Georgia and Livonia where Bummy used to train. It was a good little gym with a little dressing room and a shower, and Charley was a pretty
good featherweight in the twenties, and his brother Willie, who was even a
better fighter, fought Abe Attell and Johnny Dundee and Jack Britton and
Leach Cross and Knockout Brown.

"For 17 years I was in business," Charley said. "Seventeen times they stuck
me up."

He looked at Froike, and then he pointed with his two hands at his mouth
and his ears and his eyes.

"I had guns here and here and here," he said. "All I ever saw was guns."

The worst part was that Charley knew all the guys. A week after they'd
heist him they'd be back for a little contribution, maybe a C note. They'd be
getting up bail for one of the boys, and they just wanted Charley to know
there were no hard feelings about the heist, and that as long as he kept his
dues up they'd still consider him friendly to the club. That's how tough
Brownsville was.

Bummy had two brothers, and they were a big help. They were a lot older
than Bummy, and the one they called Little Gangy and the other they called
Duff. Right now Gangy is doing 20 to 40, just to give you an idea, and
Bummy took a lot of raps for them, too, because there were some people
who couldn't get back at Gangy and Duff so they took it out on the kid.

When Bummy was about seven his father used to run a candy and cigar
store and did a little speaking on the side. In other words, he always had a
bottle in the place, and he had Bummy hanging around in case anybody
should say cop. When the signal would go up Bummy would run behind the
counter and grab the bottle, and he was so small nobody could see him over
the counter and he'd go out the back.

One day Bummy was going it down the street with the bottle under his coat and some real smart guy stuck out his foot. Bummy tripped and the bottle broke, and Bummy looked at the bottle and the whiskey running on the sidewalk and at the guy and his eyes got big and he started to scream. The guy just laughed and Bummy was lying right on the sidewalk in the whiskey and broken glass, hitting his head on the sidewalk and banging his fists down and screaming. A crowd came around and they watched Bummy, with the guy laughing at him, and they shook their heads and they said this youngest Davidoff kid must be crazy at that.

Davidoff was his straight name. Abraham Davidoff. In Yiddish they made Abraham into Ahvron and then Ahvron they sometimes make Bommy. All his family called him Bommy, so you can see they didn't mean it as a knock. The one who changed it to Bummy was Johnny Attell.

Johnny Attell used to run the fights at the Ridgewood Grove, a fight club in Brooklyn where some good fighters like Sid Terris and Ruby Goldstein and Tony Canzoneri learned to fight, and Johnny and a nice guy named Lew Burston managed Bummy. When Bummy turned pro and Johnny made up the show card for the fight with Frankie Reese he put the name on it as A1 (Bummy) Davis, and when Bummy saw it he went right up to John's office.

"What are you doing that for?" he hollered at Johnny. "I don't want to be called Bummy."

"Take it easy," Johnny said. "You want to make money fighting, don't you? People like to come to fights to see guys they think are tough."

They sure liked to come to see Bummy all right. They sure liked to come to see him get his brains knocked out.

The first time Johnny Attell ever heard of Bummy was one day when Johnny was coming out of the Grove and Froike stopped him. Froike used to run the gym at Beecher's and handle kids in the amateurs, and he was standing there talking to Johnny under the Myrtle Avenue El.

"Also I got a real good ticket seller for you," he said to Johnny after a while.

"I could use one," Johnny said.

"Only I have to have a special for him," Froike said. "No eliminations."

"What's his name?" Johnny said.

"Giovanni Pasconi," Froike said.

"Bring him around," Johnny said.

The next week Johnny put the kid in with a tough colored boy named Johnny Williams. The kid got the hell punched out of him, but he sold $200 worth of tickets.

"He didn't do too bad," Johnny said to Froike after the fight. "I'll put him back next week."

"Only this time get him an easier opponent," Froike said.

"You get him your own opponent," Johnny said. "As long as he can sell that many tickets I don't care who he fights."

The next week Johnny put him back and he licked the guy. After the fight Johnny was walking out and he saw the kid and Froike with about 20 people around them, all of them talking Yiddish.

"Come here, Froike," Johnny said.

"What's the matter?" Froike said.

"What is this guy," Johnny said, "a Wop or a Jew?"

"He's a Jew," Froike said. "His right name's Davidoff. He's only 15, so we borrowed Pasconi's card."

"He can sure sell tickets," Johnny said.

Bummy could sell anything. That's the way Bummy learned to fight, selling. He used to sell off a pushcart on Blake Avenue. He used to sell berries in the spring and tomatoes and watermelons in the summer and apples in the fall and potatoes and onions and beans in the winter, and there are a lot of pushcarts on Blake Avenue and Bummy used to have a fight to hold his spot.

"I was the best tomato salesman in the world," Bummy was bragging once.

It was right after he knocked out Bob Montgomery in the Garden. He stiffened him in 63 seconds and he was getting $15,000, and when the sports writers came into his dressing room all he wanted to talk about was how good he could sell tomatoes.

"You go over to Jersey and get them yourself," he was telling the sports writers. "Then you don't have to pay the middle guy. You don't put them in boxes, because when you put them in boxes it looks like you're getting ready to lam. When you only got a few around it looks like you can't get rid of them so what you gotta do is pile them all up and holler: 'I gotta get rid of these. I'm gonna give 'em away!'"

The sports writers couldn't get over that. There was a lot they couldn't get over about Bummy.

When Johnny turned Bummy pro he wasn't impressed by his fighting, only his following. Every time Bummy fought for Johnny in the Grove he'd bring a couple of hundred guys with him and they'd holler for Bummy. Everybody else would holler for the other guy, because now they knew Bummy was Jewish and the Grove is in a German section of Ridgewood, and this was when Hitler was starting to go good and there was even one of those German beer halls right in the place where the waiters walked around in those short leather pants and wearing fancy vests and funny hats.

The fight that started Bummy was the Friedkin fight. Bummy was just beginning to bang guys out at the Grove and Friedkin was already a hot fighter at the Broadway Arena and they lived only blocks apart. Friedkin was a nice kid, about three years older than Bummy, kind of a studious guy they called Schoolboy Friedkin, and there was nothing between him and Bummy except that they were both coming up and the neighborhood made the match.

Like one day Bummy was standing in the candy store and a couple of guys told him Friedkin was saying he could stiffen Bummy in two heats. Then they went to Friedkin and said Bummy said Friedkin was afraid to fight. At first this didn't take, but they kept it up and one day Bummy was standing with a dame on the corner of Blake and Alabama and Friedkin came along.

"So why don't you two fight?" the dame said.

"Sure, I'll fight," Bummy said, spreading his feet.

"Right here?" Friedkin said. "Right now?"

"Sure," Bummy said.

"I'll fight whenever my manager makes the match," Friedkin said, and he walked away.

Bummy couldn't understand that, because he liked to fight just to fight. He got right in the subway and went over to see Lew Burston in Lew's office on Broadway.

"Never mind making that Friedkin match," he said to Lew.

"Why not?" Lew said.

"Because when I leave here," Bummy said, "I'm going right around to Friedkin's house and I'm gonna wait for him to come out, and we're gonna find out right away if I can lick him or he can lick me."

"Are you crazy?" Lew said.

By the time Johnny Attell made the fight outdoors for Dexter Park there was really a fire under it. They had show cards advertising it on the pushcarts on Blake Avenue and Friedkin's old man and Bummy's old man got into an argument on the street, and everybody was talking about it and betting it big. Then it was rained out five nights and Johnny sold the fight to Mike Jacobs and Mike put it into Madison Square Garden.

When Bummy started working for the fight Lew Burston came over to Beecher's to train him. When Bummy got into his ring clothes they chased everybody out of the gym, and Lew told Bummy to hit the big bag. Bummy walked up to the bag and spread his feet and pulled back his left to start his hook and Lew stopped him.

"Throw that hook away," Lew said.

"Why?" Bummy said. "What's wrong with it?"

"Nothing's wrong with it," Lew said, "only for this fight you'll have to lose that hook."

Before that Bummy was nothing but a hooker, but for weeks Lew kept him banging the big bag with rights. Then the night of the fight after Bummy was all taped and ready, Lew took him into the shower off the dressing room and he talked to Bummy.

"Now remember one thing," he said to Bummy. "I can tell you exactly how that other corner is thinking. They've got that other guy eating and sleeping with your hook for weeks. I want you to go out there and I don't want you to throw one right hand until I tell you. If you throw one right before I say so I'll walk right out on you. Do you understand?"

Bummy understood all right. He was like a kid with a new toy. He was a kid with a secret that only Bummy and Lew knew, and he went out there and did like Lew told him. Friedkin came out with his right glued along the side of his head, and for three rounds Bummy just hooked and hooked and Friedkin blocked, and a lot of people thought Friedkin was winning the fight.

"All right," Lew said, after the third round. "Now this time go right out and feint with the left, but throw the right and put everything on it."

"Don't worry," Bummy said.

Bummy walked out and they moved around for almost a minute and then Bummy feinted his hook. When he did Friedkin moved over and Bummy threw the right and Friedkin's head went back and down he went with his legs in the air in his own corner. That was all the fighting there was that night.

Now Bummy was the biggest thing in Brownsville. Al Buck and Hype Igoe and Ed Van Every and Lester Bromberg were writing about him in the New York papers, saying he was the best hooker since Charley White and could also hit with his right, and he had dough for the first time in his life.

He got $14,000 for the Friedkin fight. When he walked down the street the kids followed him, and he bought them leather jackets and baseball gloves and sodas, just to show you what money meant and how he was already looking back at his own life.

When Bummy was a kid nobody bought him anything and he belonged to a gang called the Cowboys. They used to pull small jobs, and the cops could never find them until one night. One night the cops broke into the flat where the kids used to live with some dames, and they got them all except Bummy who was with his mother that night.

Sure, Bummy was what most people call tough, but if he felt sorry for you and figured you needed him he couldn't do enough. That was the way Bummy met Barbara and fell in love.

Bummy was 19 then and one day he and Shorty were driving around and Shorty said he wanted to go to Kings County Hospital and visit a friend of his who was sick, and there was this girl about 16 years old. They sat around for a while and Shorty did all the talking and then the next time they went to see the girl Shorty was carrying some flowers and he gave them to her.

"From him," Shorty said, meaning Bummy.

When the girl left the hospital Shorty and Bummy drove her home, and then every day for a couple of weeks they used to take her for a ride and to stop off for sodas. One day the three of them were riding together in the front seat and Bummy wasn't saying anything.

"Say, Bobby," Shorty said all of a sudden, "would you like to get married?"

The girl didn't know what to say. She just looked at Shorty.

"Not to me," Shorty said. "To him."

That was the way Bummy got married. That was Bummy's big romance.

After the Friedkin fight Bummy won about three fights quick, and then they made him with Mickey Farber in the St. Nick's. Farber was out of the East Side and had a good record, and one day when Bummy finished his training at Beecher's he was sitting in the locker room soaking his left hand in a pail of ice and talking with Charley.

That was an interesting thing about Bummy's left hand. He used to bang so hard with it that after every fight and after every day he boxed in the gym it used to swell up.

"I think I'll quit fighting," Bummy said to Charley.

"You think you'll quit?" Charley said. "You're just starting to make dough."

"They're making me out a tough guy," Bummy said. "All the newspapers make me a tough guy and I don't like it and I think I'll quit."

"Forget it," Charley said.

When Charley walked out Murder, Inc., walked in. They were all there—Happy and Buggsy and Abie and Harry and the Dasher—and they were looking at Bummy soaking his hand in the ice.

"You hurt your hand?" Buggsy said.

"No," Bummy said. "It's all right."

They walked out again, and they must have gone with a bundle on Farber because the day after Bummy licked Farber he was standing under the El in front of the gym and the mob drove up. They stopped the car right in front of him and they piled out.

"What are you, some wise guy?" Buggsy said.

"What's wrong with you?" Bummy said.

"What's all this you gave us about you had a bad hand?" Buggsy said.

"I didn't say I had a bad hand," Bummy said.

"You did," Buggsy said.

"Listen," Bummy said, spreading his feet the way he used to do it, "if you guys want a fight let's start it."

Buggsy looked at the others and they looked at him. Then they all got in the car and drove off, and if you could have been there and seen that you would have gone for Bummy for it.

That was the bad part about Bummy's rap. Not enough people knew that part of Bummy until it was too late. The people who go to fights don't just go to see some guy win, but they go to see some guy get licked, too. All they knew about Bummy was some of the things they read, and he was the guy they always went to see get licked.

Even the mob that followed Bummy when he was a big name didn't mean anything to him, because he could see through that. He could see they were always grabbing at him for what they could get, and that was the thing he never got over about the time he was training in Billy West's place up in Woodstock, New York.

Bummy went up there after he came out of the Army, just to take off weight, and there are a lot of artists around there. Artists are different people, because they don't care what anybody says about a guy and they either like him or they don't like him for what they think he is. They all liked him up there, and Billy used to say that Bummy could have been Mayor of Woodstock.

Billy had a dog that Bummy never forgot, either. Bummy used to run on the roads in the mornings and Billy's dog used to run with him. Every morning they'd go out together and one day another dog came out of a yard and went for Bummy and Billy's dog turned and went after the other dog and chased it off.

"Gee, this dog really likes me," Bummy said, when he got back to the house, and he said it like he couldn't believe it. "He's really my friend."

The fight that really started everybody hating Bummy, though, was the Canzoneri fight in the Garden. It was a bad match and never should have been made, but they made it and all Bummy did was fight it.

Canzoneri was over the hill, but he had been the featherweight champion and the lightweight champion and he had fought the best of his time and they loved him. When Bummy knocked him out it was the only time Tony was knocked out in 180 fights, and so they booed Bummy for it and they waited for him to get licked.

They didn't have to wait too long. After he knocked out Tippy Larkin in five they matched him with Lou Ambers. Just after he started training for

Ambers he was in the candy store one day when an argument started between. Bummy and a guy named Mersky. Nobody is going to say who
started the argument but somebody called Bummy a lousy fighter and it
wasn't Bummy. Somebody flipped a piece of hard candy in Bummy's face,
too, and that wasn't Bummy either, and after Bummy got done bouncing
Mersky up and down Mersky went to the hospital and had some pictures
taken and called the cops.

The first Johnny Attell heard about it was the night after it happened. He
was walking down Broadway and he met a dick he knew.

"That's too bad about your fighter," the cop said.

"What's the matter with him?" Johnny said.

"What's the matter with him?" the cop said. "There's an eight-state alarm
out for him. The newspapers are full of it. He damn near killed a guy in a
candy store."

The cops couldn't find Bummy but Johnny found him. He dug up Gangy,
and Gangy drove him around awhile to shake off any cops, and finally Gangy
stopped the car in front of an old wooden house and they got out and went
in and there was Bummy.

Bummy was sitting in a pair of pajama pants, and that was all he had on.
There were four or five other guys there, and they were playing cards.

"Are you crazy?" Johnny said.

"Why?" Bummy said, playing his cards, but looking up.

"If the cops find you here they'll kill you," Johnny said. "You better come
with me."

After Johnny talked awhile Bummy got dressed and he went with Johnny.
Johnny took him back to New York and got him a haircut and a shave and he
called Mike Jacobs. Jacobs told Johnny to take Bummy down to Police
Headquarters, and when Johnny did that Sol Strauss, Mike's lawyer, showed
up and he got an adjournment in night court for Bummy until after the Ambers fight.

The night Bummy fought Ambers there was Mersky right at ringside. He
had on dark glasses and the photographers were all taking his picture and
when Ambers beat the hell out of Bummy the crowd loved it.

The crowd, more than Ambers, hurt Bummy that night. He didn't like the
licking Ambers gave him, but the hardest part was listening to the crowd and
the way they enjoyed it and the things they shouted at him when he came
down out of the ring.

"I quit," he said to Johnny in the dressing room. "You know what you can
do with fighting?"

Johnny didn't believe him. Johnny was making matches for Jacobs in the Garden then and he matched Bummy with Tony Marteliano, but Bummy wouldn't train.

Only Johnny and Gangy knew this, and one day Johnny came out to Bummy's house and talked with Bummy. When that didn't do any good Lew Burston came out and he talked for four hours, and when he finished Bummy said the same thing.

"I don't want to be a fighter," Bummy said. "I like to fight. I'll fight Marteliano on the street right now, just for fun, but when I'm a fighter everybody picks on me. I want them to leave me alone. All I wanted was a home for my family and I got that and now I just want to hang around my mob on the street."

Johnny still didn't believe it. They put out the show cards, advertising the fight, and one day Bummy saw one of the cards in the window of a bar and he phoned Johnny in Jacobs' office.

"What are you advertising the fight for?" he said, and he was mad. "I told you I'm not gonna fight."

Before Johnny could say anything Jacobs took the phone. Johnny hadn't told him Bummy didn't want to fight.

"How are you, kid?" Jacobs said. "This is Mike."

"Listen, you toothless—," Bummy said. "What are you advertising me for? I'm not gonna fight."

He hung up. Mike put the phone back and turned around and when he did Bummy was suspended and Johnny was out of the Garden and back in the Ridgewood Grove.

When Bummy heard what had happened to Johnny he went over to the Grove to see him. All the time Johnny was in the Garden Bummy was a little suspicious of him, like he was a capitalist, but now he was different.

"I came over to tell you something," he said to Johnny. "I'm gonna fight."

"Forget it," Johnny said. "You can't fight."

"Who says I can't fight?" Bummy said.

"The New York Boxing Commission," Johnny said. "You're suspended."

"Let's fight out of town," Bummy said. "We'll fight where I'm not suspended."

Johnny did it better. He took Bummy back to Mike and Bummy apologized and Bummy fought Marteliano. For nine rounds they were even, and with ten seconds to go in the last round Bummy landed the hook. Marteliano went down and the referee counted nine and the bell rang and it was another big one for Bummy and he was going again.

It was Johnny's idea to get Marteliano back, but Bummy saw Fritzie Zivic lick Henry Armstrong for the welterweight title and he wanted Zivic. If you knew the two guys you knew this was a bad match for Bummy, because he just didn't know how to fight like Zivic.

There were a lot of people, you see, who called Bummy a dirty fighter, but the Zivic fight made them wrong. The Zivic fight proved that Bummy didn't know how to do it.

When he came out of the first clinch Bummy's eyes were red and he was rubbing them and the crowd started to boo Zivic. In the second clinch it was the same thing, and at the end of the round Bummy was roaring.

"He's trying to blind me," he kept saying in the corner. "He's trying to blind me."

When it started again in the second round Bummy blew. He pushed Zivic off and he dropped his hands and that crazy look came on that wide face of his and they could hear him in the crowd.

"All right, you—," he said, "if you want to fight dirty, okay."

He walked right into Zivic and he started belting low. There was no trying to hide anything, and the crowd started to roar and before it was over people were on their chairs throwing things and the cops were in the ring and Bummy was fined $2,500 and suspended for life.

They meant it to be for life—which wouldn't have been very long at that, when you figure Bummy lived to be all of 26—but it didn't work out that way. About three weeks after the fight Bummy walked into Johnny's office with Shorty and Mousie, and they sat around for a time and Johnny could see Bummy was lost.

"You know what you ought to do?" Johnny said. "You ought to join the Army for a while until this blows over."

This was in December of 1940, before we got into the war. For a while Bummy sat there thinking, not saying anything.

"Could my buddies go with me?" he said.

"Sure," Johnny said.

So Johnny called up the recruiting officer and Bummy and Shorty and Mousie showed up and there were photographers there and it was a big show. Everybody was for it, and Ed Van Every wrote a story in *The Sun* in which he said this was a great move because the Army would teach Bummy discipline and get him in good physical shape.

That was a laugh. The first thing the Army did was split Bummy and Shorty and Mousie up and send them to different camps.

They sent Bummy to Camp Hulen, Texas, and their idea of discipline was to have Bummy cleaning latrines with a toothbrush.

"You got me into this," Bummy used to write Johnny. "I'm going crazy, so before I slug one of these officers you better get me out."

Johnny didn't get him out, but he got Mike Jacobs to get Bummy a leave to fight Zivic in the Polo Grounds for Army Emergency Relief. Bummy used to fight best at about 147 pounds, and when he came back from Texas he weighed close to 200.

"You look sharp in that uniform, Al," Zivic said to him when they signed for the bout.

"I'm glad you like it," Bummy said. "You put me in it."

You can imagine how Bummy was looking to get back at Zivic, but he couldn't do it. He hadn't fought for eight months, and Zivic was a real good fighter and he put lumps all over Bummy and in the tenth round the referee stopped it. They had to find Bummy to take him back to camp. They found him with his wife and they shipped him back, but then the Japs bombed Pearl Harbor and the Army decided it had enough trouble without Bummy and they turned him loose.

Bummy fought some of his best fights after that. He couldn't get his license back in New York but he fought in places like Holyoke and Bridgeport and Washington and Philadelphia and Elizabeth, New Jersey, and Boston. He didn't like it in those places, but he had to live, and so no matter where he fought he would always drive back to Brownsville after the fight and sometimes it would be four o'clock in the morning before he and Johnny would get in.

It's something when you think about Bummy and Brownsville, when you think of the money he made, almost a quarter of a million dollars, and the things he had thrown at him and the elegant places he could have gone. It was like what Lew Burston said, though, when he said the Supreme was Bummy's Opera, and the Supreme is a movie house on Livonia Avenue.

You have to remember, too, that Brownsville is only a subway ride from Broadway, but Bummy had never seen a real Broadway show until Chicky Bogad sent Bummy and Barbara to see *Hellzapoppin* the night before the second Farber fight.

"How long has this been going on?" Bummy said when they came out.

"How long has what been going on?" Chicky said.

"People like that on a stage," Bummy said.

"People on a stage?" Chicky said. "For years and years. For long before they had movies."

"Is that right? I'll have to see more of that," Bummy said, but he never did.

All of those fights Bummy had out of town were murders, too, because Bummy wasn't hard to hit, but the people liked to see him get hit and when the Republicans got back in power in New York, Fritzie Zivic put in a word for Bummy, saying he guessed he had egged the kid on, and Bummy got his license back. That's when they matched him with Montgomery.

"What you have to do in this one," they kept telling Bummy, "is walk right out, throw your right, and miss with it. Montgomery will grab your right arm, and that will turn you around southpaw and then you hit him with the hook."

They knew that was the only chance Bummy had, because if Montgomery got by the first round he figured to move around Bummy and cut him up. They drilled Bummy on it over and over, and they kept talking about it in the dressing room that night.

"Now what are you going to do?" Johnny Attell said to Bummy.

"I'm gonna walk right out and miss with my right," Bummy said. "He'll grab my arm and that'll turn me around southpaw and I'll throw my hook."

"Okay," Johnny said. "I guess you know it."

Bummy sat down then on one of the benches. He had his gloves on and his robe over him and he was ready to go when there was a knock on the door.

"Don't come out yet, Davis," one of the commission guys said through the door. "They're selling some War Bonds first."

When Bummy heard that he looked up from where he was sitting and you could see he was sweating, and then he keeled right over on the floor on his face. Johnny and Freddie Brown rushed over and picked him up and they stretched him on the rubbing table and Freddie brought him to, and now they weren't worried about whether Bummy would do what they told him. All they were worried about was whether they could get him in the ring.

They got him in the ring and Burston had him repeat what he was supposed to do. When the bell rang he walked right out and threw his right and missed around the head. Montgomery grabbed the arm and turned Bummy around, and when he did Bummy threw the hook and Montgomery went down. When he got up Bummy hit him again and that's all there was to it.

Montgomery was 10 to 1 over Bummy that night and they couldn't believe it. Bummy got $15,000 for that fight and he borrowed $1,500 from Jacobs and the next day when Mike paid him off he told Bummy to forget the grand and a half.

"Take it out," Bummy said, throwing the dough on the desk. "You know damn well if he kayoed me like you thought he would you were gonna take it out."

Bummy thought he'd never be broke again. He got $34,000 the night Beau Jack beat him and $15,000 when Armstrong stopped him. Then somebody sold him the idea of buying that bar and grill and somebody else sold him a couple of race horses and even after Dudy bought the bar and grill from him he was broke.

He should have been in training for Morris Reif the night he was shot. Johnny wanted him to fight Reif, just for the dough and to go as far as he could, but Bummy said that a lot of his friends would bet him and he didn't think he could beat Reif, so instead he was sitting in the back of Dudy's drinking beer and singing.

Bummy used to think he could sing like a Jewish cantor. He couldn't sing, but he was trying that night, sitting with some other guys and a cop who was off duty, when he looked through that lattice work at the bar and he saw the four guys with the guns.

"What the hell is this?" he said.

He got up and walked out and you know what happened. When Bummy stiffened the first guy one of the others fired and the bullet went into Bummy's neck. Then the three picked up the guy Bummy hit and they ran for the car. One of the guys with Bummy stuffed his handkerchief in the collar of Bummy's shirt to stop the blood, and Bummy got up and ran for the car. When he did they opened up from the car, and Bummy went flat on his face in the mud.

When the car started to pull away the cop who had been in the back ran out and fired. He hit one guy in the spine, and that guy died in Texas, and he hit another in the shoulder. The guy with the slug in his shoulder walked around with it for weeks, afraid to go to a doctor, and then one night a cop in plain clothes heard a couple of guys talking in a bar.

"You know that jerk is still walking around with the bullet in his shoulder?" the one said. "What bullet?" the second one said.

"The Bummy Davis bullet," the first said.

The cop followed them out, and when they split up he followed the first guy and got it out of him. Then the cops picked up the guy with the bullet and he sang. They picked up the other two in Kansas City and they're doing 20 to life. They were just punks, and they called themselves the Cowboys, the same as Bummy's old gang did.

It was a big funeral Bummy had. Johnny and Lew Burston paid for it. The papers had made Bummy a hero, and the newsreels took pictures outside the funeral parlor and at the cemetery. It looked like everybody in Brownsville was there.

The Rocky Road of Pistol Pete

from *True*

"Out in Los Angeles," says Garry Schumacher, who was a New York baseball writer for 30 years and is now assistant to Horace Stoneham, president of the San Francisco Giants, "they think Duke Snider is the best center fielder they ever had. They forget Pete Reiser. The Yankees think Mickey Mantle is something new. They forget Reiser, too."

Maybe Pete Reiser was the purest ballplayer of all time. I don't know. There is no exact way of measuring such a thing, but when a man of incomparable skills, with full knowledge of what he is doing, destroys those skills and puts his life on the line in the pursuit of his endeavor as no other man in his game ever has, perhaps he is the truest of them all.

"Is Pete Reiser there?" I said on the phone.

This was last season, in Kokomo. Kokomo has a population of about 50,000 and a ball club, now affiliated with Los Angeles and called the Dodgers, in the Class D Midwest League. Class D is the bottom of the barrel of organized baseball, and this was the second season that Pete Reiser had managed Kokomo.

"He's not here right now," the woman's voice on the phone said. "The team played a double-header yesterday in Dubuque, and they didn't get in on the bus until 4:30 this morning. Pete just got up a few minutes ago and he had to go to the doctor's."

"Oh?" I said. "What has he done now?"

In two and a half years in the minors, three seasons of Army ball and ten years in the majors, Pete Reiser was carried off the field 11 times. Nine times

17

he regained consciousness either in the clubhouse or in hospitals. He broke a bone in his right elbow, throwing. He broke both ankles, tore a cartilage in his left knee, ripped the muscles in his left leg, sliding. Seven times he crashed into outfield walls, dislocating his left shoulder, breaking his right collarbone and, five times, ending up in an unconscious heap on the ground. Twice he was beaned, and the few who remember still wonder today how great he might have been.

"I didn't see the old-timers," Bob Cooke, who is sports editor of the New York *Herald Tribune*, was saying recently, "but Pete Reiser was the best ballplayer I ever saw."

"We don't know what's wrong with him," the woman's voice on the phone said now. "He has a pain in his chest and he feels tired all the time, so we sent him to the doctor. There's a game tonight, so he'll be at the ball park about 5 o'clock."

Pete Reiser is 39 years old now. The Cardinals signed him out of the St. Louis Municipal League when he was 15. For two years, because he was so young, he chauffeured for Charley Barrett, who was scouting the Midwest. They had a Cardinal uniform in the car for Pete, and he used to work out with the Class C and D clubs, and one day Branch Rickey, who was general manager of the Cardinals then, called Pete into his office in Sportsman's Park.

"Young man," he said, "you're the greatest young ballplayer I've ever seen, but there is one thing you must remember. Now that you're a professional ballplayer you're in show business. You will perform on the biggest stage in the world, the baseball diamond. Like the actors on Broadway, you'll be expected to put on a great performance every day, no matter how you feel, no matter whether it's too hot or too cold. Never forget that."

Rickey didn't know it at the time, but this was like telling Horatius that, as a professional soldier, he'd be expected someday to stand his ground. Three times Pete sneaked out of hospitals to play. Once he went back into the lineup after doctors warned him that any blow on the head would kill him. For four years he swung the bat and made the throws when it was painful for him just to shave and to comb his hair. In the 1947 World Series he stood on a broken ankle to pinch hit, and it ended with Rickey, then president of the Dodgers, begging him not to play and guaranteeing Pete his 1948 salary if he would just sit that season out.

"That might be the one mistake I made," Pete says now. "Maybe I should have rested that year."

"Pete Reiser?" Leo Durocher, who managed Pete at Brooklyn, was saying recently. "What's he doing now?"

"He's managing Kokomo," Lindsey Nelson, the TV sportcaster, said.

"Kokomo?" Leo said.

"That's right," Lindsey said. "He's riding the buses to places like Lafayette and Michigan City and Mattoon."

"On the buses," Leo said, shaking his head and then smiling at the thought of Pete.

"And some people say," Lindsey said, "that he was the greatest young ballplayer they ever saw."

"No doubt about it," Leo said. "He was the best I ever had, with the possible exception of Mays. At that, he was even faster than Willie." He paused. "So now he's on the buses."

The first time that Leo ever saw Pete on a ball field was in Clearwater that spring of '39. Pete had played one year of Class D in the Cardinal chain and one season of Class D for Brooklyn. Judge Kenesaw Mountain Landis, who was then Baseball Commissioner, had sprung Pete and 72 others from what they called the "Cardinal Chain Gang," and Pete had signed with Brooklyn for $100.

"I didn't care about money then," Pete says. "I just wanted to play."

Pete had never been in a major-league camp before, and he didn't know that at batting practice you hit in rotation. At Clearwater he was grabbing any bat that was handy and cutting in ahead of Ernie Koy or Dolph Camilli or one of the others, and Leo liked that.

One day Leo had a chest cold, so he told Pete to start at shortstop. His first time up he hit a homer off the Cards' Ken Raffensberger, and that was the beginning. He was on base his first 12 times at bat that spring, with three homers, five singles and four walks. His first time against Detroit he homered off Tommy Bridges. His first time against the Yankees he put one over the fence off Lefty Gomez.

Durocher played Pete at shortstop in 33 games that spring. The Dodgers barnstormed North with the Yankees, and one night Joe McCarthy, who was managing the Yankees, sat down next to Pete on the train.

"Reiser," he said, "you're going to play for me."

"How can I play for you?" Pete said. "I'm with the Dodgers."

"We'll get you," McCarthy said. "I'll tell Ed Barrow, and you'll be a Yankee."

The Yankees offered $100,000 and five ballplayers for Pete. The Dodgers turned it down, and the day the season opened at Ebbets Field, Larry

MacPhail, who was running things in Brooklyn, called Pete on the club-house phone and told him to report to Elmira.

"It was an hour before game time," Pete says, "and I started to take off my uniform and I was shaking all over. Leo came in and said: 'What's the matter? You scared?' I said: 'No. MacPhail is sending me to Elmira.' Leo got on the phone and they had a hell of a fight. Leo said he'd quit, and MacPhail said he'd fire him—and I went to Elmira.

"One day I'm making a throw and I heard something pop. Every day my arm got weaker and they sent me to Johns Hopkins and took X rays. Dr. George Bennett told me: 'Your arm's broken.' When I came to after the operation, my throat was sore and there was an ice pack on it. I said: 'What happened? Your knife slip?' They said: 'We took your tonsils out while we were operating on your arm.'"

Pete's arm was in a cast from the first of May until the end of July. His first two weeks out of the cast he still couldn't straighten the arm, but a month later he played ten games as a left-handed outfielder until Dr. Bennett stopped him.

"But I can't straighten my right arm," Pete said.

"Take up bowling," the doctor said.

When he bowled, though, Pete used first one arm and then the other. Every day that the weather allowed he went out into the back yard and practiced throwing a rubber ball left-handed against a wall. Then he went to Fairgrounds Park and worked on the long throw, left-handed, with a baseball.

"At Clearwater that next spring," he says, "Leo saw me in the outfield throwing left-handed, and he said: 'What do you think you're doin'?' I said: 'Hell, I had to be ready. Now I can throw as good with my left arm as I could with my right.' He said: 'You can do more things as a right-handed ballplayer. I can bring you into the infield. Go out there and cut loose with that right arm.' I did and it was okay, but I had that insurance."

So at 5 o'clock I took a cab from the hotel in Kokomo to the ball park on the edge of town. It seats about 2,200, 1,500 of them in the white-painted fairgrounds grandstand along the first base line, and the rest in chairs behind the screen and in bleachers along the other line.

I watched them take batting practice; trim, strong young kids with their dreams, I knew, of someday getting up there where Pete once was, and I listened to their kidding. I watched the groundskeeper open the concession booth and clean out the electric popcorn machine. I read the signs on the outfield walls, advertising the Mid-West Towel and Linen Service, Basil's

Nite Club, the Hoosier Iron Works, UAW Local 292 and the Around the Clock Pizza Café. I watched the Dubuque kids climbing out of their bus, carrying their uniforms on wire coat hangers.

"Here comes Pete now," I heard the old guy setting up the ticket box at the gate say.

When Pete came through the gate he was walking like an old man. In 1941 the Dodgers trained in Havana, and one day they clocked him, in his baseball uniform and regular spikes, at 9.8 for 100 yards. Five years later the Cleveland Indians were bragging about George Case and the Washington Senators had Gil Coan. The Dodgers offered to bet $1,000 that Reiser was the fastest man in baseball, and now it was taking him forever to walk to me, his shoulders stooped, his whole body heavier now, and Pete just slowly moving one foot ahead of the other.

"Hello," he said, shaking hands but his face solemn. "How are you?"

"Fine," I said, "but what's the matter with you?"

"I guess it's my heart," he said.

"When did you first notice this?"

"About eleven days ago. I guess I was working out too hard. All of a sudden I felt this pain in my chest and I got weak. I went into the clubhouse and lay down on the bench, but I've had the same pain and I'm weak ever since."

"What did the doctor say?"

"He says it's lucky I stopped that day when I did. He says I should be in a hospital right now, because if I exert myself or even make a quick motion I might go—just like that."

He snapped his fingers. "He scared me," he said. "I'll admit it. I'm scared."

"What are you planning to do?"

"I'm going home to St. Louis. My wife works for a doctor there, and he'll know a good heart specialist."

"When will you leave?"

"Well, I can't just leave the ball club. I called Brooklyn, and they're sending a replacement for me, but he won't be here until tomorrow."

"How will you get to St. Louis?"

"It's about 300 miles," Pete says. "The doctor says I shouldn't fly or go by train, because if anything happens to me they can't stop and help me. I guess I'll have to drive."

"I'll drive you," I said.

Trying to get to sleep in the hotel that night I was thinking that maybe, standing there in that little ball park, Pete Reiser had admitted out loud for the first time in his life that he was scared. I was thinking of 1941, his first full year with the Dodgers. He was beaned twice and crashed his first wall and still hit .343 to be the first rookie and the youngest ballplayer to win the National League batting title. He tied Johnny Mize with 39 doubles, led in triples, runs scored, total bases and slugging average, and they were writing on the sports pages that he might be the new Ty Cobb.

"Dodgers Win On Reiser HR," the headlines used to say. "Reiser Stars As Brooklyn Lengthens Lead."

"Any manager in the National League," Arthur Patterson wrote one day in the New York *Herald Tribune*, "would give up his best man to obtain Pete Reiser. On every bench they're talking about him. Rival players watch him take his cuts during batting practice, announce when he's going to make a throw to the plate or third base during outfield drill. They just whistle their amazement when he scoots down the first base line on an infield dribbler or a well-placed bunt."

He was beaned the first time at Ebbets Field five days after the season started. A sidearm fast ball got away from Ike Pearson of the Phillies, and Pete came to at 11:30 that night in Peck Memorial Hospital.

"I was lying in bed with my uniform on," he told me once, "and I couldn't figure it out. The room was dark, with just a little night light, and then I saw a mirror and I walked over to it and lit the light and I had a black eye and a black streak down the side of my nose. I said to myself: 'What happened to me?' Then I remembered.

"I took a shower and walked around the room, and the next morning the doctor came in. He looked me over, and he said: 'We'll keep you here for five or six more days under observation.' I said: 'Why?' He said: 'You've had a serious head injury. If you tried to get out of bed right now, you'd fall down.' I said: 'If I can get up and walk around this room, can I get out?' The doc said: 'All right, but you won't be able to do it.'"

Pete got out of bed, the doctor standing ready to catch him. He walked around the room. "I've been walkin' the floor all night," Pete said.

The doctor made Pete promise that he wouldn't play ball for a week, but Pete went right to the ball park. He got a seat behind the Brooklyn dugout and Durocher spotted him.

"How do you feel?" Leo said.

"Not bad," Pete said.

"Get your uniform on," Leo said.

"I'm not supposed to play," Pete said.

"I'm not gonna play you," Leo said. "Just sit on the bench. It'll make our guys feel better to see that you're not hurt."

Pete suited up and went out and sat on the bench. In the eighth inning it was tied, 7–7. The Dodgers had the bases loaded, and there was Ike Pearson again, coming in to relieve.

"Pistol," Leo said to Pete, "get the bat."

In the press box the baseball writers watched Pete. They wanted to see if he'd stand right in there. After a beaning they are all entitled to shy, and many of them do. Pete hit the first pitch into the center-field stands, and Brooklyn won, 11 to 7.

"I could just barely trot around the bases," Pete said when I asked him about it. "I was sure dizzy."

Two weeks later they were playing the Cardinals, and Enos Slaughter hit one and Pete turned in center field and started to run. He made the catch, but he hit his head and his tail bone on that corner near the exit gate.

His head was cut, and when he came back to the bench they also saw blood coming through the seat of his pants. They took him into the clubhouse and pulled his pants down and the doctor put a metal clamp on the cut.

"Just don't slide," he told Pete. "You can get it sewed up after the game."

In August of that year big Paul Erickson was pitching for the Cubs and Pete took another one. Again he woke up in a hospital. The Dodgers were having some pretty good beanball contests with the Cubs that season, and Judge Landis came to see Pete the next day.

"Do you think that man tried to bean you?" he asked Pete.

"No sir," Pete said. "I lost the pitch."

"I was there," Landis said, "and I heard them holler: 'Stick it in his ear.'"

"That was just bench talk," Pete said. "I lost the pitch."

He left the hospital the next morning. The Dodgers were going to St. Louis after the game, and Pete didn't want to be left in Chicago.

Pete always says that the next year, 1942, was the year of his downfall, and the worst of it happened on one play. It was early July and Pete and the Dodgers were tearing the league apart. In a fourth-game series in Cincinnati he got 19 for 21. In a Sunday double-header in Chicago he went 5 for 5 in the first game, walked three times in the second game and got a hit the one time they pitched to him. He was hitting .381, and they were writing in the papers that he might end up hitting .400.

When they came into St. Louis the Dodgers were leading by ten and a half games. When they took off for Pittsburgh they left three games of that lead and Pete Reiser behind them.

"We were in the twelfth inning, no score, two outs and Slaughter hit it off Whit Wyatt," Pete says. "It was over my head and I took off. I caught it and missed that flagpole by two inches and hit the wall and dropped the ball. I had the instinct to throw it to Peewee Reese, and we just missed gettin' Slaughter at the plate, and they won, 1–0.

"I made one step to start off the field and I woke up the next morning in St. John's Hospital. My head was bandaged, and I had an awful headache."

Dr. Robert Hyland, who was Pete's personal physician, announced to the newspapers that Pete would be out for the rest of the season. "Look, Pete," Hyland told him. "I'm your personal friend. I'm advising you not to play any more baseball this year."

"I don't like hospitals, though," Pete was telling me once, "so after two days I took the bandage off and got up. The room started to spin, but I got dressed and I took off. I snuck out, and I took a train to Pittsburgh and I went to the park.

"Leo saw me and he said: 'Go get your uniform on, Pistol.' I said: 'Not tonight, Skipper.' Leo said: 'Aw, I'm not gonna let you hit. I want these guys to see you. It'll give 'em that little spark they need. Besides, it'll change the pitching plans on that other bench when they see you sittin' here in uniform.'"

In the fourteenth inning the Dodgers had a runner on second and Ken Heintzelman, the left-hander, came in for the Pirates. He walked Johnny Rizzo, and Durocher had run out of pinch hitters.

"Damn," Leo was saying, walking up and down. "I want to win this one. Who can I use? Anybody here who can hit?"

Pete walked up to the bat rack. He pulled out his stick. "You got yourself a hitter," he said to Leo.

He walked up there and hit a line drive over the second baseman's head that was good for three bases. The two runs scored, and Pete rounded first base and collapsed.

"When I woke up I was in a hospital again," he says. "I could just make out that somebody was standin' there and then I saw it was Leo. He said: 'You awake?' I said: 'Yep.' He said: 'By God, we beat 'em! How do you feel?' I said: 'How do you think I feel?' He said: 'Aw, you're better with one leg, and one eye than anybody else I've got.' I said: 'Yeah, and that's the way I'll end up—on one leg and with one eye.'

"I'd say I lost the pennant for us that year," Pete says now, although he still hit 310 for the season. "I was dizzy most of the time and I couldn't see fly balls. I mean balls I could have put in my pocket, I couldn't get near. Once in Brooklyn when Mort Cooper was pitching for the Cards I was seeing two baseballs coming up there. Babe Pinelli was umpiring behind the plate, and a couple of times he stopped the game and asked me if I was all right. So the Cards beat us out the last two days of the season."

The business office of the Kokomo ball club is the dining room of a man named Jim Deets, who sells insurance and is also the business manager of the club. His wife, in addition to keeping house, mothering six small kids, boarding Pete, an outfielder from Venezuela and a shortstop from the Dominican Republic, is also the club secretary.

"How do you feel this morning?" I asked Pete. He was sitting at the dining-room table, in a sweat shirt and a pair of light-brown slacks, typing the game report of the night before to send it to Brooklyn.

"A little better," he said.

Pete has a worn, green 1950 Chevy, and it took us eight and a half hours to get to St. Louis. I'd ask him how the pain in his chest was and he'd say that it wasn't bad or it wasn't so good, and I'd get him to talking again about Durocher or about his time in the Army. Pete played under five managers at Brooklyn, Boston, Pittsburgh and Cleveland, and Durocher is his favorite.

"He has a great mind, and not just for baseball," Pete said. "Once he sat down to play gin with Jack Benny, and after they'd played four cards Leo read Benny's whole hand to him. Benny said: 'How can you do that?' Leo said: 'If you're playin' your cards right, and I give you credit for that, you have to be holding those others.' Benny said: 'I don't want to play with this guy.'

"One spring at Clearwater there was a pool table in a room off the lobby. One night Hugh Casey and a couple of other guys and I were talking with Leo. We said: 'Gee, there's a guy in there and we've been playin' pool with him for a couple of nights, but last night he had a real hot streak.' Leo said: 'How much he take you for?' We figured it out and it was $2,000. Leo said: 'Point him out to me.'

"We went in and pointed the guy out and Leo walked up to him and said: 'Put all your money on the table. We're gonna shoot for it.' The guy said: 'I never play like that.' Leo said: 'You will tonight. Pick your own game.' Leo took him for $4,000, and then he threw him out. Then he paid us back what we'd gone for, and he said: 'Now, let that be a lesson. That guy is a hustler from New York. The next time it happens I won't bail you out.' Leo hadn't had a cue in his hands for years."

It was amazing that they took Pete into the Army. He had wanted to enlist in the Navy, but the doctors looked him over and told him none of the services could accept him. Then his draft board sent him to Jefferson Barracks in the winter of 1943, and the doctors there turned him down.

"I'm sittin' on a bench with the other guys who've been rejected," he was telling me, "and a captain comes in and says: 'Which one of you is Reiser?' I stood up and I said: 'I am.' In front of everybody he said: 'So you're trying to pull a fast one, are you? At a time like this, with a war going on, you came in here under a false name. What do you mean, giving your name as Harold Patrick Reiser? Your name's Pete Reiser, and you're the ballplayer, aren't you?' I said: 'I'm the ballplayer and they call me Pete, but my right name is Harold Patrick Reiser.' The captain says: 'I apologize. Sergeant, fingerprint him. This man is in.'"

They sent him to Fort Riley, Kansas. It was early April and raining and they were on bivouac, and Pete woke up in a hospital. "What happened?" he said.

"You've got pneumonia," the doctor said. "You've been a pretty sick boy for six days. You'll be all right, but we've been looking you over. How did you ever get into this Army?"

"When I get out of the hospital," Pete was telling me, "I'm on the board for a discharge and I'm waitin' around for about a week, and still nobody there knows who I am. All of a sudden one morning a voice comes over the bitch box in the barracks. It says: 'Private Reiser, report to headquarters immediately.' I think: 'Well, I'm out now.'

"I got over there and the colonel wants to see me. I walk in and give my good salute and he says: 'Sit down, Harold.' I sit down and he says: 'Your name really isn't Harold, is it?' I say: 'Yes, it is, sir.' He says: 'But that isn't what they call you where you're well known, is it? You're Pete Reiser the ballplayer, aren't you?' I say: 'Yes, sir.' He says: 'I thought so. Now, I've got your discharge papers right there, but we've got a pretty good ball club and we'd like you on it. We'll make a deal. You say nothing, and you won't have to do anything but play ball. How about it?' I said: 'Suppose I don't want to stay in?'

"He picked my papers up off his desk," Pete was saying, "and he tore 'em right up in my face. I can still hear that 'zip' when he tore 'em. He said: 'You see, you have no choice.'

"Then he picked up the phone and said something and in a minute a general came in. I jumped up and the colonel said: 'Don't bother to salute, Pete.' Then he said to the general: 'Major, this is Pete Reiser, the great Dodger ballplayer. He was up for a medical discharge, but he's decided to stay here and play ball for us.'

"So, the general says: 'My, what a patriotic thing for you to do, young man. That's wonderful. Wonderful.' I'm sittin' there, and when the general goes out the colonel says: 'That major, he's all right.' I said: 'But he's a general. How come you call him a major?' The colonel says: 'Well, in the regular Army he's a major and I'm a full colonel. The only reason I don't outrank him now is that I've got heart trouble. He knows it, but I never let him forget it. I always call him major.' I thought: 'What kind of an Army am I in?'"

Joe Gantenbein, the Athletics' outfielder, and George Scharein, the Phillies' infielder, were on that team with Pete, and they won the state and national semipro titles. By the time the season was over, however, the order came down to hold up all discharges.

The next season there were 17 major-league ballplayers on the Fort Riley club, and they played four nights a week for the war workers in Wichita. Pete hit a couple of walls, and the team made such a joke of the national semipro tournament that an order came down from Washington to break up the club.

"Considering what a lot of guys did in the war," Pete says, "I had no complaints, but five times I was up for discharge, and each time something happened. From Riley they sent me to Camp Livingston. From there they sent me to New York Special Services for twelve hours and I end up in Camp Lee, Virginia, in May of 1945.

"The first one I meet there is the general. He says: 'Reiser, I saw you on the list and I just couldn't pass you up.' I said: 'What about my discharge?' He says: 'That will have to wait. I have a lot of celebrities down here, but I want a good baseball team.'"

Johnny Lindell, of the Yankees, and Dave Philley, of the White Sox, were on the club and Pete played left field. Near the end of the season he went after a foul fly for the third out of the last inning, and he went right through a temporary wooden fence and rolled down a 25-foot embankment.

"I came to in the hospital, with a dislocated right shoulder," he says, "and the general came over to see me and he said: 'That was one of the greatest displays of courage I've ever seen, to ignore your future in baseball just to win a ball game for Camp Lee.' I said: 'Thanks.'

"Now it's November and the war is over, but they're still shippin' guys out, and I'm on the list to go. I report to the overseas major, and he looks at my papers and says: 'I can't send you overseas. With everything that's wrong with you, you shouldn't even be in this Army. I'll have you out in three hours.' In three hours, sure enough, I've got those papers in my hand, stamped, and I'm startin' out the door. Runnin' up to me comes a Red Cross guy. He says: 'I can get you some pretty good pension benefits for the physical and mental injuries you've sustained.' I said: 'You can?' He said: 'Yes, you're entitled to them.' I said: 'Good. You get 'em. You keep 'em. I'm goin' home.'"

When we got to St. Louis that night I drove Pete to his house and the next morning I picked him up and drove him to see the heart specialist. He was in there for two hours, and when he came out he was walking slower than ever.

"No good," he said. "I have to go to the hospital for five days for observation."

"What does he think?"

"He says I'm done puttin' on that uniform. I'll have to get a desk job."

Riding to the hospital I wondered if that heart specialist knew who he was tying to that desk job. In 1946, the year he came out of the Army, Pete led the league when he stole 34 bases, 13 more than the runner-up Johnny Hopp of the Braves. He also set a major-league record that still stands, when he stole home eight times.

"Nine times," he said once. "In Chicago I stole home and Magerkurth hollered: 'You're out!' Then he dropped his voice and he said: '____, I missed it.' He'd already had his thumb in the air. I had nine out of nine."

I suppose somebody will beat that some day, but he'll never top the way Pete did it. That was the year he knocked himself out again trying for a diving catch, dislocated his left shoulder, ripped the muscles in his left leg and broke his left ankle.

"Whitey Kurowski hit one in the seventh inning at Ebbets Field," he was telling me. "I dove for it and woke up in the clubhouse. I was in Peck Memorial for four days. It really didn't take much to knock me out in those days. I was comin' apart all over. When I dislocated my shoulder they popped it back in, and Leo said: 'Hell, you'll be all right. You don't throw with it anyway.'"

That was the year the Dodgers tied with the Cardinals for the pennant and dropped the play-off. Pete wasn't there for those two games. He was in Peck Memorial again.

"I'd pulled a Charley horse in my left leg," Pete was saying. "It's the last two weeks of the season, and I'm out for four days. We've got the winning run on third, two outs in the ninth and Leo sends me up. He says: 'If you don't hit it good, don't run and hurt your leg.'

"The first pitch was a knockdown and, when I ducked, the ball hit the bat and went down the third base line, as beautiful a bunt as you've ever seen. Well, Ebbets Field is jammed. Leo has said: 'Don't run.' But this is a big game. I take off for first, and we win and I've ripped the muscles from my ankle to my hip. Leo says: 'You shouldn't have done it.'

"Now it's the last three days of the season and we're a game ahead of the Cards and we're playin' the Phillies in Brooklyn. Leo says to me: 'It's now or never. I don't think we can win it without you.' The first two up are outs and

I single to right. There's Charley Dressen, coachin' on third, with the steal sign. I start to get my lead, and a pitcher named Charley Schanz is workin' and he throws an ordinary lob over to first. My leg is stiff and I slide and my heel spike catches the bag and I hear it snap.

"Leo comes runnin' out. He says: 'Come on. You're all right.' I said: 'I think it's broken.' He says: 'It ain't stickin' out.' They took me to Peck Memorial, and it was broken."

We went to St. Luke's Hospital in St. Louis. In the main office they told Pete to go over to a desk where a gray-haired, semistout woman was sitting at a typewriter. She started to book Pete in, typing his answer on the form. "What is your occupation, Mr. Reiser?" she said.

"Baseball," Pete said.

"Have you ever been hospitalized before?"

"Yes," Pete said.

In 1946 the Dodgers played an exhibition game in Springfield, Missouri. When the players got off the train there was a young radio announcer there, and he was grabbing them one at a time and asking them where they thought they'd finish that year.

"In first place," Reese and Casey and Dixie Walker and the rest were saying. "On top" . . . "We'll win it."

"And here comes Pistol Pete Reiser!" the announcer said. "Where do you think you'll finish this season, Pete?"

"In Peck Memorial Hospital," Pete said.

After the 1946 season Brooklyn changed the walls at Ebbets Field. They added boxes, cutting 40 feet off left field and dropping center field from 420 to 390 feet. Pete had made a real good start that season in center, and on June 5 the Dodgers were leading the Pirates by three runs in the sixth inning when Culley Rikard hit one.

"I made my turn and ran," Pete says, "and, where I thought I still had that thirty feet, I didn't."

"The crowd," Al Laney wrote the next day in the New York *Herald Tribune*, "which watched silently while Reiser was being carried away, did not know that he had held onto the ball . . . Rikard circled the bases, but Butch Henline the umpire, who ran to Reiser, found the ball still in Reiser's glove. . . . Two outs were posted on the scoreboard after play was resumed. Then the crowd let out a tremendous roar."

In the Brooklyn clubhouse the doctor called for a priest, and the Last Rites of the Church were administered to Pete. He came to, but lapsed into unconsciousness again and woke up at 3 A.M. in Peck Memorial.

For eight days he couldn't move. After three weeks they let him out, and he made that next western trip with the Dodgers. In Pittsburgh he was working out in the outfield before the game when Clyde King, chasing a fungo, ran into him and Pete woke up in the clubhouse.

"I went back to the Hotel Schenley and lay down," he says. "After the game I got up and had dinner with Peewee. We were sittin' on the porch, and I scratched my head and I felt a lump there about as big as half a golf ball. I told Peewee to feel it and he said: 'Gosh!' I said: 'I don't think that's supposed to be like that.' He said: 'Hell, no.'"

Pete went up to Rickey's room and Rickey called his pilot and had Pete flown to Johns Hopkins in Baltimore. They operated on him for a blood clot.

"You're lucky," the doctor told him. "If it had moved just a little more you'd have been gone."

Pete was unable to hold even a pencil. He had double vision and, when he tried to take a single step, he became dizzy. He stayed for three weeks and then went home for almost a month.

"It was August," he says, "and Brooklyn was fightin' for another pennant. I thought if I could play the last two months it might make the difference, so I went back to Johns Hopkins. The doctor said: 'You've made a remarkable recovery.' I said: 'I want to play.' He said: 'I can't okay that. The slightest blow on the head can kill you.'"

Pete played. He worked out for four days, pinch hit a couple of times and then, in the Polo Grounds, made a diving catch in left field. They carried him off, and in the clubhouse he was unable to recognize anyone.

Pete was still having dizzy spells when the Dodgers went into the 1947 Series against the Yankees. In the third game he walked in the first inning, got the steal sign and, when he went into second, felt his right ankle snap. At the hospital they found it was broken.

"Just tape it, will you?" Pete said.

"I want to put a cast on it," the doctor said.

"If you do," Pete said, "they'll give me a dollar-a-year contract next season."

The next day he was back on the bench. Bill Bevens was pitching for the Yankees and, with two out in the ninth, it looked like he was going to pitch the first no-hitter in World Series history.

"Aren't you going to volunteer to hit?" Burt Shotton, who was managing Brooklyn, said to Pete.

Al Gionfriddo was on first and Bucky Harris, who was managing the Yankees, ordered Pete walked. Eddie Miksis ran for him, and when Cookie Lavagetto hit that double, the two runs scored and Brooklyn won, 3–2.

"The next day," Pete says, "the sports writers were second-guessing Harris for putting me on when I represented the winning run. Can you imagine what they'd have said if they knew I had a broken ankle?"

At the end of that season Rickey had the outfield walls at Ebbets Field padded with one-inch foam rubber for Pete, but he never hit them again. He had headaches most of the time and played little. Then he was traded to Boston, and in two seasons there he hit the wall a couple of times. Twice his left shoulder came out while he was making diving catches. Pittsburgh picked Pete up in 1951, and the next year he played into July with Cleveland and that was the end of it.

Between January and September of 1953, Pete dropped $40,000 in the used-car business in St. Louis, and then he got a job in a lumber mill for $100 a week. In the winter of 1955 he wrote Brooklyn asking for a part-time job as a scout, and on March 1, Buzzy Bavasi, the Dodger vice-president, called him on the phone.

"How would you like a manager's job?" Buzzy said.

"I'll take it," Pete said.

"I haven't even told you where it is. It's Thomasville, Georgia, in Class D."

"I don't care," Pete said. "I'll take it."

At Vero Beach that spring, Mike Gaven wrote a piece about Pete in the New York *Journal American*.

"Even in the worn gray uniform of the Class D Thomasville, Georgia, club," Mike wrote, "Pete Reiser looks, acts and talks like a big leaguer. The Dodgers pitied Pete when they saw him starting his comeback effort after not having handled a ball for two and a half years. They lowered their heads when they saw him in a chow line with a lot of other bushers, but the old Pistol held his head high. . . ."

The next spring, Sid Friedlander, of the New York *Post*, saw Pete at Vero and wrote a column about him managing Kokomo. The last thing I saw about him in the New York papers was a small item out of Tipton, Indiana, saying that the bus carrying the Kokomo team had collided with a car and Pete was in a hospital in Kokomo with a back injury.

"Managing," Pete was saying in that St. Louis hospital, "you try to find out how your players are thinking. At Thomasville one night one of my kids made a bad throw. After the game I said to him: 'What were you thinking while that ball was coming to you?' He said: 'I was saying to myself that I hoped I could make a good throw.' I said: 'Sit down.' I tried to explain to him the way you have to think. You know how I used to think?"

"Yes," I said, "but you tell me."

"I was always sayin': 'Hit it to me. Just hit it to me. I'll make the catch. I'll make the throw.' When I was on base I was always lookin' over and sayin': 'Give me the steal sign. Give me the sign. Let me go.' That's the way you have to think."

"Pete," I said, "now that it's all over, do you ever think that if you hadn't played it as hard as you did, there's no telling how great you might have been or how much money you might have made?"

"Never," Pete said. "It was my way of playin'. If I hadn't played that way I wouldn't even have been whatever I was. God gave me those legs and the speed, and when they took me into the walls that's the way it had to be. I couldn't play any other way."

A technician came in with an electrocardiograph. She was a thin, dark-haired woman and she set it up by the bed and attached one of the round metal disks to Pete's left wrist and started to attach another to his left ankle.

"Aren't you kind of young to be having pains in your chest?" she said.

"I've led a fast life," Pete said.

On the way back to New York I kept thinking how right Pete was. To tell a man who is this true that there is another way for him to do it is to speak a lie. You cannot ask him to change his way of going, because it makes him what he is.

Three days after I got home I had a message to call St. Louis. I heard the phone ring at the other end and Pete answered. "I'm out!" he said.

"Did they let you out, or did you sneak out again?" I said.

"They let me out," he said. "It's just a strained heart muscle, I guess. My heart itself is all right."

"That's wonderful."

"I can manage again. In a couple of days I can go back to Kokomo."

If his voice had been higher he would have sounded like a kid at Christmas.

"What else did they say?" I said.

"Well, they say I have to take it easy."

"Do me a favor," I said.

"What?"

"Take their advice. This time, please take it easy."

"I will," he said. "I'll take it easy."

If he does it will be the first time.

The Ghost of
the Gridiron

from *True*

When I was ten years old I paid ten cents to see Red Grange run with a football. That was the year when, one afternoon a week, after school was out for the day, they used to show us movies in the auditorium, and we would all troop up there clutching our dimes, nickels or pennies in our fists.

The movies were, I suppose, carefully selected for their educational value. They must have shown us, as the weeks went by, films of the Everglades, of Yosemite, of the Gettysburg battlefield, of Washington, D.C., but I remember only the one about Grange.

I remember, in fact, only one shot. Grange, the football cradled in one arm, started down the field toward us. As we sat there in the dim, flickering light of the movie projector, he grew larger and larger. I can still see the rows and rows of us, with our thin little necks and bony heads, all looking up at the screen and Grange, enormous now, rushing right at us, and I shall never forget it. That was thirty-three years ago.

"I haven't any idea what film that might have been," Grange was saying now. "My last year at Illinois was all confusion. I had no privacy. Newsreel men were staying at the fraternity house for two or three days at a time."

He paused. The thought of it seemed to bring pain to his face, even at this late date.

"I wasn't able to study or anything," he said. "I thought and I still do, that they built me up out of all proportion."

Red Grange was the most sensational, the most publicized, and, possibly, the most gifted football player and greatest broken field runner of all time. In high school, at Wheaton, Illinois, he averaged five touch-downs a game.

In twenty games for the University of Illinois, he scored thirty-one touchdowns and ran for 3,637 yards, or, as it was translated at the time, 2 miles and 117 yards. His name and his pseudonyms—The Galloping Ghost and The Wheaton Iceman—became household words, and what he was may have been summarized best by Paul Sann in his book *The Lawless Decade*.

"Red Grange, No. 77, made Jack Dempsey move over," Sann wrote. "He put college football ahead of boxing as the Golden Age picked up momentum. He also made the ball yards obsolete; they couldn't handle the crowds. He made people buy more radios: how could you wait until Sunday morning to find out what deeds Red Grange had performed on Saturday? He was 'The Galloping Ghost' and he made the sports historians torture their portables without mercy."

Grange is now 55 years old, his reddish brown hair marked with gray, but he was one with Babe Ruth, Jack Dempsey, Bobby Jones and Bill Tilden.

"I could carry a football well," Grange was saying now, "but I've met hundreds of people who could do their thing better than I. I mean engineers, and writers, scientists, doctors—whatever.

"I can't take much credit for what I did, running with a football, because I don't know what I did. Nobody ever taught me, and I can't teach anybody. You can teach a man how to block or tackle or kick or pass. The ability to run with a ball is something you have or you haven't. If you can't explain it, how can you take credit for it?"

This was last year, and we were sitting in a restaurant in Syracuse, New York. Grange was in town to do a telecast with Lindsey Nelson of the Syracuse-Penn State game. He lives now in Miami, Florida, coming out of there on weekends during the football season to handle telecasts of college games on Saturdays and the Chicago Bears' games on Sundays. He approaches this job as he has approached every job, with honesty and dedication, and, as could be expected, he is good at it. As befits a man who put the pro game on the map and made the whole nation football conscious, he has been making fans out of people who never followed the game before. Never, perhaps, has any one man done more for the game. And it, of course, has been good to him.

"Football did everything for me," he was saying now, "but what people don't understand is that it hasn't been my whole life. When I was a freshman at Illinois, I wasn't even going to go out for football. My fraternity brothers made me do it."

He was three times All-American. Once the Illinois students carried him two miles on their backs. A football jersey, with the number 77 that he made famous and that was retired after him, is enshrined at Champaign. His fellow students wanted him to run for Congress. A Senator from Illinois led him into the White House to shake hands with Calvin Coolidge. Here, in its entirety, is what was said.

"Howdy," Coolidge said. "Where do you live?"

"In Wheaton, Illinois," Grange said.

"Well, young man," Coolidge said, "I wish you luck."

Grange had his luck, but it was coming to him because he did more to popularize professional football than any other player before or since. In his first three years out of school he grossed almost $1,000,000 from football, motion pictures, vaudeville appearances and endorsements, and he could afford to turn down a Florida real estate firm that wanted to pay him $120,000 a year. Seven years ago the Associated Press, in selecting an All-Time All-American team in conjunction with the National Football Hall of Fame, polled one hundred leading sportswriters and Grange received more votes than any other player.

"They talk about the runs I made," he was saying, "but I can't tell you one thing I did on any run. That's the truth. During the depression, though, I took a licking. Finally I got into the insurance business. I almost starved to death for three years, but I never once tried to use my football reputation. I never once opened a University of Illinois year book and knowingly called on an alumnus. I think I was as good an insurance man as there was in Chicago. On the football field I had ten other men blocking for me, but I'm more proud of what I did in the insurance business, because I did it alone."

Recently I went down to Miami and visited Grange in the white colonial duplex house where he lives with his wife. They met eighteen years ago on a plane, flying between Chicago and Omaha, on which she was a stewardess, and they were married the following year.

"Without sounding like an amateur psychologist," I said, "I believe you derive more satisfaction from what you did in the insurance business, not only because you did it alone, but also because you know how you did it, and, if you had to, you could do it again. You could never find any security in what you did when you ran with a football because it was inspirational and creative, rather than calculated."

"Yes," Grange said, "you could call it that. The sportswriters used to try to explain it, and they used to ask me. I couldn't tell them anything."

I have read what many of those sportswriters wrote, and they had as much trouble trying to corner Grange on paper as his opponents had trying to tackle him on the field. . . .

Grange had blinding speed, amazing lateral mobility, and exceptional change of pace and a powerful straight-arm. He moved with high knee action, but seemed to glide, rather than run, and he was a master at using his blockers. What made him great, however, was his instinctive ability to size up a field and plot a run the way a great general can map not only a battle but a whole campaign.

"The sportswriters wrote that I had peripheral vision," Grange was saying. "I didn't even know what the word meant. I had to look it up. They asked me about my change of pace, and I didn't even know that I ran at different speeds. I had a cross-over step, but I couldn't spin. Some ball carriers can spin but if I ever tried that, I would have broken a leg."

Harold Edward Grange was born on June 13, 1903, in Forksville, Pennsylvania, the third of four children. His mother died when he was five, and his sister Norma died in her teens. The other sister, Mildred, lives in Binghamton, New York. His brother, Garland, two and a half years younger than Red, was a 165-pound freshman end at Illinois and was later with the Chicago Bears and is now a credit manager for a Florida department store chain. Their father died at the age of 86.

"My father," Grange said, "was the foreman of three lumber camps near Forksville, and if you had known him, you'd know why I could never get a swelled head. He stood six-one and weighed 210 pounds, and he was quick as a cat. He had three hundred men under him and he had to be able to lick any one of them. One day he had a fight that lasted four hours."

Grange's father, after the death of his wife, moved to Wheaton, Illinois, where he had relatives. Then he sent the two girls back to Pennsylvania to live with their maternal grandparents. With his sons, he moved into a five-room apartment over a store where they took turns cooking and keeping house.

"Can you recall," I said, "the first time you ever ran with a football?"

"I think it started," Grange said, "with a game we used to play without a football. Ten or twelve of us would line up in the street, along one curb. One guy would be in the middle of the road and the rest of us would run across the street to the curb on the other side. When the kid in the middle of the street tackled one of the runners, the one who was tackled had to stay in the middle of the street with the tackler. Finally, all of us, except one last runner, would be in the middle of the street. We only had about thirty yards to maneuver in and dodge the tackler. I got to be pretty good at that. Then somebody got a football and we played games with it on vacant lots."

In high school Grange won sixteen letters in football, basketball, track and baseball. In track he competed in the 100 and 220 yard dashes, low and high hurdles, broad jump and high jump and often won all six events. In his sophomore year on the football team, he scored 15 touch-downs, in his junior year 36—eight in one game—and in his senior year 23. Once he was kicked in the head and was incoherent for 48 hours.

"I went to Illinois," he was saying, "because some of my friends from Wheaton went there and all the kids in the state wanted to play football for Bob Zuppke and because there weren't any athletic scholarships in those days and that was the cheapest place for me to go to. In May of my senior year in high school I was there for the Interscholastic track meet, and I just got through broad jumping when Zup came over. He said, 'Is your name Grainche?' That's the way he always pronounced my name. I said, 'Yes.' He said, 'Where are you going to college?' I said, 'I don't know.' He put his arm around my shoulders and he said, 'I hope here. You may have a chance to make the team here.' That was the greatest moment I'd known."

That September, Grange arrived at Champaign with a battered second-hand trunk, one suit, a couple of pairs of trousers and a sweater. He had been working for four summers on an ice wagon in Wheaton and saving some money, and his one luxury now that he was entering college was to pledge Zeta Phi fraternity.

"One day," he was saying, "they lined us pledges up in the living room of the fraternity house. I had wanted to go out for basketball and track—I thought there would be too much competition in football—but they started to point to each one of us and tell us what to go out for: 'You go out for cheerleader. You go out for football manager. You go out for the band.' When they came to me, they said, 'You go out for football.'

"That afternoon I went over to the gym. I looked out the window at the football practice field and they had about three hundred freshman candidates out there. I went back to the house and I said to one of the seniors, 'I can't go out for football. I'll never make that team.'

"So he lined me up near the wall, with my head down, and he hit me with this paddle. I could show you the dent in that wall where my head took a piece of plaster out—this big."

With the thumb and forefinger of his right hand, he made a circle the size of a half dollar.

"Do you remember the name of that senior?" I said.

"Johnny Hawks," Grange said. "He was from Goshen, Indiana, and I see him now and then. I say to him. 'Damn you. If it wasn't for you, I'd never have gone out for football.' He gets a great boot out of that."

"So what happened when you went out the next day?"

"We had all these athletes from Chicago I'd been reading about. What chance did I have, from a little farm town and a high school with three hundred students? I think they cut about forty that first night, but I happened to win the wind sprints and that got them at least to know my name."

It was a great freshman team. On it with Grange was Earl Britton, who blocked for Grange and did the kicking throughout their college careers, and Moon Baker and Frank Wickhorst, who transferred to Northwestern and Annapolis, respectively, where they both made All-American. After one week of practice, the freshman team played the varsity and were barely nosed out, 21–19, as Grange scored two touch-downs, one on a 60 yard punt return. From then on, the freshmen trimmed the varsity regularly and Zuppke began to give most of his time to the freshmen.

"That number 77," I said to Grange, "became the most famous number in football. Do you remember when you first got it?"

"It was just handed to me in my sophomore year," he said. "I guess anybody who has a number and does well with it gets a little superstitious about it, and I guess that began against Nebraska in my first varsity game."

That game started Grange to national fame. This was 1923, and the previous year Nebraska had beaten Notre Dame and they were to beat "The Four Horsemen" later this same season. In the first quarter Grange sprinted 35 yards for a touchdown. In the second quarter he ran 60 yards for another. In the third period he scored again on a 12 yard burst, and Illinois won, 24–7. The next day, over Walter Eckersall's story in the Chicago *Tribune*, the headline said: GRANGE SPRINTS TO FAME.

From the Nebraska game, Illinois went on to an undefeated season. Against Butler, Grange scored twice. Against Iowa, he scored the only touchdown as Illinois won, 9–6. In the first quarter against Northwestern, he intercepted a pass and ran 90 yards to score the first of his three touchdowns. He made the only touchdown in the game with the University of Chicago and the only one in the Ohio State game, this time on a 34 yard run.

"All Grange can do is run," Fielding Yost, the coach at Michigan, was quoted as saying.

"All Galli-Curci can do is sing," Zuppke said.

Grange had his greatest day in his first game against Michigan during his junior year. On that day Michigan came to the dedication of the new $1,700,000 Illinois Memorial Stadium. The Wolverines had been undefeated in twenty games and for months the nation's football fans had been waiting for this meeting. There were 67,000 spectators in the stands, then the largest crowd ever to see a football game in the Midwest.

Michigan kicked off. Grange was standing on his goal line, with Wally McIlwain, whom Zuppke was to call "the greatest open field blocker of all time" on his right, Harry Hall, the Illinois quarterback, on his left, and Earl Britton in front of him. Michigan attempted to aim the kickoff to McIlwain, but as the ball descended, Grange moved over under it.

"I've got it," he said to McIlwain.

He caught it on the 5 yard line. McIlwain turned and took out the first Michigan man to get near him. Britton cut down the next one, and Grange started underway. He ran to his left, reversed his field to avoid one would-be tackler, and, then, cutting back again to the left, ran diagonally across the field through the oncoming Michigan players. At the Michigan 40 yard line he was in the open and on the 20 yard line, Tod Rockwell, the Michigan safety man, made a futile dive for him. Grange scored standing up. Michigan never recovered.

In less than twelve minutes, Grange scored three more touchdowns on runs of 67, 56 and 44 yards. Zuppke took him out to rest him. In the third period, he re-entered the game, and circled right end for 15 yards and another touchdown. In the final quarter, he threw a pass for another score. Illinois won, 39–14. Against a powerful, seasoned and favored team, Grange had handled the ball twenty-one times, gained 402 yards running, scored five touchdowns and collaborated, as a passer, in a sixth.

"This was," Coach Amos Alonzo Stagg, the famous Chicago mentor, later wrote, "the most spectacular singlehanded performance ever made in a major game."

"Did Zuppke tell you that you should have scored another touchdown?" I asked Grange.

"That's right," Grange said. "After the fourth touchdown we called a time-out, and when Matt Bullock, our trainer, came with the water, I said to him, 'I'm dog tired. You'd better tell Zup to get me out of here.' When I got to the bench Zup said to me, You should have had five touchdowns. You didn't cut right on one play.' Nobody could get a swelled head around him."

"And you don't recall," I said, "one feint or cut that you made during any one of those runs?"

"I don't remember one thing I ever did on any run I made. I just remember one vision from that Michigan game. On that opening kickoff runback, as I got downfield I saw that the only man still in front of me was the safety man, Tod Rockwell. I remember thinking then, 'I'd better get by this guy, because after coming all this way, I'll sure look like a burn if he tackles me.' I can't tell you, though, how I did get by him."

When Grange started his senior year, Illinois had lost seven regulars by graduation and Harry Hall, its quarterback, who had a broken collarbone.

Zuppke shifted Grange to quarterback. Illinois lost to Nebraska, Iowa and Michigan and barely beat Butler before they came to Franklin Field in Philadelphia on October 31, 1925, to play Pennsylvania.

The previous year Penn had been considered the champion of the East. They had now beaten Brown, Yale and Chicago, among others. Although Grange's exploits in the Midwest had been widely reported in Eastern papers, most of the 65,000 spectators and the Eastern sportswriters—Grantland Rice, Damon Runyon and Ford Frick among them—came to be convinced.

It had rained and snowed for 24 hours, with only straw covering the field. At the kickoff, the players stood in mud. On the third play of the game, the first time he carried the ball, Grange went 55 yards for his first touchdown. On the next kickoff he ran 55 yards again, to the Penn 25 yard line, and Illinois worked it over the goal line from there. In the second period, Grange twisted 12 yards for another score and in the third period he ran 20 yards to a touchdown. Illinois won, 24–2, with Grange carrying the ball 363 yards, and scoring three touchdowns and setting up another one, in thirty-six rushes.

Two days later when the train carrying the Illinois team arrived in Champaign, there were 20,000 students, faculty members and towns-people waiting at the station. Grange tried to sneak out of the last car but he was recognized and carried two miles to his fraternity house.

"Do you remember your feelings during those two miles?" I asked him.

"I remember that I was embarrassed," he said. "You wish people would understand that it takes eleven men to make a football team. Unless they've played it, I guess they'll never understand it, but I've never been impressed by individual performances in football, my own or anyone else's."

"Do you remember the last touchdown you scored in college?"

"To tell you the truth, I don't," he said. "It must have been against Ohio State. I can't tell you the score. I can't tell you the score of more than three or four games I ever played in."

I looked it up. Grange's last college appearance, against Ohio State, attracted 85,500 spectators at Columbus. He was held to 153 yards on the ground but threw one touchdown pass as Illinois won, 14–9. The following afternoon, in the Morrison Hotel in Chicago, he signed with Charles C. (Cash and Carry) Pyle to play professional football with the Chicago Bears, starting immediately, and he quit college. Twenty-five years later, however, he was elected to the University of Illinois Board of Trustees for a six-year term.

"I had a half year to finish when I quit," he said. "I had this chance to make a lot of money and I couldn't figure where having a sheepskin would pull any more people into football games."

"How were your marks in college?"

"I was an average student. I got B's and C's. I flunked one course, economics, and I made that up in the summer at Wheaton College. I'd leave the ice wagon at 11 o'clock in the morning and come back to it at 1 o'clock. There was so much written about my job on the ice wagon, and so many pictures of me lugging ice, that people thought it was a publicity stunt. It wasn't. I did it for eight summers, starting at 5 o'clock every morning, for two reasons. The pay was good—$37.50 a week—and I needed money. I didn't even have any decent clothes until my junior year. Also, it kept me in shape. After carrying those blocks of ice up and down stairs six days a week, my legs were always in shape when the football season started. Too many football players have to play their legs into shape in the first four or five games."

Grange played professional football from 1925 through the 1934 season, first with the Bears, then with the New York Yankees in a rival pro league that Pyle and he started, and then back with the Bears again. He was immobilized during the 1928 season with arm and knee injuries, and after that he was never able to cut sharply while carrying the ball. He did, however, score 162 touchdowns as a professional and kicked 86 conversion points, for a total of 1,058 points.

What the statistics do not show, however, is what Grange, more than any other player, did to focus public attention and approval on the professional game. In 1925, when he signed with the Bears, professional football attracted little notice on the sports pages and few paying customers. There was so little interest that the National Professional Football League did not even hold a championship playoff at the end of the season.

In ten days after he left college Grange played five games as a pro and changed all that. After only three practice sessions with the Bears, he made his pro debut against the Chicago Cardinals on Thanksgiving Day, November 26. The game ended 0–0 but 36,000 people crowded into Wrigley Field to see Grange. Three days later, on a Sunday, 28,000 defied a snowstorm to watch him perform at the same field. On the next Wednesday, freezing weather in St. Louis held the attendance down to 8,000 but on Saturday 40,000 Philadelphians watched him in the rain at Shibe Park. The next day the Bears played in the Polo Grounds against the New York Giants.

It had been raining for almost a week, and, although advance sales were almost unknown in pro football in those days, the Giants sold almost 60,000 before Sunday dawned. It turned out to be a beautiful day. Cautious fans who had not bought seats in advance stormed the ticket booths. Thousands of people were turned away but 73,651 crammed into the park. Grange did not score but the Bears won, 19–7.

That was the beginning of professional football's rise to its present popularity. At the end of those first ten days, Grange picked up a check for $50,000. He got another $50,000 when the season ended a month later.

"Can you remember," I asked him now, "the last time you ever carried a football?"

"It was in a game against the Giants in Gilmore Stadium in Hollywood in January of 1935. It was the last period, and we had a safe lead and I was sitting on the bench. George Halas said to me, 'Would you like to go in, Red?' I said, 'No, thanks.' Everybody knew this was my last year. He said, 'Go ahead. Why don't you run it just once more?'

"So I went in, and we lined up and they called a play for me. As soon as I got the ball and started to go I knew that they had it framed with the Giants to let me run. The line just opened up for me and I went through and started down the field. The farther I ran, the heavier my legs got and the farther those goal posts seemed to move away. I was thinking, 'When I make that end zone, I'm going to take off these shoes and shoulder pads for the last time.' With that something hit me from behind and down I went on about the 10 yard line. It was Cecil Irvin, a 230-pound tackle. He was so slow that, I guess, they never bothered to let him in on the plan. But when he caught me from behind, I knew I was finished."

Grange, who is 5 feet 11 and [fr3/4] inches, weighed 180 in college and 185 in his last game with the Bears. Now he weighs 200. On December 15, 1951, he suffered a heart attack. This motivated him to give up his insurance business and to move to Florida where he and his wife own, in addition to their own home in Miami, land in Orlando and Melbourne and property at Indian Lake.

"Red," I said, "I'll bet there are some men still around whose greatest claim to fame is that they played football with you or against you. I imagine there are guys whose proudest boast is that they once tackled you. Have you ever run into a guy who thought he knew everything about football and didn't know he was talking with Red Grange?"

"Yes," he said. "Once about fifteen years ago, on my way home from work, I dropped into a tavern in Chicago for a beer. Two guys next to me and the bartender were arguing about Bronco Nagurski and Carl Brumbaugh. On the Bears, of course, I played in the backfield with both of them. One guy doesn't like Nagurski and he's talking against him. I happen to think

Nagurski was the greatest football player I ever saw, and a wonderful guy. This fellow who is knocking him says to me, 'Do you know anything about football? Did you ever see Nagurski play?' I said, 'Yes, and I think he was great.' The guy gets mad and says, 'What was so great about him? What do you know about it?' I could see it was time to leave, but the guy kept at me. He said, 'Now wait a minute. What makes you think you know something about it? Who are you, anyway?' I reached into my wallet and took out my business card and handed it to him and started for the door. When I got to the door, I looked back at him. You should have seen his face."

Mrs. Grange, who had been listening to our talk, left the room and came back with a small, gold-plated medal that Grange had won in the broad jump at the Interscholastic track meet on the day when he first met Zuppke.

"A friend of mine just sent that to me," Grange said. "He wrote: 'You gave me this away back in 1921. I thought you might want it.' Just the other day I got a letter from a man in the Midwest who told me that his son just found a gold football inscribed, 'University of Illinois, 1924' with the initials H. G. on it. I was the only H. G. on that squad so it must have been mine. I guess I gave it to somebody and he lost it. I wrote the man back and said: 'If your son would like it, I'd be happy to have him keep it.'"

Mrs. Grange said, "We have a friend who can't understand why Red doesn't keep his souvenirs. He has his trophies in another friend's storage locker in Chicago. The clipping books are nailed up in a box in the garage here and Red hasn't looked at them in years."

"I don't like to look back," Grange said. "You have to look ahead."

I remembered that night when we ate in the restaurant in Syracuse. As we stood in line to get our hats and coats, Grange nudged me and showed me his hat check. In the middle of the yellow cardboard disk was the number 77.

"Has this ever happened to you before?" I said.

"Never," he said, "as far as I know."

We walked out into the cold night air. A few flakes of snow were falling.

"That jersey with the 77 on it that's preserved at Illinois," I said, "is that your last game jersey?"

"I don't know," Grange said. "It was probably a new jersey."

"Do you have any piece of equipment that you wore on the football field?"

"No," he said. "I don't have anything."

The traffic light changed, and we started across the street. "I don't even have an I-sweater," he said.

We walked about three paces.

"You know," Grange said, "I'd kind of like to have an I-sweater now."

Death of a Racehorse

from the *New York Sun*

They were going to the post for the sixth race at Jamaica, two year olds, some making their first starts, to go five and a half furlongs for a purse of four thousand dollars. They were moving slowly down the backstretch toward the gate, some of them cantering, others walking, and in the press box they had stopped their working or their kidding to watch, most of them interested in one horse.

"Air Lift," Jim Roach said. "Full brother of Assault."

Assault, who won the triple crown . . . making this one too, by Bold Venture, himself a Derby winner, out of Igual, herself by the great Equipoise. . . . Great names in the breeding line . . . and now the little guy making his first start, perhaps the start of another great career.

They were off well, although Air Lift was fifth. They were moving toward the first turn, and now Air Lift was fourth. They were going into the turn, and now Air Lift was starting to go, third perhaps, when suddenly he slowed, a horse stopping, and below in the stands you could hear a sudden cry, as the rest left him, still trying to run but limping, his jockey—Dave Gorman—half falling, half sliding off.

"He broke a leg!" somebody, holding binoculars to his eyes, shouted in the press box. "He broke a leg!"

Down below they were roaring for the rest, coming down the stretch now, but in the infield men were running toward the turn, running toward the colt and the boy standing beside him, alone. There was a station wagon moving around the track toward them, and then, in a moment, the big green van that they call the horse ambulance.

"Gorman was crying like a baby," one of them, coming out of the jockey room said. "He said he must have stepped in a hole, but you should have seen him crying."

"It's his left front ankle," Dr. J. G. Catlett, the veterinarian, was saying. "It's a compound fracture; and I'm waiting for confirmation from Mr. Hirsch to destroy him."

He was standing outside one of the stables beyond the backstretch, and he had just put in a call to Kentucky where Max Hirsch, the trainer, and Robert Kleberg, the owner, are attending the yearling sales.

"When will you do it?" one of them said.

"Right as soon as I can," the doctor said. "As soon as I get confirmation. If it was an ordinary horse I'd done it right there."

He walked across the road and around another barn to where they had the horse. The horse was still in the van, about twenty stable hands in dungarees and sweat-stained shirts, bare-headed or wearing old caps, standing around quietly and watching with Dr. M. A. Gilman, the assistant veterinarian.

"We might as well get him out of the van," Catlett said, "before we give him the novocaine. It'll be a little better out in the air."

The boy in the van with the colt led him out then, the colt limping, tossing his head a little, the blood running down and covering his left foreleg. When they saw him, standing there outside the van now, the boy holding him, they started talking softly.

"Full brother of Assault." . . . "It don't make no difference now. He's done." . . . "But damn, what a grand little horse." . . . "Ain't he a horse?"

"It's a funny thing," Catlett said. "All the cripples that go out, they never break a leg. It always happens to a good-legged horse."

A man, gray-haired and rather stout, wearing brown slacks and a blue shirt walked up.

"Then I better not send for the wagon yet?" the man said.

"No," Catlett said. "Of course, you might just as well. Max Hirsch may say no, but I doubt it."

"I don't know," the man said.

"There'd be time in the morning," Catlett said.

"But in this hot weather—" the man said.

They had sponged off the colt, after they had given him the shot to deaden the pain, and now he stood, feeding quietly from some hay they had placed at his feet. In the distance you could hear the roar of the crowd in the grandstand, but beyond it and above it you could hear thunder and see the occasional flash of lightning.

When Catlett came back the next time he was hurrying, nodding his head and waving his hands. Now the thunder was louder, the flashes of lightning brighter, and now rain was starting to fall.

"All right," he said, shouting to Gilman. "Max Hirsch talked to Mr. Kleberg. We've got the confirmation."

They moved the curious back, the rain falling faster now, and they moved the colt over close to a pile of loose bricks. Gilman had the halter and Catlett had the gun, shaped like a bell with the handle at the top. This bell he placed, the crowd silent, on the colt's forehead, just between the eyes. The colt stood still and then Catlett, with the hammer in his other hand, struck the handle of the bell. There was a short, sharp sound and the colt toppled onto his left side, his eyes staring, his legs straight out, the free legs quivering.

"Aw—" someone said.

That was all they said. They worked quickly, the two vets removing the broken bones as evidence for the insurance company, the crowd silently watching. Then the heavens opened, the rain pouring down, the lightning flashing, and they rushed for the cover of the stables, leaving alone on his side near the pile of bricks, the rain running off his hide, dead an hour and a quarter after his first start, Air Lift, son of Bold Venture, full brother of Assault.

Out of ten years of daily journalism, four of them covering sports, this is the sole piece that, I feel, deserves an afterlife, although I am not sure. Some months after the column ran, the editors of *Cosmopolitan* wrote to inform me that I had been chosen as one of "twelve leading American columnists," each of us invited to grant reprint rights to his "favorite column" as part of a new monthly feature. As the five hundred dollars they were to pay me for work already done was more than four times what my impecunious employers were rewarding me for a whole week's labor, this column went out in the return mail. When the reply came back no check fell out, the column rejected because they doubted "that women would understand it."

Vince Lombardi

"What's charisma?" he said, suddenly and looking up from his desk.

"What?" I said, stalling.

"You're the writer," he said. "I keep reading that I've got charisma. What the hell is it?"

"Relax," I said. "It's not a disease."

"Smart ass," he said.

He couldn't find it in his Webster's nor his thesaurus, where he searched regularly for the new to him that he hoped would be yet other tools in his obsessive attempt to shape all others into the best performers he could make them and they could be. Nor, fortunately, could Vince Lombardi find it when he looked in the mirror, for what looked back was the same compulsive perfectionist he had seen all his life, a man who inspired and moved people who knew him, or didn't, as none other in his profession but Knute Rockne a quarter century before.

There was, of course, his appearance, that which struck people first. He looked rock-solid, more a bear than a lion of a man, although his roar could rattle his environment and shake the nerves of any who didn't know that inside was a being as soft as one of those stuffed animals they named after the first Roosevelt.

"All right!" he was saying in the Green Bay Packer dressing room right after they had pulled an early season game out in the last thirty-three seconds. "That was a great team effort! It was. . . ."

The room had fallen absolutely silent, but he had stopped. He had to, because he was fighting to hold back the tears.

"Yeah, coach!" they were hollering, rescuing him. "Coach! Coach!"

What they knew about him, those who had stood up to the temper tantrums and the insults and so had come to know him, was that his intent was as pure and honest as his emotions. The gimmick play was no more a part of his game plans that it was of his life plan, and he went with his great-

est strength, which was the truth of his team and of himself as best he could
determine it.

"What each and every one of you must understand," he was telling them
in one of those opening orations at the first team meeting the evening before
summer training, "is that, as talented individuals, you have an absolute moral
responsibility to perfect those talents with which you have been gifted and
entrusted."

Here he was—he who a quarter century before started out teaching
physics, algebra and Latin and coaching football for $1,700 a year at St. Ce-
celia's Prep in Englewood, New Jersey—standing in front of yet another
class in yet another classroom. There they were—men, sports page celebrities, some of them heads of families, all of them previously pampered in one
way or another because of their physical prowess—wedged yet again into
those oak chairs with those writing arms, and they were being transfixed by a
lecture on moral responsibity.

"And I will tell you this!" he was saying, the voice rising, the right hand
cupped and beating the cadence at them, the eyes moving from one to another and boring into them. "And I will promise you this! With every fiber
in my body I will try . . . and try . . . and try . . . in every way I know . . . to
make each and every one of you . . . the very best football player . . . he . . .
can . . . be!"

"I don't care how many of those opening speeches I listened to," Bart
Stsrr, his quarterback, would say, and he listened to nine. "Every time I
heard one I could feel the hairs standing up again on the back of my neck."

That promise he made in meeting, on the practice field became a reality
painful even to observe. He pushed them harder than anyone else ever had.
He ranted at them and ran at them screaming. One of them, who towered
over him and who, he later said, could have driven him into the ground like a
stake, he pummeled with his fists.

"Everybody pushes him around," he told me later, "and he smiles. If I
could just get him angry once I might be able to prove to him what kind of
football player, with his physical capabilities, he could be."

I think he saw it as at least a minor sin against the Maker he worshipped
daily at Mass when they did not dedicate themselves to th e perfection of
those gifts He had given them. Thus it was his duty to lead them, or to drive
them, to that purpose, and each one he led, or drove, as he did no other for
he was acutely sensitive to their individual needs, to what would stimulate
one and stop another.

"Communication," he said. "If you put all the coaches in the National
Football League in the same room and gave them the same questions: how

to defeat the 4–3, the 5–1, the Zone—you'd get the same answers. The difference is in how they organize—and communicate."

"And when Vin gets one he thinks can be a real good ballplayer," Marie, his wife, would tell me, "I feel sorry for that boy. Vin will just open a hole in that boy's head and pour everything he knows into it, and there's no way out. I just don't want to watch it."

"And you'd like to give all your time to that one," he said, when I put it to him, "but you can't because of all of the time you have to give to your weakest one. A team is like a chain, no stronger than its weakest member."

Out of all those disparate members, then, with their separate strengths and weaknesses, he built units that were so true to the principles of the game and so tuned in execution that he and they could call their shots. His contemporaries, half in disgust but half in admiration, used to complain that, game after game, season after season, he showed them exactly what he was going to do to them, and then, so near perfect was the execution, that they couldn't stop him from doing it.

"I guess I got it from my father," he said. "He was a perfectionist. Around the house, when I was a kid, if we were doing any repairs—pouring a new cement floor or whatever—you had to do it his way and do it absolutely right, or he'd take your head off."

His father, born in Italy, became a moderately successful butcher in the New World. From the Old World, like so many before and with him in the history of this country, he brought those principles that perhaps it takes at least some degree of poverty, or the fear of it, to appreciate and to stoke what Vince Lombardi used to call "that fire on Sunday."

Now, a quarter century after his death, in a country where profit-taking persists as the dominant drive, he survives as a symbol of that other, Old World, old-fashioned way. He proved that perfectionism and pride in product will win in the end—and may even get a man accused of having charisma.

G.I. Lew

from *Argosy*

There is a major general named Robert N. Young. He had the 2nd Infantry Division in Korea, and now he is commandant of the Infantry Center and the Infantry School at Fort Benning, Georgia. We were sitting in his office and he was just back from Korea and I think he felt a little out of place with the wall-to-wall carpeting and the air conditioning and the paneled walls.

"I brought two fine combat men back with me," he said. "I had places for a staff, but I didn't have a staff, so I picked two good combat sergeants. I brought back a sergeant named Adams and a sergeant named Jenkins."

"I know the sergeant named Jenkins," I said.

"He's a great combat soldier," the general said. "He's famous up and down the front."

I knew the sergeant named Jenkins, all right. It was one of those blue and pink evenings they were getting in that summer of 1944 off the Channel coast of France. We were tied up with a Coast Guard LST several hundred yards off the beach, and it was quiet and the air was soft and the water was almost flat and had in it those colors of the sky.

The Army had pushed inland and I was coming back from England, trying to get with the Army. I was sitting in my jeep among the other jeeps on the forward deck, reading, when I heard them talking off to the right.

"You want to know something?" the first one said, in the high voice of a kid.

"Sure," the second one said.

"You know who's on this tub tied up with us?"

"Sure," the second said. "Betty Grable."

"Lew Jenkins," the first one said. "He was the lightweight champion of the world."

"Why don't you—" the second one said.

I think this is the way to start telling you about Lew Jenkins, but I am not sure. Maybe I should tell you about the time he was in the peacetime Army in Japan and this big mess cook picked on him. He stood about six feet two and weighed about two hundred forty pounds and Lew stands five feet seven and goes to about a hundred forty-five now. Lew put his right hand in his back pocket and kept it there. He cut the big guy to ribbons and knocked him down a half-dozen times with left hooks before the big guy quit.

"But he wasn't a bad guy," Lew said. "After that he didn't bother us and he'd give us anything we wanted. He was an all right guy."

Anyway, I don't think anybody who ever became big in sports lived as wildly as this man and I don't know of anybody who ever came off the sports pages and stood up like this man in war. I want to tell you how they used to have to feed him whiskey from the water bottle to keep him from coming off a drunk in the middle of a round and falling on his face on the canvas, and I want to tell you how he won the Silver Star in Korea long after they made him a bum in the newspapers and long after I knew he would do it or die trying, if we ever had another war.

"Lew," I said to him, "how's the Coast Guard?"

All I had to do was step from our ship to his and there we were sitting on the deck in the natural beauty of that early summer of 1944. There was the quiet, with just the water lapping a little between the two ships, and the clean air and, all around us, the pastel colors.

"I guess it's all right," Lew said, in that Texas drawl. "But I don't like it."

"Why?"

"I don't want to knock the Coast Guard, or the Navy, either," he said, "but we don't fight."

There he was sitting on a deck housing with me, and he had on a pair of dirty blue jeans and a faded blue shirt and a dirty white cap stuck on the back of that wild bush of hair. There he was, a skinny little guy with the heavy brows of a fighter and those pale, sunken eyes and that sad face, and he had put the 1st Division ashore at Sicily and the 36th Division ashore at Salerno. He had put the British ashore behind the Japanese lines in Burma and the British ashore here in Normandy on D-Day. He had been up and down many beaches in the small boats, bombed and strafed and shelled, and with them getting killed all around him, and now he was telling me it wasn't fighting.

"Sure, the Coast Guard and the Navy been in there," he said, looking at me in that sad way. "We ain't always had it easy, but we take the Army in there and then we go away and leave 'em. It ain't the same as the Army."

"I know," I said.

"When I say the Army," he said, "I mean the soldier. I mean like the First Division. Before we took them in, I talked with them and when I talked with them I knew this was the greatest army in the world. Then I took them in and I seen them get killed, and you know what I'd do now if I had a house?"

"No," I said.

Of course, he didn't have a house. When he was a guy making $25,000 in one night fighting Henry Armstrong in the Polo Grounds, he had two houses. He had one in Sweetwater, Texas, where he came from, and one in Florida, but while he was running those LCVPs up on the beaches and his only home was a tired old LST, they sold him out of both houses.

"If I had a house," he said, "and a soldier didn't have a house, I'd give it to him. If I didn't, I'd be stealin', because he earned it. There ain't nothin' they shouldn't give a soldier if he's a soldier like in the First Division or the Thirty-sixth or one of them."

"I know what you mean," I said.

"I see sometimes that a landing was easy," he said. "Sometimes they say that a landing was easy, and I remember some soldier I saw get killed. I think about how, back home, some person is goin' to hear that this soldier got killed and that person is goin' to be just as miserable as if our whole Army got killed. I think about that a long time."

"I know," I said. "Many times I've thought the same thing."

"When they told us we were takin' the British in here," he said, "my heart wasn't in it. You know where my heart was?"

"No."

"My heart was with the First Division here. I wanted to be with them I knew. Then I saw the Limeys get killed and then I liked them, too."

"There's no difference between any of them, Lew," I said.

"You know what got to me?" Lew said.

"No."

"When I put the Thirty-sixth Division in at Salerno. That's the Texas Division and it was two or three in the mornin' and I put them on the beach and they were just mowin' them down. Just everybody was gettin' killed, and I'd walk up there to see who wanted to go back and they were just piled up.

"My mind and soul was with the soldiers on the beach, and they'd load me up with wounded and I'd go from ship to ship and the medics would say, 'Take 'em away. We can't handle any more here.' There'd be men with their legs blown off and there'd be men with their sides blown open, and they wouldn't say a word. There wasn't one of them let out a moan, and I hid my head in my hands and I cried.

"I never did go for cryin' as a kid or nothin'," Lew said, "but I wanted to go and fight with them and help them, but I was afraid if I did I'd get court-martialed. I felt so cheap. My own state's men were dyin', and I felt so ashamed bein' off the beach."

He just looked at me and I looked at him. We didn't say anything.

"I just prayed," Lew said. "I just prayed for another war to start, for me to be a front-line soldier."

I never forgot this. That's why I can give it to you now, word for word. I came back off the war and Lew came back and he was broke and took a few dinky fights up around New England. Then he went back to Texas, and every now and then I used to see in the agate fight results at the bottom of the sports pages that he was fighting out there.

Then one day in the winter of 1946 there were some of us out at Lee Oma's training camp at Teddy Gleason's at Greenwood Lake, New Jersey. Oma was getting ready to fight Gus Lesnevich in the Garden, and we were standing around there where the ring was set up next to the bar, waiting for Oma to work, when Al Buck came off the phone.

Al writes boxing for the New York *Post*. He had been talking to his office.

"Do you want a laugh?" he said.

"What?" I said.

"My desk just told me," he said. "Lew Jenkins has enlisted in the Army."

"Oh?" I said.

"What is it?" somebody else said. "Is he going for that bonus they get, or is it a gag?"

I didn't try to explain it to them. They all knew Lew and they all liked him, but there were some of them who had written when Lew was champion and Red Cochrane knocked him down five times in the Garden and Lew didn't fight a lick, that he was not only a disgrace to himself and the title he held, but to the whole fight game.

They didn't know that he had three broken vertebrae in his neck after piling his motorcycle into a traffic circle in Jersey, blind drunk at three o'clock one morning less than three weeks before the fight. They knew a lot about Lew and they put it in the papers, but they didn't know the half of it.

"Here were two youngsters," Cas Adams wrote in the New York *Herald Tribune* when Lew fought a hell of a draw in the Garden with Fritzie Zivic, who was the welterweight champ, "in perfect condition and with the sole idea of knocking the other fellow out."

Lew was in perfect condition all right. At 3 A.M. on the day of the fight he was drunk on Broadway with some guys from Texas and he'd been loaded every night for a week.

"You know something, Lew?" I said to him once. "They say in the fight game that Harry Greb was the greatest liver anybody ever saw. Even Greb couldn't have lived like you."

"People who knew Greb," Lew said, "say he was a junior compared to me."

He didn't say it as a boast. He never says anything as a boast, but just as a matter of fact, and always sadly. Lew can be very funny, but even when he comes up with a line that makes you laugh out loud there is only that little weak smile around his mouth and then it goes away and there is just that sad, puzzled expression, with those deep eyes trying to find an answer somewhere off in the distance.

Take the night he fought Joey Zodda outdoors in the Meadowbrook Bowl in Newark. In the third round he hit Zodda with that straight right and down went Zodda in his own corner. There he was, stretched out, but one of his seconds was thinking and he reached up with the smelling salts and made a pass with it under Zodda's nose.

Zodda got up, and when he did Lew got mad. He moved at him again, belted him another right hand, and knocked him halfway across the ring. When Zodda went down Lew didn't even look at him, but just turned and walked to his own corner.

"Willie," he said to Willie Ketchum, who trained him when Lew would train. "He can give him all the smellin' salts he wants now. The man's gone."

Well, Willie had to laugh. Lew didn't mean it for a laugh, but the sad way in which he said it made it a laugh. There is so much about people and about life that saddens Lew, because he was born into sadness.

"Nobody," he told me once, "really knows the poor people of Texas in my time."

The way he felt about the poor people of Texas is the way he feels about the poor guys of the infantry, and he came from one and he joined the other. In between he was a champion of the world and he made enough money for you and me to retire on. All of this and his title he threw away because he had no understanding of it and it meant nothing to him. All he understands is trouble.

"The poor old private," he was telling me once. "The only time he's first is when they say, 'Take that objective there.' I stand back with them at shows. I eat with privates. The noncoms eat together in a circle, but I eat with privates. I always wanted to be with the underdog. They hold up."

It was that way with Lew when he was a fighter. He made his greatest fights when nobody believed in him and his worst when he was the favorite. He was four to one underdog the night he won the title, because only then did fighting have some meaning.

I know, you see, that he didn't enlist for Korea to win a war or save a world, but just to be a part of that misery that is the private property of the front-line soldier. He became a great front-line soldier because he came into the world in misery and because, when he was making all that money and had a chance to rise above it, he felt like a stranger and was not at home in success and so he sought his level.

Lew was born on December 4, 1916, in Milburn, Texas. There were seven kids in the family, five of them girls, and Lew was the third born, with two girls ahead of him. His old man was a black-smith in Brownwood, and for a while he tried running a second-hand clothing store. He could never make a go of anything, and every time he tapped out he would load the family in an old covered wagon and hitch up the two old mules and they'd push off in hope but knowing that nothing would ever be any different.

"I come from a poor, ridiculous family," Lew once said to Jimmy Cannon, the sports columnist, and Jimmy said that tells all of it.

From Brownwood they went to Abilene and then back to Brown-wood. They hit Big Spring and then, in 1929, Sweetwater.

"Any little old house," Lew says, "cost five dollars a month rent, so we lived in tents. We used to live in tents on the side of Highway 80."

They would pick cotton, the whole family. They would go out in the fields at sunup and they would be out there at sundown. You could pick two hundred pounds a day and, when you got good at it, maybe three hundred, but in those days they were paying only thirty-five cents a hundred.

"We'd pick fourteen hours," Lew says, "and no ten-minute break or nothin'. We'd get to the end of a row and my Dad would say, 'Come on.' In cold weather your hands would chap and the burrs would prick 'em. That's the way it was with the poor people of Texas in my time."

When Lew was sixteen he started to fight in an alley. He never had an amateur fight in his life because there was a pie shop next to the alley and the wise guys would hang around the alley and match the Mexican kids. Lew would fight the Mexicans and the winner got a pie.

It was amazing the way Lew could punch with that straight right hand. It is one of those things you either have or you don't, and if you have it you were born with it. Lew was born with it, and he had it in the alley in Sweetwater and he had it in the Garden in New York.

"Jenkins looks about as much like a fighter as a Bohemian free-verse writer," Joe Williams wrote once in the New York *World-Telegram*. "A starved cannibal wouldn't take a second look at him. He has a hatchet face, a head of wild, stringy hair, and deep, sunken eyes that seem to be continuously startled. Where he gets his punching power is baffling."

They described him as a floor mop walking on its stick end. They said you had to go back to Willie Jackson and Richie Mitchell and Charley White and Benny Leonard to remember any lightweights who could punch like him, though.

It was that same year, when Lew was sixteen, that his father died and Lew met up with the T. J. Tidwell carnival. As part of the come-on they would pair kids off to box on the ballyhoo platform and Lew went up there and belted a couple of guys out. When the carnival came back to Sweetwater in 1934, Lew joined it.

The carnival moved through Texas and New Mexico and Oklahoma, and Lew would take on all comers. He would get 10 percent of what came in to see him fight and he'd fight three times a night and make, maybe, a buck and a half.

"They weren't fighters," he says, "but neither was I. I only weighed about a hundred and twenty pounds, and some of them were heavyweights."

The carnival folded in January 1936, and Lew went to pick cotton in Mesa, Arizona. He and a couple of buddies cleaned out an old chicken house and were living in that when he read in a newspaper that Jim Braddock, who was heavyweight champion of the world, was going to box Jack McCarthy, his sparring partner, in Phoenix.

"I never seen a champion or been close to one," Lew told his pals. "I'm gonna get me a fight on that card."

One of them went with him. They bummed into Phoenix and the promoter gave Lew one dollar in advance on the five dollars he was to get for boxing four rounds. The fight was a week off and Lew's buddy starved out and caught a freight, but Lew lived on oatmeal and water and fought the guy and licked him. He picked up the four dollars and bummed to Dallas and lived for a week on doughnuts and coffee.

"You could get doughnuts and coffee for a nickel," he says, "and after I licked the guy he told them I won because I had a big steak. I could have killed him, because I had to lay back between rounds because I was exhausted and the referee had to tell me I was winnin', to keep on. Why would that guy lie that I had a steak?"

"I don't know, Lew," I said. "I don't know why."

"But why would he lie?" Lew said.

After the fight in Dallas, Lew caught a freight for El Paso and he enlisted in the cavalry at Fort Bliss. This was in 1936 and he wasn't yet twenty, and he enlisted because he was hungry and tired of sleeping out.

"They think more of a horse in the cavalry," Lew used to say, "than they do of a man. Horses cost a lot of money, and they could get all the men they wanted for twenty-one dollars a month."

While he was in the cavalry, Lew used to fight pro at El Paso and Silver City. He weighed only 136 pounds, but he was the welterweight champion of Bliss, and when he had a sixty-day furlough coming up in 1938, he decided he wanted out.

"You know what I'd like to do?" he said one night.

He was sitting and talking in barracks with a friend of his. His friend's name was Al Humphrey and this was just before Lew's furlough.

"What?" Al said.

"I'd like to get out," Lew said, "and fight Armstrong and Ambers. I'd like to go over to Dallas now and get me some fights."

"I'll give you five bucks," Al said.

Lew never forgot that. He doesn't know what ever became of Al Humphrey, but, even with all the things that have happened to Lew, he never forgot that.

"He was just a private," Lew says, "and he let me have all the money he had."

It cost him four dollars to get to Dallas. The promoter there remembered him from the night two years before when he licked the guy who said Lew had a steak, so he started putting Lew in about every other week. Lew boxed ten fights there, came off pneumonia weighing a hundred thirteen pounds, and got four bucks for two fights with a carnival. He drifted to California, Chicago, and Mexico.

In Mexico City he picked up enough of a stake to get to New York. He got fifty bucks to box a Mexican and seventy-five to blow the duke to him. The next night he got another seventy-five to carry a guy in another town, and when he hit New York in July of 1939, he had eight bucks in his pocket.

When Lew came to New York he was sent to Frank Bachman. Frank is in the printing business now but was managing fighters then, and Frank took him up to Stillman's and introduced him to Willie Ketchum.

Willie looked at Lew and Lew didn't look like anything. He was skinny and undernourished and weighed 129 pounds and looked like he was ready to fall apart. Willie looks at hundreds of fighters, and this looked like just another one to him.

There was one thing Willie saw, though, when he put Lew in the ring. Lew had one good combination. He would paw a left in your face to bring your hands up, and then he'd throw that straight right hand into the body.

"You got the right punch for these fellas around here," Willie told Lew, "but I want you to do something."

"What?" Lew said.

"Forget the right hand," Willie said.

"That's my best punch," Lew said.

"Forget it," Willie said. "Jabs and left hooks. The left is the weapon. The right comes after it."

Willie worked on that with Lew, and Willie got to like him. Lew was a little worried about the big town, and Willie put in a lot of time with him because he felt sorry for him.

Lew must have been in town a couple of weeks when Bachman made him with Baby Breese, eight rounds in the Queensboro Arena. Breese was a tough Scandinavian out of Kansas, and he weighed about 138 to Lew's 129, and in the fourth round he cut Lew over the left eye.

"I'm tired," Lew said, when he came back to the corner. "I got enough."

"Wait a minute," Willie said. "There's nothing wrong with the eye, and I'm the guy who's gonna fix it. You can't do this here. This ain't Texas. They'll suspend you and you won't get paid."

Willie pushed Lew out and he finished good and won. He licked Joey Fontana and Breese again, and then he started to put together the seven straight kayoes that got him the Ambers fight and the title.

Every fight with Lew was a war, because he wasn't what you'd call a stylist and he was hungry and there was a lot of fire in him in those days. When he fought Primo Flores in the Bronx Coliseum, Flores had him down five times before he caught Flores coming in with a right hand. Lew came to in the shower that night, and Lester Bromberg of the New York *World-Telegram* had to tell him he won.

By now Hymie Caplan had moved in on Bachman. Hymie was a pasty-faced, blue-eyed, blond little guy, and he had Ben Jeby and Lou Salica and Solly Krieger, who held titles at one time or another. Hymie knew fighters, but he never knew Lew.

"Left jab!" Hymie was hollering from the corner the night Lew was fighting Mike Belloise in the Coliseum. "Right cross! Uppercut! Underneath!"

Willie took it as long as he could. Lew was getting licked, and finally Willie turned to Hymie.

"Leave him alone, will you, Hymie?" Willie said. "He can't grasp that. He ain't that kind of a fighter."

Hymie didn't say anything and now it was the end of the sixth round and Lew came back to the corner. Willie bent over him and looked at him.

"How do you feel?" he said.

"I'm tired," Lew said.

"Do me a favor," Willie said. "Throw a couple of punches. This guy is out."

Lew went out and threw a right hand under the heart, a right on the chin and another right under the heart. The fight was over.

After that Johnny Attell, who was making matches for the Garden then, went up to the little hotel Lew was living in and signed Lew to fight Billy Marquart in the Garden. When Hymie heard it he blew his top.

Marquart was out of Winnipeg, Canada, and he had just come off stretching Billy Beauhuld in five at the Garden. Jack Hurley had him, and he was one of those hands-down, walk-in hookers like all of Jack's fighters.

"Are you out of your mind?" Hymie screamed at Lew. "This guy is a murderous puncher. He'll kill you."

"I'll kill him," Lew said. "This is goin' to be a short trip. I'll knock this guy out so they'll have to let me fight for the title."

"You're crazy," Hymie said.

Hymie tried to break the match. They wouldn't let him out of it, and the night of the fight Marquart was nine to five over Lew.

"Never mind," Hymie said to Lew in the dressing room. "Don't worry if he knocks you out, because we'll start building you up all over again."

"Ain't this awful?" Lew said, turning to the others. "There ain't anybody here believes in me. I'm the lone man who believes."

Lew was a vicious man that night. The referee was Eddie Joseph, and once he had to pull Lew off Marquart while Marquart was through the ropes and going down. It ended in the third with Joseph holding Lew off with one hand and counting Marquart out with the other.

Then they made Lew in the Garden with Tippy Larkin. Larkin was a real good stand-up boxer with a beautiful left hand, and Angelo Pucci, who had him, figured Larkin could move around Lew and stab him and cut him up and tie him up inside.

"You know what I'm gonna do to that man tonight?" Lew said to Willie in the dressing room.

"What?" Willie said.

"I'm gonna knock him out," Lew said, "and pick him up by his legs and drag him to his corner."

"Listen," Willie said. "Don't get heated up. With this Larkin everything has to go his own smooth way. You go out there and you jab him."

"Jab him?" Lew said. "Why do I want to jab him? I want to knock him out."

"Jab him," Willie said, "because he won't be looking for it. He thinks he's gonna jab you."

"I think that's crazy," Lew said.

He walked out and he jabbed Larkin, though. He hit him three stiff jabs and Larkin didn't know what to do. He backed off and made a lunge at Lew and missed. Lew jabbed him again, and when he did Larkin was so surprised he just stopped to decide what to do. When he stopped, Lew threw that right hand, on a straight line from the shoulder, and it hit Larkin on the chin. Larkin stood still for a second and then he shuddered and, as he started to go, Lew hit him three more—a left, a right, and another left—and Larkin landed on his face underneath the ropes.

When the referee started the count, Willie started up the steps. All he was afraid of was that Lew would pick Larkin up by the feet and try to drag him to his corner.

"You know something?" Lew said, sitting on the rubbing table in the dressing room. "That man was the most convinced knocked-out man I ever knocked out."

The newspapermen, crowding around him, laughed. That was another of those times when he didn't mean it for a laugh, though, and when he said it as a kind of sad fact and in his sad way.

"Shucks," he said. "That Ambers doesn't figure to be tough for me, either. The fighters up in this country ain't so hot. They were better when I read about them in the Texas newspapers."

The Ambers fight was the last time Lew was ever in shape. Nobody could see him winning it because Ambers had fought all the good men and licked Fritzie Zivic and Tony Canzoneri and Henry Armstrong and, as it was, Lew almost walked out on the fight.

Lew was training at the Long Pond Inn on the New York end of Greenwood Lake. One day they announced he would work twelve rounds, and there were a half-dozen sportswriters from New York up to see him and watching him in that pine gym near the lake. Hymie was there too and when Lew started to work Hymie started to shout.

"Jab!" Hymie was hollering. "Cross! One-two! Turn 'em off!"

Willie could see what would happen, and he was standing across the ring and he was trying to flag Hymie down. Nobody could flag Hymie down, though, and at the end of the fourth round Lew jumped through the ropes, ripped off his headgear and gloves, and headed into the dressing room.

"What's the matter with him?" Hymie said to Willie.

"I told you," Willie said. "He don't like that stuff. With all these newspapermen here he thinks you're trying to show him up."

Hymie took the newspapermen down to the bar and conned them and then he sent them off. In a couple of minutes he ran up to Willie in Willie's room.

"Quick," he said. "He's puttin' his suitcases in his car and he's leavin'!"

When Willie ran out, there was Lew pulling out into the road in his black Ford. Willie ran to Hymie's car and he got in and he chased Lew until he caught him in Suffern, New York, which is about twenty-five miles from camp.

"What are you doing?" he said to Lew after he squeezed him off the road.

"I'm goin' back to Texas," Lew said.

"But you can't," Willie said. "You're fighting for the lightweight championship of the world."

"I don't care," Lew said. "I can knock this man out, so I don't care."

It took Willie a half hour to persuade Lew to come back. He told him about all the money he could make and about how much it would mean not only to Lew but to Willie, too, and finally Lew said he'd turn around if Hymie would stay away from him and if he could train in New York.

Hymie was with Lew, though, the night of the fight. Two hours before Lew climbed into the ring with Ambers for the biggest night he would ever know as a fighter, Hymie was showing him off in the restaurants around Broadway. Two hours before a fight a fighter lies down on a hotel bed somewhere and rests, so the sportswriters never will forget this guy walking around in an old rumpled suit and a flannel shirt, with his hair sticking up and that seamed, drawn, leathery face, shaking hands and smiling that small, sad smile when somebody asked him how he figured he would do with Ambers.

"You would have thought," Frankie Graham wrote in the New York *Journal-American* long afterwards, "he was going to fight some stumblebum in an out-of-the-way fight club, for all the tension he showed."

Ambers never had a chance. He was four to one over Lew, though, because they said Lew was strictly a long puncher and Ambers would fight him in close and Lew would never hit him. Even if he hit him, they said, nothing would happen because men like Jimmy McLarnin, Canzoneri, Armstrong, and Pedro Montanez hadn't been able to stop Ambers.

Ambers was on the floor before the fight was a minute old. In the second round he came back and started to take the lead when Lew dumped him with a left hook. Just as the bell sounded, Lew hit him a right on the chin and then he belted him two more before Billy Cavanaugh, the referee, could pull him off. In the third, Lew was on top of him and knocked him down for seven. Ambers got up groggy and Lew piled in and that was the end. Lew was the light-weight champion of the world.

"But how about hitting him after the bell at the end of the second round?" one of the newspapermen asked Lew in the dressing room with everybody milling around and the noise and the photographers taking pictures.

"I didn't hear any bell," Lew said.

When the cops finally cleared everybody out, Lew sat there on the rubbing table for a minute, not saying anything. Then he looked up at Willie.

"Willie," he said, "you know damn well I heard that bell."

"I know," Willie said.

"But when they start to go," Lew said in that sad way, "they got to go."

It was then that Lew started to live. He won the title on May 10, 1940, and two months later they put him into the Polo Grounds with Armstrong, a guy who once held the featherweight, light-weight, and welterweight titles at the same time, and one of the greatest little men who ever climbed into a ring.

Armstrong was still the welterweight champion with no title going in this one and they made him nine to five over Lew. If they knew Lew was up drinking until four o'clock every morning, he'd have been ninety to one and no takers.

Lew was down seven times in six rounds. Armstrong tried to finish him in the fifth and Lew cut him over both eyes and had Henry's legs wobbling when the round ended. In the sixth, Armstrong dropped Lew twice with hooks in the body and when the bell rang Hymie had to lead him back to his stool.

"I want air," Lew was saying.

Arthur Donovan walked over and looked at Lew sitting there, gasping. He took one look and walked out to the center of the ring and threw his hands out, palms down.

"How'm I doin'?" Lew kept asking in the dressing room. "What round did I get him in?"

"You didn't," Hymie said.

"You're crazy," Lew said, his eyes firing up. "I wasn't knocked out. I wasn't hurt."

"Donovan stopped it," Hymie said.

"You mean I couldn't get up?" Lew said, and he started rambling now. "Get me another fight. Get me another shot at him."

All of a sudden he stopped talking. He looked around at those looking at him. "Say, listen," he said to Henry McLemore, the newspaperman. "Where am I?"

On September 16, Lew fought Bob Montgomery over the weight in Shibe Park in Philadelphia. The fight was postponed once when one of Lew's sisters called him from Texas and told him their mother was dying.

Lew was sitting there in the bedroom looking at his mother, who didn't recognize anyone now, when he got a call telling him he had to come back and fight or he'd be suspended and fined.

Lew had a new convertible, with less than three thousand miles on it, and he and Eddie Carroll started back. Eddie was a tall, lean welterweight from Canada, and he and Lew took turns driving right around the clock.

In Sparta, Tennessee, Eddie was driving and Lew was asleep in the back seat when they went off the side of a mountain. The car rolled down the hill and wedged against a tree and Lew was thrown out.

"When I come to," he was telling me, "Eddie was pinned behind the motor and he was bleedin' and moanin'. There was this little old Brownie camera in the car, and I grabbed that and he was moanin' and I said to him, 'Wait a minute. Hold still. This'll make a hell of a picture.'"

If you want to understand Lew Jenkins, listen to this. This is Lew Jenkins.

"But there was something wrong with the camera," Lew said. "The camera wouldn't work, but wouldn't that make a hell of a picture?"

"Yes," I said, "It would."

Lew had a cut on the top of his head and one knee was cut and there was something wrong with his hip. The next day he took a secondhand automobile guy out to look at the car.

"Ain't that a wreck?" Lew said.

"It sure is," the guy said. "I'll give you two-fifty for it."

"Make it three hundred," Lew said, "and you can have the tree, too."

"O.K.," the guy said.

When Lew got to Philly, he ached all over, so he just figured there was no sense in trying to train. He and Willie had a suite in a good hotel where there is one of those businessmen's gyms in the basement, and Lew was supposed to train in the gym.

He tried to go two rounds in the gym, but he couldn't. Herman Taylor was promoting the fight, and he was going crazy. "He's a disgrace," he kept saying to Willie.

"I know," Willie would say. "What can I do?"

Willie was living in the big suite alone. Lew would be gone all night and they got a doctor to give him some treatments on the hip, but they could never find Lew.

The fight was on a Monday and the Friday afternoon before that Lew showed up, stewed. He flopped into bed and he slept until Saturday morning.

"I'll tell you what we'll do," he said to Willie when he woke up. "Let's go on the road."

Willie got a cab and they rode out to Fairmount Park. Lew got out of the cab and disappeared. He was gone for an hour and a half.

"Where is he?" the cab driver kept saying to Willie.

"I don't know," Willie said. "Maybe he fell in the lake."

After a while they saw Lew coming down the road. His arms and his legs were going, and he was flying. He got back in the cab and they went to the hotel. He had a meal, flopped into bed, and that afternoon he worked a couple of rounds in the gym. He had another meal and he slept until Sunday morning.

Sunday morning they went out to the park again, and he disappeared for another hour and a half. He ate, went back to bed, woke up at midnight, ate, and slept until it was almost time to go to the weigh-in.

"Man," he said when he got up and stretched, "I feel good."

"You must," Willie said, looking at him. "How good can you feel?"

With that Hymie came in from New York. He waited until Lew went into the bathroom.

"Willie," he said, "what shape is he in?"

"What shape can he be in?" Willie said. "He's lucky if he can climb up the three steps to the ring."

In the third round Lew was on the floor. He had just belted Montgomery a right in the belly and Montgomery had hit him a long right on the chin and there he was, face down on the canvas.

"Well," Willie said, turning to Hymie in the corner, "that's two in a row."

"But look!" Hymie said. "He's gettin' up."

Lew got up at nine, punching. He happened to hurt Montgomery with a right hand, and Montgomery went into his shell. While he was in the shell he kept walking to Lew, though. If he had just walked away, Lew had to fall on his face, the shape he was in.

"Lew," Willie said after the ninth round, "it's the last round. That guy just about got to his corner."

"I know," Lew said, gasping, "but I can't get off this stool."

Willie pushed him off. Halfway through the round he was bleeding from the mouth and nose, but he kept throwing punches and they wrote in the papers later that this was the most savage fight in Philly since Lew Tendler and Willie Jackson, fifteen years before.

"And at the end," Willie says, "the referee walks over and he lifts Lew's hands and he says, 'The winner, Lew Jenkins!' I just stood there and I said to myself, 'Did I see this thing? Can it be true, with his hip and his knee and the way he's living?'"

"How could I do that?" Lew was asking me. "How could I even stand up for ten rounds in those fights with good men the shape I was in?"

"I don't know, Lew," I said. "Don't ask me."

After the fight, Lew went back to Sweetwater and the day he got there his mother died. He bought a new Caddy in Dallas and he drove back to New

York. Then he put the Caddy in a parking lot and took a plane to Miami. He was walking along the streets in Miami when he happened to look in a window and he saw a half-dozen new motorcycles.

"How do you turn one of these things on?" he asked the guy in the store. "And how do you turn it off?"

The guy showed him and Lew asked the price and the guy said five hundred dollars. Lew paid him, and the guy fixed up the license. Lew took the motorcycle out on the street, ran it once around the block and took off for New York.

"Man," he was telling me, "you fall off a motorcycle about ten times goin' sixty miles a hour and it raises hell with your insides. I was near shook to death by the time I got to New York."

They matched Lew to defend his title against Pete Lello in the Garden on November 22, 1940. Lello was out of Gary, Indiana, and they called him "The Gary Gunner." Lew was supposed to be training at Pompton Lakes, New Jersey. He trained there for a number of fights after that, if you want to call it training, and it was always the same deal.

"He'd disappear," Allie Stolz was saying once, "and he'd be gone three or four days. Then he'd call me up and he'd say, 'Where have you been?' I'd say, 'Me? Where have *you* been?' He'd say, 'Don't go away. I'll be right out.' Sometimes he'd come out that day. Sometimes it would be another three or four days."

Allie Stolz was a real good lightweight. He was telling Frankie Graham and a few of us about it one time up in the Garden.

"After a while he had three motorcycles," Allie said. "He had one for straight speeding and one for hill climbing, and one that, so help me, ran in curves and circles. One day he was missing from camp and just about when it was time for him to box we heard a terrific clatter out on the road that runs past the camp, and there he was at the head of about fifty guys on motorcycles, waving to us as they roared past."

Lew also had a guitar and a phonograph and a stack of cowboy records. He'd play them over and over again, and then take the guitar and strum it and sing songs.

"Don't I sound like him?" he'd say.

"No," Allie would say.

Then he'd write a couple of songs a day. No matter what the words were, though, the tune was always the same.

"Listen to this one," he'd say, and he'd start out strumming and singing.

"I heard that one yesterday," Allie would say.

"No you didn't," Lew would say. "I just wrote it. I hear fellas get a lot of money for writing songs. I'm gonna write some more and sell them and make a lot of money."

One night Allie went with Lew to some roadside joint around Pompton. Just before they got to the place, Lew took a wad of bills out of his pocket, and this will show you how much he needed to make more money writing songs.

"I got five hundred," he said to Allie, handing him some bills. "Here. You take this two-fifty and keep it for me. I don't wanta spend it all tonight."

They walked into the joint and there were a lot of people there and everybody knew Lew. Everybody was saying hello to him and calling him "Champ" and he was buying everybody a drink.

"See what those people over there will have," he would say to the waiter, and then guys started to come up to touch him for a saw-buck or two.

"Say, Allie," Lew said after a while. "Give me that money I gave you."

"Nope," Allie said. "You gave it to me to keep for you and that's what I'm gonna do."

"Give me that money," Lew said. "It's mine, and you got no right to keep it."

"Drop dead," Allie said.

Lew kept after him, though. He kept arguing with Allie, and he put on such a hurt that finally Allie gave him the other two-fifty.

The next morning the two of them got up in camp, and Lew went through his pockets. He didn't have a dime.

"Did you give me that money back last night?" he said to Allie.

"Yep," Allie said.

"What did I do with it?" Lew said.

"You spent it."

"You—," Lew said. "What did you give it to me for?"

At the weigh-in for the Lello fight, Lew did a funny thing. He asked Lello for an autographed picture, and Lello gave him one. This was the first time anybody ever heard of a fighter, especially a champion, asking the other fighter for an autographed picture, but Lew is a lot like a small boy.

The afternoon of the Lello fight the cops picked up Hymie. Hymie was one of five they grabbed and Bill O'Dwyer was King's County DA then, before he became Mayor of New York and Ambassador to Mexico, and he described it as a $4,000,000 marked-card swindle.

There was a real-estate dealer who was taken for $150,000 and a Park Avenue doctor for $18,000. Two manufacturers from Philly had lost $40,000 and $25,000 apiece and some jeweler went for $75,000 and some yarn manu-facturer for $100,000. There were thirty-eight other businessmen who said they lost $700,000 in two years, and the cops said Hymie was the godfather and had been putting up the dough for the expensive establishments.

Hymie went to Sing Sing for it, but it was always around town that he took the rap for somebody else. When he was dying of cancer about three years ago, I went over to see him in the hospital in Brooklyn, and I wanted to ask him then about it, but I never did.

"I'll get him off," Lew said, when he heard they had Hymie.

They were holding Hymie in a Brooklyn hotel, and when Lew got on the phone with the dicks he knew he wasn't going to get Hymie off. He pleaded with them just to bring Hymie to the fight, so he could see it, and when they wouldn't do that he asked them to put Hymie on the phone.

"Listen, Hymie," he told him on the phone, "When you hear the building shake, that's Lello hittin' the floor."

He hit the floor, too. In the second round they were coming out of a clinch and Lew threw a hook and Lello started down. Lew was mad about Hymie, and he was right on top of Lello and he chopped a right into him as he was going. Lello rolled over on the canvas and got up at nine. The crowd was roaring now and Arthur Donovan moved in to wipe Lello's gloves, but as he lifted them Lew belted Lello a right and down he went again. Donovan waved Lew back and he picked up Lello to give him a breather, and Lew hit Lello another right and another left and dumped him for eight. When he got up, Lew knocked him down again with another right for nine. He staggered toward Lew and Lew hit him with a straight right and a hook and Lello went to his knees in Lew's corner and Donovan caught him as he was about to pitch forward on his face and stopped it.

"Did you miss Hymie?" one of the newspapermen asked Lew later.

"I missed Hymie," Lew said, with that sad, faraway look in his eyes, "but I didn't miss Lello."

"Against Lello, Jenkins looked like a great champion," Dan Parker wrote in the New York *Daily Mirror.* "Certainly no light-weight within the mem-ory of this present generation of fans could hit like this bag of bones."

Fritzie Zivic had just won the welterweight title from Armstrong, and so they put Lew and Fritzie together in the Garden on December 20. This fig-ured to be a tough fight for Lew, even if he bothered to get in shape, because Fritzie knew everything there was to know about handling himself in a ring, and Sugar Ray Robinson told me once that he learned more fighting Fritzie than he ever learned fighting any other man.

The fight was on a Friday night, and the Saturday before that Lew and Willie were coming out of a movie in Pompton late in the afternoon. Lew had on his old roadwork clothes, and it was cold and there was ice on the ground.

"Willie," he said, "I wanna see somebody in this little bar down here."

"Please," Willie said. "Why do you want to see somebody?"

"I just want to see him," Lew said.

They went into the bar and Lew had a beer. Then the bartender bought him one back. Lew said the guy wasn't there, so they went to another bar. He bought and the bartender bought. They drove over to Paterson to the New York Bar and he had five or six more. At midnight they were in the Top Hat in Jersey City, where somebody loaned Lew a jacket and tie so he could get in, and at 4 A.M. the place closed down so Lew was standing outside gabbing with a ring of guys.

Willie was standing there, too, but he got tired of waiting. He went across the street to get the car and turn it around, and when he got back Lew had gone. He didn't show up again until the next Monday night, and then he decided to finish training in New York.

Every night he was out until 2 or 3 A.M., and Willie could never find him. On the morning of the fight he left him at three o'clock on Broadway, and at ten-thirty Willie was in the lobby of the hotel waiting for Lew to go to the weigh-in, but there wasn't any Lew.

"You waiting for Lew Jenkins?" a bellhop said to Willie finally, about eleven.

"Sure," Willie said.

"He's gone an hour and a half ago," the bellhop said.

"Are you kidding?" Willie said.

"No," the bellhop said. "I saw him go out with a pair of ice skates."

Willie went down to the boxing commission and tried to stall them. Zivic was there waiting and so were the newspapermen, and when Lew finally walked in at one o'clock, General John J. Phelan, who was the boxing commissioner then, was ready to fall out of his shoes.

"I got lost in the subway," Lew said.

Lew was never any good with a lie, though. It seemed like he always had to get it off his chest.

"You know, Willie," he said, when they were alone later, "I didn't get lost in no subway."

"I know," Willie said.

"I went ice skatin'," Lew said.

"Why?" Willie said. "Why on the day of a fight?"

"Well," Lew said, "somebody told me it's good for your legs."

After the weigh-in they went to eat, and they went up to the suite in the Astor. Lew took a cigarette—he always smoked three or four in the dressing room before he got into the ring—and he just sort of fell back on the bed with his hat and his coat and his shoes on, and he went to sleep.

Willie took the cigarette out of his hand, and there must have been twenty guys in the room, smoking cigars and hollering to be heard. Every now and then the phone would ring, but nothing bothered Lew until seven o'clock when Willie woke him.

"Man, I feel good," he said, stretching, and that was the night he and Zivic fought that great draw and Cas Adams wrote about the two finely conditioned young athletes. How would he know?

It was after they made Lew with Ambers again over-the-weight that he and Al Dunbar, a welterweight, were in the auto wreck. Early one morning they hit that bridge going into Paterson on Route 4.

"He's been in an auto accident," Mike Jacobs said, calling Willie on the phone and getting him out of bed. "They think he's dead."

He didn't have a scratch on him, but that same day he was back in New York and riding a cab. The cab hit the back of another car, and Lew pitched forward and came up with a bad knee.

"You see," he said to Willie. "I smash that car to pieces and nobody would think I'd come out of it alive. Now I'm ridin' in a cab and mindin' my own business and I hurt my knee. It don't pay you to mind your own business."

Two weeks before the Ambers fight he got the grippe. For seven days he was running a fever and in bed, but Willie always said it won him the fight.

"This is one guy," Willie said, "that the grippe helped. He rested or seven days."

When they came in from Pompton for the weigh-in it was snowing. About two o'clock in the afternoon they were sitting in Lindy's and Lew had had his big meal.

"Willie," he said, "I got to deliver some tickets."

"Lew, it's bad weather," Willie said. "Let me deliver them."

"No," Lew said, shaking his head. "These are personal friends, and I got to deliver them myself."

Off he went, and Willie went to the suite in the Astor to wait. At eight o'clock they were supposed to be in the Garden, and at eight-fifteen Lew came in.

"Whatta ya know?" he said, with a big smile on his face.

"Oh-oh," Willie said. "You're drunk."

"Willie," Lew said, "I like you. You're a man."

The blizzard had closed down all the cabs, so they walked the eight blocks to the Garden through deep snow. They had to sneak him into the room, and then send out for mouthwash to get rid of the smell of drink in case General Phelan should drop in to see him.

In the first round he had Ambers on the ropes and he had Ambers out. Arthur Donovan broke them and Lew pinned Ambers again and twice more Donovan broke them.

"Man," Lew said, when he came back to the corner, "that man ain't lettin' me knock him out. He's disturbin' me. I'll hit that man."

"Please, Lew," Willie said. "Don't."

It took him four rounds to sweat the drink out, and in the sixth he had Ambers going and in the seventh he finished him. He was a great finisher, and he must have hit Ambers thirty punches, and that was the night Al Weill retired Ambers.

"Willie," Lew said in the dressing room, "how come I didn't knock him out as quick as I did the last time?"

"I don't know," Willie said, looking at him amazed. "I can't imagine."

The story they like to tell about Lew, though, has to do with the second Montgomery fight. After knocking out Ambers again Lew was still a big draw, and when Jacobs made Lew and Montgomery for a return in the Garden there was a pretty good gate involved.

Mike had his office in the Brill Building then, on Broadway just south of 50th Street. It was a couple of days before the fight that Mike was coming out of the building to have lunch across the street at Lindy's when he heard this motorcycle roaring through the traffic. He was standing on the curb now, and he looked up and there was Lew on his cycle swinging into Broadway from 50th.

"Hey, Mike!" Lew hollered. "Look! No hands!"

Montgomery gave Lew an awful cuffing around, and after it was over they had to put twenty stitches over Lew's eyes and across his nose. A little thing like being stitched up never bothered Lew, though. In September of 1941 he was in Minneapolis to fight Cleo McNeil, and he had an abscess in his throat. He had trouble swallowing and couldn't eat, so Willie took him to a doctor. The doctor lanced the infection and Lew just swallowed.

"That's fine," he said. "I'm hungry."

Lew knocked McNeil out in the third round. He hit him so hard that the punch ripped McNeil's cheek and upper lip open like it had been done with a knife.

"That guy had something in his glove," McNeil said when he came to his corner.

"Sure," one of his seconds said. "His fist was in there."

Lew was to fight Cochrane in the Garden three weeks later, and he had driven his car to Minneapolis. Willie didn't want him bouncing back in the car so he drove the car back and he sent Lew back by train. Willie drove to Pittsburgh to see Harry Bobo fight Bill Poland, and that morning he turned on the radio in his hotel room to listen to the news while he was shaving.

"Lew Jenkins," he heard the man say, "the lightweight champion of the world, is in critical condition in a New Jersey hospital as the result of a motorcycle crash."

At that time Benny Goodman was playing at Frank Daley's Meadowbrook in Jersey, and Peggy Lee was singing with the band. Lew used to ride his cycle out there from Pompton Lakes, and he'd sit in the back with the band after they came off the stand and he'd drink. About three o'clock in the morning he got on his cycle to find an all-night spot, and he hit a traffic circle.

Lew woke up eight hours later in a hospital. He was so bad they had already put down the dough to hold the room for a week, and they had his arms and back and neck taped. Two hours after he came to, he had them carry him back to camp, and he stripped all the bandages off.

"I had to train," he told me, "but I couldn't even wash my own face."

After the Cochrane fight, when Red knocked him down five times and Lew couldn't figure it out, they discovered the broken vertebrae in a clinic in Fort Worth. They put a cast on, and Lew went out the back door while the newspapermen were waiting at the front door because he was matched to defend his title against Sammy Angott in the Garden in a month.

When Lew got out of the place he took the cast off. He never told Willie what was wrong with him, but Willie could see he had nothing and Angott won fourteen out of the fifteen rounds. Nineteen months after he had won the lightweight title, Lew had lost it. Adding the Cochrane and Angott fights, Lew lost nine in a row and eleven out of twelve before he enlisted in the Coast Guard in 1943.

One night he woke up in the waiting room of the railroad station in St. Louis with two cops beating on his skull with billies. He was drunk, and it cost him ten dollars to get out of the can and get to Pittsburgh where Zivic stopped him in ten rounds.

He was in New Orleans on the night of August 17, 1942, to fight Cosby Linson. The fight was in Victory Arena, outdoors, and Lew walked up to the gate and showed his ticket.

"You can't go through here, Mac," the guy on the gate said. "Fighters go around the side."

"But I'm fightin' the main event," Lew said, "and I just saw the guy I'm fightin' go through here."

"I don't know nothin' about that," the guy at the gate said. "All I know is, you gotta go around the side."

What Lew said I won't repeat. He went down the street and into a bar and he started loading up. There couldn't be any fight without him, so in about an hour they came looking for him. Linson licked him, but he made them take him through the front gate.

Ten days later he was in Detroit to fight Carmen Notch. At 4 A.M. on the day of the fight he was blind drunk in the hotel lobby with his bags packed and hollering that he was going home. They had to get him a bottle to keep him in his room, and that was one of the times when they had to give him whiskey between rounds for fear he'd sober up. He got licked, but he made one of his greatest fights that night.

The next month he fought Al Tribuani in Wilmington, Delaware. The week of the fight he was drunk on Broadway, and he got into a bar fight with a couple of sailors. He grabbed a glass and cut his left hand across the palm, and it took thirteen stitches to close it.

"This will heal all right," the doctor told him, "but I've got bad news for you."

"What?" Lew said.

"You'll never be able to close the index finger of that hand."

"Then how can I punch?" Lew said. "How can I make a fist?"

"I don't know," the doctor said. "I'm afraid you can't."

Lew and Willie walked out of the doctor's office together. Lew didn't say anything for a while.

"Don't worry, Willie," he said, suddenly, "I know what we'll do."

"What?" Willie said.

"We'll cut it off, and we'll make it even with the knuckles."

"You're out of your mind, Lew," Willie said. "Don't even talk about it."

"But you have to, Willie," Lew said. "Please, Willie. You got to cut it off."

"All right," Willie told him. "I'll cut it off."

Lew was up at Stillman's and he was training with one hand. They got another doctor to take the stitches out, and the cut reopened. They bandaged it up and Willie sent Lew and a sparring partner to Wilmington with Artie Rose, the second. At midnight Artie called Willie at his apartment in New York.

"You got to come out here quick, Willie," Artie said. "They're drunk and they're breaking up the town."

"I thought you were gonna keep an eye on him," Willie said.

"I did," Artie said, "but they went into the diner on the train and when they came back they were drunk."

"Forget it," Willie said. "There's nothing you can do. Go back to sleep."

Lew and his sparring partner had had a bottle of gin apiece on them when they went in to eat. Lew was still rummed up when Willie got to Wilmington the next day, and he was just starting to come out of it in the dressing room.

"Get me in there," he kept saying. "I'm gonna die."

Willie sent Artie out to get him a bottle of whiskey. Then it came time to bandage Lew's hands.

"Now we got to face it," Willie said. "I can't bandage you, Lew, with this stiff finger."

"Give it to me," Lew said. "I'll fix it."

He walked up to the wall with his finger sticking out straight. He put it against the wall and he pressed it and Willie says he couldn't watch it. Willie says he felt himself getting sick, but Lew pressed until he closed the finger and he's been closing it ever since.

"You see?" he said. "There it is."

Willie bandaged him, and he put a sponge in the left glove to keep the blood from the cut from running down Lew's arm as Lew punched and the cut opened. As they were about to leave the dressing room Lew was good and high with the whiskey, and he hit the door with his right fist and Willie says he split it just like it had been hit with an axe.

"I'm ready," he said.

Of course he wasn't ready. Tribuani didn't discover this, though, until the third round, and from then on he knocked Lew down six times in the next seven rounds. The crowd was booing and calling Lew a bum, and when Lew and Willie got back to the dressing room Willie called it quits.

"Lew, you got to quit," Willie was saying, and the tears were coming into his eyes and starting down his cheeks. "If you don't quit I'm through, anyway. I can't stand it to see a great fighter like you gettin' licked by guys like this. I can't stand it."

Well, that was Lew's fighting career. He had forty fights after that, between wars, but they were little fights and didn't mean anything because he was done. Then I met him that beautiful evening off Normandy. In war he had finally found a meaning in living, and then I lost him again to hear, out at Oma's camp, that he had reenlisted.

"You remember," he was telling me, "how they were all saying in '46 that we were gonna fight the Russians? I read all that in the papers and I went right to Baltimore to enlist and I told them I wanted to be in it."

At the time they were hoping to throw Lew in with Charlie Fusari in Jersey City. Charlie is a Jersey boy and was going good then, and they were talking about giving Lew six thousand dollars, with it being sure that Charlie would belt him out.

"I got a chance to make this six thousand," Lew told the colonel at the enlistment center. "If I sign up now, can I get off to make that fight?"

"No," the colonel said. "I'm afraid you can't. When you're in the Army, you're in. Why don't you fight that fight and get the six thousand, and then come back and enlist?"

"No," Lew said. "I'm afraid if I wait I might talk myself out of it. You better give me that paper. I'll sign it now."

He signed it, but no war came. At the end of 1948 he was discharged after two years in Japan. He fought around Philly, training by playing the guitar in Big Bill's nightclub and singing songs like "I'm a Plain Old Country Boy" and "Take an Old Cold 'Tater (and Wait)." Then came the invasion of South Korea, and Lew stood up to what he told me about praying for another war.

"There's nobody can know what it's like," he was telling me right after the general brought him back. "There's nobody but the front-line soldier knows, with the shellin' and the woundin' and goin' without food and bein' so tired that you want to die. The poor front-line soldier, he knows, but nobody knows if they ain't been there."

Lew arrived in Pusan on July 2, 1951, when the 2nd Infantry was in reserve. On the 15th they went into the line to relieve the Marines around the reservoir near Bloody Ridge and Heartbreak Ridge, and they held there until August 8th when they attacked Hill 772.

Lew was a platoon sergeant in George Company and they moved out about four miles while it was still dark. Charley Company took over their positions, and at dawn they started up the hill. The hill was mined and they lost twenty-one men to mines. They were getting shelled from beyond the hill and then they began to get small arms and mortars, but by noon they were within fifty yards of the top. By six o'clock that night they had been forced off.

"I ain't so young any more," Lew was telling me, and he'll be thirty-six this December. "And my legs ain't so good. I'd get to the top of a hill and I'd be so tired I'd holler, 'Dig in! Dig in, everybody!' Then I'd just turn around and I'd holler, 'Kill me, you—! Kill me! I'm so tired I don't care!' I was too tired to dig in, but there was only one fella ever beat me to the top of a hill and he was twenty-two years old and from Philadelphia and a squad sergeant. I just had to do it, and you know why?"

"No," I said.

"I had my pride," he said sadly, in that way of his. "I was Lew Jenkins, and the rest of them were kids and they looked up to me."

That is the truth, and they say that the kids used to flock to Lew for courage. He says he was as scared as any of them, but he couldn't let them know it.

"We'd have to take a hill," he told me, "and I'd be scared, but they'd all be watchin' me so I'd make up a rhyme about the hill so rough and tough, we'll get them gooks, sure enough. Then they'd all holler, 'Listen to old Lew, he's singin'! There he goes!' Then they'd all follow me, and we'd take that hill."

On the 17th day of August they set up a roadblock and they held it for ten days against the Chinese Reds. Sixty-eight out of a company of two hundred eventually got out, and Lew said he'd have gone back to battalion with the rest of them but he was too tired to make it.

"They were shootin' them down all around me," he told me. "It was rainin' and I lay in a creek bottom and I didn't care if I got killed, and I could see 'em takin' prisoners and killin' our guys. I remember one kid was nineteen years old and with his leg blown off and when they started to take him out they went by me and he said, 'So long, Lew. I'll see you.'

"I had a kid in my platoon, one of those screw-off kids you give details to. He got it through the leg and the arm when it was man eat man and this kid was about seventeen and he come limpin' out two or three miles in the rain. Then I got a letter from him later from the hospital and it was signed: 'Your Buddy, the Detail Kid.' He wanted to know who got out and who got killed, and that shows you he was a real man.

"When they had us surrounded there was another kid I could see was breakin'. I told an officer about him and he said, 'He's fine. He's bigger and stronger than I am.' The kid wasn't even in my platoon, but he used to come to me. This second day he come to me he started to scream. He was hollerin', 'We'll all get killed! They'll kill us all.' I patted him on the shoulder and I told him tanks were comin' up to get us and they were goin' to give us artillery for support.

"Hell," Lew said, "none of that was goin' to happen, but I had to tell him somethin'. Then I saw him walk over to some trees, and I heard a shot and I walked over to the trees. There was the kid and he had put his rifle under his chin and he pulled the trigger. I looked at him with the blood runnin all over and his face blown and I got sick and I threw up right there."

When Lew was telling me this there wasn't anything I could say. I would say that I knew, but I didn't know.

"We'd have to attack sometimes through the gook dead," he said, "and there'd be so many of them I'd get sick to my stomach there."

In the ten days at the roadblock Lew formed a company of Americans and some remnants of the 36th ROK regiment and they sent another company down to him. That is what he got the Silver Star for, and the citation says that George Company and Fox Company were being withdrawn when Lew went up a draw with the 4th Platoon and that they held there and saved the battalion from being surrounded.

The last I heard of Lew was late in July and he was still at Benning but in the hospital. He had malaria and a fever of 105.6 and he was delirious. They said he was hollering about wanting to go back to Korea, but that wasn't because he was out of his mind. When I was with him and we'd sit and drink two and three glasses of iced tea at a time in the EM canteen, trying to get cool on those hot, muggy Georgia afternoons, he'd tell me the same thing.

"It ain't soldierin' here," he'd tell me. "I got to go back to the front lines. The poor front-line soldier, he's just miserable. They need me there."

You know he means it, too. Here's a guy who's had it good and had it bad. I've known lots of them who have been up and down, but I never before knew one who liked it better down than up. Not like this one.

I keep trying to figure him out. I often think of how much was written about Lew when he was a fighter and the lightweight champion of the world, and of how many people knew his name. I think of how they used to boo him and rip him apart in the newspapers because he gave them plenty of reason. Then I think of how little they really knew about him.

I keep saying I don't understand him, but now that I've seen Lew again and written all this, I can't help wondering if it doesn't all tie in to a kid picking cotton.

I'm not too sure, but I think the way he lived when he was champion shows you he was ashamed of success, as he was ashamed that evening off Normandy when the front-line soldier had less and was giving more.

He was born to misery and it kept drawing him back again like a magnet. Once, when he was picking cotton on his own and all he owned was in his burlap sack and the clothes on his back, he gave his sack to another picker so the guy could get a start. To do something like that you have to be what Lew Jenkins calls a guy when he likes him. He calls him a man.

He used to write to me, sometimes on Army requisition forms and sometimes on lined paper torn from a spiral notebook. The letters came from Hawaii and Germany and Fort Ord, California, and he was disillusioned and unhappy.

"It ain't the same, old pal," he wrote once, and ahead of his time. "If you could see what's happening to our Army now it would make you sick, but I just mind my own business and I do my job until I can get out."

After he had put in his twenty years he got out, and he and Lupie settled in California. He tried it as a car salesman, but Lupie said that he felt sorry for the poor people who had to trade for the trucks and cars. He worked on a golf course as a greenskeeper, and then drove a laundry truck until a heart attack slowed him.

Five years ago I visited them in their condominium in Concord. He was amazed that he had lived to celebrate, some months before, his sixtieth birthday. He hadn't had a drink in twenty-five years.

"I just had to quit," he said. "I was just bein' crazy. I said to myself, 'I can't go on. I got a son and a wonderful wife, and my wife and son are doin' without.'"

Lew II is now in his mid-thirties, married and the father of three small children. He has an engineering degree and heads his own computer firm, and it was obvious that he and his family were a joy to his parents who had been hurt by what they saw as the disintegration of America around them.

"There's no honesty in anything," Lew said, "and there's no faith in anything anymore."

"I don't know the answer, Lew," I said. "I guess we just have to ride with the punches."

"And it's comin'," he said, "and the Man upstairs better say somethin'."

When I left them I tried to say that, obviously, the problems of peace are more complex than the problems of war. I said that the willingness of man to sacrifice himself for others is still inherent in man, and to be drawn upon if man can find a way in peace. Then, in the parting, I said I just wanted to thank him again for all he had done in two wars.

"Hell, what I did was nothin'," he said, "compared to all them that got killed. They gave their lives, and it's such a goddamn shame."

That which he had found in war, though, he tried to express in peace, and on the corner of Ygnacio Valley Road and Michigan Street in Concord now there is a traffic light. The residents, who know the story that goes with it, call it "The Lew Jenkins Light."

"Kids were gettin' run over on their way to school," Lew was telling me one night on the phone. "One got killed and so many almost got killed that I just had to do somethin', and I appointed myself a crossing guard.

"Every day, for five or six years, I went out there from seven A.M. to eight-thirty, and at the beginnin' the cops didn't like it. They wanted me to stop, and I told them, 'Why don't you do it? Then I'll stay home.' After a while, though, they understood and they left me alone.

"Then this last Christmas," he said, "the young ones, they brought me presents—cookies and candies, all wrapped up, and cards. It made you want to cry, the poor little things."

When his heart could no longer make it on its own, a pacemaker was implanted. He lived with that for some months, until Lew II called to tell me that his father, hospitalized again, was slipping away and then, the next night, to let me know that he had just died. On November 6, 1981, Lew Jenkins was buried, among those to whom he had so belonged as to no others, in Arlington National Cemetery.

The Greatest,
Pound for Pound

from *Once They Heard the Cheers*

> It is when we try to grapple with another man's intimate need that we
> perceive how incomprehensible, wavering and misty are the beings that
> share with us the sight of the stars and the warmth of the sun.
>
> **—Joseph Conrad, *Lord Jim***

"When I am old," I wrote more than twenty years ago, "I shall tell them
about Ray Robinson. When I was young, I used to hear the old men talk of
Joe Gans and Terry McGovern and Kid McCoy. They told of the original
Joe Walcott and Sam Langford, of Stanley Ketchel and Mickey Walker and
Benny Leonard. How well any of them really knew those men I'm not sure,
but it seemed to me that some of the greatness of those fighters rubbed off
on these others just because they lived at the same time.

"That is the way," I wrote, "I plan to use Sugar Ray. When the young assault me with their atomic miracles and reject my Crosby records and find
comical the movies that once moved me, I shall entice them into talking
about fighters. Robinson will be a form of social security for me, because
they will have seen nothing like him, and I am convinced that they never
will."

I am still sure today that they will never be able to match Robinson because of the social changes that were altering life in this country while he
fought. The prejudice that drove the black—as before him it drove the Irish,
the Jew, and then the Italian—to the ring in desperation is becoming a part
of our past. In an age of reason fewer men are forced to fight with their fists,
the amateurs are not what they used to be, the bootleg circuit, where Robin-

son received his intermediate schooling, is long gone, and the professional game has been on the decline for twenty-five years.

Ray Robinson—and Archie Moore, the venerable Sage of San Diego and the greatest ring mechanic I ever saw—were the last of the old-fashioned fighters because they fought from the end of one era through the beginning of another, and because they were the products of poverty as well as prejudice. Robinson was eight years old when his mother brought him and his two older sisters from Detroit to New York, and tried to support them on the fifteen dollars a week she made working in a laundry. Robinson sold firewood he gathered in a wagon under the West Side Highway and as far south as the Bowery. On Saturdays and Sundays he shined shoes, and at night he danced for coins on the sidewalks off Broadway. For him, as for all those others of that time, the fight game was a court of last resort.

"You may find this hard to believe," he told me a couple of times, "but I've never loved fightin'. I really dislike it. I don't believe I watch more than two fights a year, and then it has to be some friend of mine fightin'."

"Fightin', to me, seems barbaric," he said. "It seems to me like the barbarous days when men fought in a pit and people threw money down to them. I really don't like it."

"But at the same time," I said, "I must believe that fighting has given you the most satisfying experiences you have ever known."

"That's right," he said. "I enjoy out-thinkin' another man and out-maneuverin' him, but I still don't like to fight."

I believed him then, and I still do, because of something else he once told me and that one of his sisters confirmed. On the streets of Detroit and New York he ran from fights.

"I would avoid fightin'," he said, "even if I had to take the short end. I'd even apologize when I knew I was right. I got to be known as a coward, and my sisters used to fight for me. They used to remark that they hoped that some day I'd be able to take care of myself."

How able he became is in the record. He began fighting when he was fifteen, and he had 160 amateur and bootleg-amateur fights before he turned pro. As a professional he not only won the welterweight championship of the world, but he won the middle-weight title for the fifth time when he was thirty-seven and he went fifteen rounds trying for it again when he was forty. He was forty-five when he finally retired in 1965, and in 362 fights, amateur and pro, over thirty years, he failed to finish only once. On that June night in 1952, when he boxed Joey Maxim for the light-heavyweight title, giving away fifteen pounds, it was 104 degrees under the Yankee Stadium ring lights, so brutally hot and humid that Ruby Goldstein, the referee, had to be replaced in the eleventh round. Robinson was giving Maxim a boxing lesson, and seemed on his way to winning yet another title, when he collapsed in his corner at the end of the thirteenth.

While Willie Pep was the greatest creative artist I ever saw in a ring, Sugar Ray Robinson remains the greatest fighter, pound-for-pound and punch-for-punch, of more than a half century, or since Benny Leonard retired with the lightweight title in 1924. Perhaps it is foolish to try to compare them, for Pep was a poet, often implying, with his feints and his footwork, more than he said, as that night when he won a round without even throwing a punch. Robinson was the master of polished prose, structuring his sentences, never wasting a word, and, as he often did, taking the other out with a single punch. That was the Robinson, however, that most Americans, enthralled by him as they were but who came to follow boxing on television, never saw. His talent had peaked between 1947 and 1950, before the era of TV boxing and before it saddened me to watch him years later on the screen struggling with fighters like Gene Fullmer and Paul Pender whom once he would have handled with ease.

"The public don't know it," he told me when I brought it up as far back as 1950, fifteen years before he retired, "but I do. The fighter himself is the first one to know."

"And how does he know it?" I said.

"You find you have to think your punches," he said. "The punches you used to throw without thinkin', you now have to reason."

It is something that happens to all of us, once the instinctive inventions and discoveries have been made. Then we reach back into the library of our experience, and what was once the product of inspiration is now merely the result of reason.

"How are you, old buddy?" he said on the phone, when I called him before flying out to Los Angeles. "When are you comin' out?"

"I'm fine," I said, "and I want to come out next week if you'll be there. How about next Friday?"

"Let me check that," he said, and then, "I'll be here. I'll be lookin' for you, because you're my man."

In his 202 professional fights, he hit fifty or more towns, and I imagine that in most, if not in all, there are still writers today whom he annointed as his "man." He was as smooth outside the ring as he was in it, and under pressing interrogation he was as elusive, but until you found that out he was a charmer.

I met him first in the spring of 1946. Already unquestionably the best welterweight in the world, he was unable to get a shot at the title, and he had hired a press agent named Pete Vaccare. We were sitting, late one morning, in Vaccare's office in the old Brill Building on Broadway, waiting for Robinson as, I was to find out, one almost inevitably did, when we heard singing out in the hall. Then the door opened, and they came in, Robinson and Junius ("June") Clark, whom he called his secretary, both of them in heavy road clothes topped off by red knitted skating caps, for they had been running on the Harlem Speedway, and they finished the song. It was "The Very Thought of You," with Robinson carrying the melody and Clark improvising, and they ended it with a soft-shoe step and a hand flourish, and amid the laughter, we were introduced. We talked, with Robinson telling how he once stole so much from a grocery store that the owner gave him a job as a delivery boy to protect his stock, and how the minister who caught him in a crap game on the steps of the Salem Methodist Episcopal Church took him inside and introduced him to boxing.

"I've just met Ray Robinson," I said to Wilbur Wood when I got back to the office that afternoon. "He's quite a guy."

"Oh, no," Wilbur said. "He conned you too."

"What do you mean, conned me?" I said.

"Hang around the fight game a little longer," Wilbur said, "and you'll find out."

In the fight game they like fighters who will fight anybody anywhere at any time and leave the business end to their managers. After he won the welterweight title, with George Gainford doing the dickering, Robinson made his own deals, and I knew a New York boxing writer who had collected two dozen complaints against him from promoters around the country.

"The trouble with Robinson," another one told me one day at lunch in Lindy's, "is that every time I get ready to bomb him, he shows up at some hospital or at the bedside of some sick kid. He's always one move ahead of you."

"As he is in the ring," I said.

There was about him an air of humble superiority, a contrariety that annoyed and frustrated those who tried to come to know him. He would plead humility and reserve a pew in church for Easter Sunday. At big fights, when other notables gathered for their introductions in the ring before the main event, Robinson would wait beyond the ringside rows and receive his applause apart as he came down the aisle and, all grace, vaulted through the ropes. He was a man who was trying to find something he had lost even before he turned professional.

"The biggest thrill I ever got," he told me once, "was when I won the Golden Gloves and they streamed that light down on me in Madison Square

Garden and said, 'The Golden Gloves feather-weight champion, Sugar Ray Robinson!' I bought the papers. I read about it over and over. It was more of a thrill than when I won the welterweight championship of the world.

"Once I read," he said—and he even read law, fascinated by its contradictions—"something that King Solomon said. He said, 'The wiser a man gets the less beauty he finds in life.' If I try to explain that to people they don't understand. It's like the first time you go to Coney Island and you ride the chute-the-chute and you get a big thrill. The second time it isn't so much."

Few fighters have been as disliked within their profession and by its press as was Robinson while he was struggling to make his way, and the fight game was, in part, responsible for that. In this country, from the turn of the century on, boxing gave the black man, because it needed him, a better break than he received in any other sport, but it only gave him what it had to. For years, while Mike Jacobs ran big-time boxing, he refused Robinson that chance at the welterweight title.

"Mike explained that to me," Robinson told me once. "He explained that I'd kill the division. He said, 'I got to have two or three guys fightin' for the title. You'd darken the class.' I understand that. That's good business."

I am sure he understood it, but he did not have to like it. In his early days, in order to get fights, he had to take less money than the opponents he knocked out. Once, after he had trained three weeks for a fight, the promoter ran out. A couple of years later, Jacobs promised him $2,000 beyond his small purse if he would box for a Boston promoter to whom Jacobs owed a favor. When, after the fight, Robinson showed up for his money, Jacobs ridiculed him.

"You didn't think I'd go into my own kick," Mike said, "for some other guy's fight."

They tried to do it to him in the ring too. There was the story that Duke Stefano, then a manager of fighters, was telling me one afternoon in Stillman's Gym.

"I remember Robinson one night when he was just starting out as a pro," Duke said. "Just before the fight, Robinson complained that he had a bad ear, and he didn't want to go through with the fight. It was his left ear, and they looked in it, and you could see it was red and swollen.

"The other guy's manager—he was from New Jersey—looked at it and he said, 'Look, my guy is just an opponent. Go through with the fight, and I promise you he won't touch the ear.' Robinson said, 'Okay, long as he stays away from the ear.' Well, the bell rang, and the other guy came out of his corner and winged a right hand at the ear. Robinson just turned his head and looked at the corner. The guy did it a second time, and Robinson looked at the manager again. The third time the guy tried it, Robinson stepped in with a hook and flattened him.

"The manager," Duke said, "turned right around and went back to New Jersey. He didn't even second another kid he had in the next bout. Fritzie Zivic did it to him too, as he did to many others. He was the recently dethroned welterweight champion of the world when Robinson, in only his second year as a pro, outpointed him over ten rounds in Madison Square Garden. Ten weeks later he would knock Zivic out in ten.

"Fritzie Zivic," Robinson told me once, "taught me more than anybody I ever fought."

"What did he teach you?" I said.

"He taught me that a man can make you butt open your own eye," he said, and I appreciated the phrasing. He was one of the cleanest of fighters, and what he had learned from Zivic was not something that you did to another man, but that he could do to you.

"And how does a man do that?" I said.

"He slipped one of my jabs," Robinson said, "and reached his right glove around behind my head and pulled my head down on his."

Young Otto, who boxed the best lightweights during the first two decades of this century and was a great student of the science, refereed that first fight. One day in Stillman's I asked him about it.

"In the sixth round," he said, "Robinson said to me, 'He's stickin' his thumbs in my eyes.' I said, 'You ain't no cripple.' After that he give it back to Zivic better than Zivic was givin' it to him. I said to myself then, 'This kid is gonna be a great fighter.'"

So they tried to use him and abuse him, and sometimes succeeded, in and out of the ring. When, in self-defense, he retaliated, he acquired the reputation that provoked *The Saturday Evening Post* to ask me to do a piece they were to entitle, "Why Don't They Like Ray Robinson?"

"This is a tough assignment for me," I said to him.

"How's that?" he said.

We were sitting in his office at Ray Robinson Enterprises, Inc., in Harlem, and he had his feet up on his triangular glass-topped desk. He owned most of the block on the west side of Seventh Avenue from 123rd to 124th streets, and he had $250,000 tied up in the five-story apartment house, Sugar Ray's Bar and Restaurant, Edna Mae's Lingerie Shop, and Sugar Ray's Quality Cleaners, with its five outlets.

"I have to ask you the tough questions," I said.

"That's all right," he said. "Go ahead."

"I will," I said, "but I want to explain something first. I think this piece can do you a lot of good. You're unquestionably the greatest fighter since Benny Leonard, and there are some old-timers who say you may be the best since Joe Gans, who died ten years before you were born."

"They say that?" he said, as if he hadn't known. "I appreciate that."

"My point is," I said, "that you should be the most popular fighter of your time, but you're not. There are raps against you in the fight game, and they keep bringing up your Army record and you've never made the money that you should. A fighter like Graziano, who's a beginner compared to you and has a dishonorable discharge from the Army while you have an honorable one, has made twice as much as you have."

"That's right," he said.

"Part of that is style," I said. "All his fights are wars, and that's what the public likes, but it's style outside the ring, too. He's open and frank, and you're not, really. What I want to do is explain you. I want you to tell me what it's like to have a fine mind and great physical talents, to be a great artist but to be colored and to have that used against you in the fight game and out of it. It can explain a lot about you, and I'll understand. If I understand, I can make the readers understand, and as I said, that can mean a lot to you, if you'll level with me."

I really believed it. I believed it for about five minutes.

"If you can do that," he said, "I'll appreciate it. Nobody's ever done that for me before. You just ask me the questions, what you want to know."

"All right," I said. "Let's get the Army thing out of the way first."

It wasn't any good. We went around and around, as in a ring, and when Robinson couldn't counter my leads or even slip them, he professed only astonishment that I should hold such documented assertions to be facts.

There was something to be celebrated in his Army record. He had been a member of Casual Detachment 7, known as "The Joe Louis Troupe." Joe and he and four other fighters spent seven months touring camps in this country and putting on boxing exhibitions. In Florida, Robinson refused to box unless black troops were allowed to attend, and he, an enlisted man, faced down a general. At Camp Sibert, Alabama, a white M.P. saw Louis emerge from a phone booth in so-called white territory, and he threatened to club Joe. Robinson took him on, the two rolling on the ground, and there was rioting by black troops before apologies were made to the two fighters.

It was a matter of Army record and common knowledge, however, that when the troupe sailed for Europe, from Pier 90, New York, on March 31, 1944, Robinson was not aboard. It was also in the record that he had previously declared his intention not to go, and that the Articles of War as they applied to the punishment for desertion had been explained to him.

"But why would a man say such a thing?" he said when I had read to him from the affidavit.

"He not only said it," I said, "but he swore to it."

"I can't understand that," Robinson said. "I never met that officer, and he never read me such things."

Years later, in his autobiography, he would state that he had been suffering from amnesia following a fall, and had been hospitalized for that before his honorable discharge as a sergeant on June 3, 1944. It was a book he had wanted me to write after he had retired for the first time in 1952. Because he preferred to avoid using elevators, as he also preferred not to fly, we had met late one afternoon with my agent and another, not in my agent's office on the twentieth floor of the Mutual of New York Building, but in the cocktail lounge of the Park Sheraton.

"I just can't do it, Ray," I said, after we had talked for a while, the others listening, and I had tried again. "There are those conflicting versions of those events in your life, in and out of boxing, and we tried two years ago in your office and we've tried again now, and we still can't resolve them. I'm sorry, but I just can't do the book."

"That's all right, old buddy," he said. "I understand."

I doubt that he did—why couldn't we just put it all down the way he said, and possibly even believed it had been, and ignore the conflicts? And when I would see him after that it would always be in camp before his fights and I would be with others. Now I had heard that he was heading up a youth project in Los Angeles, and at ten o'clock on that Friday morning the taxi driver and I found it, finally, on West Adams Boulevard with the sign—Sugar Ray's Youth Foundation—fronting the one-story building.

"He's in conference with Mr. Fillmore right now," the woman said across the counter, and I had missed her name when she had introduced herself. "I don't think he'll be long, though."

"That's all right," I said. "I have plenty of time."

"Maybe while you're waiting," she said, "you'd like to look at some of our material."

"That would be fine," I said.

She introduced me then to Mel Zolkover, who had arisen from behind one of the desks beyond the counter. He is a middle-aged retired mechanical engineer and the foundation's administrative director, and we shook hands.

She went back to a desk, and while I waited I could hear the even tones of Robinson's voice, still familiar after all the years, in an office on the left.

When she came back she handed me the several sheets of publicity and a folder from the 1976–77 "Miss Sugar Ray Teen Pageant." From a photograph I identified her as Thelma Smith, the executive secretary, and elsewhere I noted that Bob Hope is the foundation's honorary chairman, Robinson the chairman, and Wright Fillmore the president. I read about arts and crafts projects, costume making, karate instruction, talent shows, art classes, and workshops in beauty and personal development, drama, band and combo repertory, and dance.

"Old buddy!" he said, smiling and his face fuller and shaking hands across the counter. "How's my old buddy?"

"Fine," I said. "And you?"

"Just fine," he said. "Come on in here and sit down and we'll talk."

I followed him to the middle desk at the back. He was wearing a blue leisure suit, the jacket over a dark blue-and-fuschia sports shirt. Once I had checked his wardrobe. He owned thirty-four suits, twenty-six pairs of shoes, nine sports jackets and as many pairs of slacks, six overcoats and four topcoats, most of which apparel he said he had never worn even once.

"You've gained some weight," I said.

As a fighter he was one of the most lithe and handsome of men. He moved with such grace and rhythm, in the ring and out, that watching him made me think of rubbing silk or satin between one's hands. During his first retirement, in fact, he tried it as a dancer, opening at the French Casino in New York for $15,000 a week. After that, it was downhill.

"Robinson was a good dancer, for a fighter," a Broadway booking agent told me, after Robinson had come back to knock out Bobo Olson and win the middleweight title the second time. "Maybe no other fighter ever danced as well, but the feature of his act was his change of clothes. He looked good in everything he put on."

He was leaning back now in the high-backed desk chair. Not only was his face fuller, but at fifty-six he was a lot heavier across the shoulders and chest and at the waist.

"Yeah, I'm heavier," he said now. "You see, I sit here with something on my mind, and I don't get the exercise I should. Every day, though, I try to take a five-mile walk."

"How heavy are you?"

"Oh, 183–84," he said, and he fought best at 147. "You see, you've got a certain ego about having been a champion, and you'd like to keep like that, but it's so difficult. There are temptations, and it takes will power. When you're fightin' you have to live by the rules, because when that bell rings condition is the name of the game. Even then, in camp, Joe Louis and I would go out in the boat and have quarts of ice cream and our trainers would get mad."

He reached into a desk drawer, and he brought out a package of Danish pastries. He tore one end off the transparent wrapper and took out one and, leaning back again, began eating.

"My breakfast," he said. "You know, the most important meal is breakfast."

"And that's your breakfast?"

"That's right," he said, "and Jack Blackburn used to get after Joe and me." Blackburn was Louis's discoverer, teacher, and trainer. He developed Louis so precisely in the image of what he himself had been as a fighter that Louis had the same flaw that Blackburn had of dropping the left arm after a jab. It was what made Louis vulnerable to a straight right counter over the jab.

"Blackburn," Robinson was saying, "used to tell us, 'You got to eat breakfast.' Then they used to squeeze blood from the meat, and I'd drink that. From Monday through Friday I'd drink it. You have to get that from a slaughter house, and they put this blood in a can and I used to go down there and get it. I'll tell you, that's the most potent thing there is."

"I remember that you used to do that," I said. "Do you ever drink it now?"

"Every now and then I think I'll do it," he said, "but I don't."

He had finished the pastry and folded over the end of the package. He put the package back in the desk drawer.

"What brought you out here to California?" I said.

"My wife is from out here," he said. When he was fighting he was married to Edna Mae Holly. She had been a dancer and they had two sons, and I had not known he had remarried. "Joe Louis was goin' with a girl out here, and I met Millie through the recommendation of this other girl. You know, like a dog. You see something, and the ears go bong! We were married in 1965, and that's how I met Mr. Fillmore, and we started this foundation."

"Tell me about that."

"We went to London," he said, "and she was having her thirty-third or thirty-fourth birthday party, and . . . "

"Who was?" I said.

"Queen Elizabeth," he said. "Millie and I, we were invited and we went to the party. It was a wonderful ceremony, and Prince Phillip and I were talkin'. You remember those strikes?"

"What strikes?"

"I think it started in Berkeley," he said.

"The student protests?"

"That's right," he said. "We were talkin', and he said, 'Sugar, I believe you could help that.' I said, 'What do you mean?' He said, 'Youngsters look up to you, and I've got an idea.' I had met Mr. Fillmore, and of all the people I've met—all the Popes and all—I never met a man who believes in God and lives it more than Mr. Fillmore. You never hear the guy say a harsh word, even a loud word, and I want you to meet him."

"I'd like to," I said.

"I came back to New York," he said, "and I was goin' with my present wife. She lived upstairs out here and Mr. Fillmore lived downstairs. I talked with him, and we went to the Council of Churches and asked them to help us, and they gave us money. The county saw the potential and funded us. Now we hope to have the State Junior Olympics, and Jimmy Carter was out and I met with him, and he's a nice guy and likes what we're doing, and we hope for Federal funding. We work with the Board of Education and the Department of Parks and Recreation, and there has never been a paid member of the board of trustees. Every dollar goes in, and I'm about the poorest cat on the board."

"What happened to all that property you owned in Harlem?"

"I sold that even at a loss," he said, "just to get out. I fell in love with my wife out here, and Harlem was goin' down hill so bad, and now if you see a white face there, you know it's a cop."

"Did you get clipped?"

One day, sitting in his office in Harlem, he had told me that he felt he was destined to make a great success in business. It was that afternoon in 1950, when he spoke of how he knew his ring skills were starting to decline.

"After a man attains all the things he likes," he had said then, "he has to find some other form of happiness. I feel I'm gonna find that in business. I'm not cocky within myself. I'm an extreme Christian within myself. I just believe. My faith is so strong that I know that someday I'm gonna be the head of some real big business. I thank God for the success I've had, and the investments I've made."

"Yeah, I got clipped," he said now. "It happened to Joe, too, but that's a part of life. I didn't get out with too much, but I didn't lose too much, either."

"As you say," I said, "it happened to Joe, too, and it happens so often. They talk about the dirty fight game, but a fighter makes a fortune in it, and when he gets out into the nice clean world of American business they take it all from him."

"You're so right," he said. "What other fighters are you seeing for the book?"

"I just saw Willie Pep last month."

"He was a great one," he said. "When I beat him in the amateurs in Connecticut, they took me to the police station."

"I remember that story," I said. "Willie's all right. He's working for the Athletic Commission in Connecticut, and he's married for the fifth time."

"You know how that is," he said, smiling. "When Joe was the champion and I used to go to the airport, they came off that plane like it was a parade."

"And I saw Billy Graham," I said. "He's doing fine, working for Seagram's."

"Billy Graham?" he said. "He's my man. He beat me in the first fight I lost."

"When you were ninety-pound kids," I said.

He had reached into the desk drawer again. He brought out the Danish, and started on another one.

"There are so many of your fights I remember," I said. "The night you won the middleweight title from Jake LaMotta in Chicago . . . "

"Jake wasn't smart," he said, "but he was in condition. He was 'The Bull.'"

"I know," I said. "I remember that, after your first fight with him, you were passing blood for days."

"That's right," he said.

"When you fought him in Chicago for the title in '51," I said, "I watched it at a neighbor's house on TV. Ted Husing was announcing the fight, and in the early rounds he was filled with LaMotta. He kept saying that we were seeing an upset, that LaMotta was running the fight."

"He said that?"

"Yes, and I said to my neighbor, 'Husing doesn't know what he's talking about. Watch what Robinson does the next time the referee breaks them, or Robinson backs off from an exchange.' You would back off so far that sometimes you went out of the camera range, right off the screen. I said, 'LaMotta had trouble making the weight, and Robinson is walking the legs off him. When he gets ready to turn it on, Jake won't have much left.' In the thirteenth round you turned it on, and the referee had to stop it."

"That's right," he said, nodding. "That's exactly what I did. You remember that?"

"Another fight I remember," I said, "was the one with "Flash" Sebastian, and that one scared me."

"That scared me, too," he said.

On June 24, 1947, Robinson knocked out Jimmy Doyle in the eighth round in Cleveland, and the next day Doyle died of brain injury. At the coroner's inquest, Robinson was asked, "Couldn't you tell from the look on Doyle's face that he had been hurt?" Robinson said, "Mister, that's what my business is, to hurt people." Because he was absolutely frank, he caught the criticism. He set up a $10,000 trust fund for Doyle's mother, and two months later he took little more than his expenses to fight Sebastian, the welterweight champion of the Philippines, on an American Legion show in Madison Square Garden.

"It was right after that Doyle fight," I said now.

"I know," he said. "The night before the Doyle fight I dreamed what was gonna happen, and I got up the next day and I called the commission and I told them. They said that they'd sold all the tickets, and they went so far as to get a Catholic priest to talk to me."

"In that Sebastian fight," I said, "you came out of your corner for the first round and he threw a wide hook, and you brought your right glove up and blocked it. He backed off, and came in again and did the same thing. This time you threw the right hand inside the hook and followed it with a hook of your own, and he went back on his head. Then he tried to get up, and he fell forward on his face, and the photographers at ringside were hollering, 'Get this! Get this! This guy may die, too!'"

"I know," he said. "I said, 'Oh, Lord, don't let it happen again.'"

"In the dressing room later," I said, "Sebastian was hysterical. Whitey Bimstein had seconded him, and he took a towel and soaked it in ice water and snapped it in Sebastian's face to bring him out of it. I said to Whitey, 'What kind of a fighter is this they brought all the way from the Philippines to almost be killed?' Whitey said, 'I never saw him before tonight, but they asked me to work with him. After I got him taped, I told him to warm up. He threw one punch, and I stopped him. I said, "Look, fella. When you throw that hook, don't raise your head. You're fightin' Ray Robinson. You do that with him, and he'll take your head right off your shoulders."'"

"Then sometime later I was talking with Ruby Goldstein. You remember Ruby was the referee that night, and Ruby said, 'That Sebastian threw that first hook, and Robinson brushed it away. I was just thinkin' to myself that if he did that again Robinson would cross a right. The next thing I knew he did, and I was saying, 'One . . . two . . . three.'"

"I was lucky that night," Robinson said now.

"And Sebastian was, too," I said, "and I'll tell you another night when you were lucky."

"When was that?" he said.

"When you got the title back from Randy Turpin."

In August of 1950 Robinson carried Charley Fusari over fifteen rounds of what was ostensibly a fight for Robinson's welterweight title but was, on Robinson's part, just one of the greatest boxing exhibitions I have ever seen.

He gave his entire purse to the Damon Runyan Cancer Fund, of which Dan Parker, the sports editor and columnist of the *New York Daily Mirror*, was president. This act of charity had the effect, however unintended, of silencing Parker who, whenever the word got out that Robinson intended to go to Europe, would recall that he had missed that opportunity when he had failed to sail with the "Joe Louis Troupe."

The following May, Robinson left for Paris—Parker merely pointing out that it was "by boat"—and took along his fuschia Cadillac and George Gainford's black one. Included in the party of eleven were Robinson's golf pro, and his barber, and in Paris they acquired an Arabian midget who spoke five languages. They occupied most of one floor of the Claridge, and seldom left to eat in restaurants. There was an almost constant flow of room-service waiters through the suites, and the bill at the end was staggering.

"You know how the French are," Lew Burston, who had lived for many years in Paris and ran the foreign affairs of the Mike Jacobs boxing empire, said to me one day following Robinson's return. "In the old days they used to see the maharajas arrive with their retinues, and they basically believe that another man's business is his own. At the end of Robinson's stay, though, even the French were somewhat stunned."

Robinson fought a half-dozen times in Europe, in Paris and elsewhere, and on July 10 in London he defended his middle-weight title against Randy Turpin, the British and European champion. Turpin out-pointed him over the fifteen rounds in an upset so startling that in the fight game on this side of the ocean they found it hard to believe.

"You may remember," I was saying to him now, "what Lew Burston said after the first Turpin fight. He said, 'Robinson had Paris in his legs.'"

"That was one of the few fights," he said, nodding, "where I took a chance. Remember what I told you—about temptation and will power? Then he had one of the most unorthodox styles, too. You remember the second fight?"

Two months after the London fight they met again in the Polo Grounds in New York. Robinson won the early rounds, but then Turpin, awkward, sometimes punching off the wrong foot, lunging with his jab, chopping with his right in close and eight years younger, began to come on. By the tenth round, Robinson seemed spent, and then a wide cut opened over his left eye and, obviously fearful that the fight might be stopped and with the blood gushing out of the cut, he took the big gamble. He walked in with both hands going. He shook Turpin with a right, pushed him off and dropped him in the middle of the ring with another right. When Turpin got up at nine, Robinson drove him to the ropes, and there he must have thrown forty punches. Turpin, reeling now and trying to cover, was half sitting on the middle rope, and there were 61,000 people there, and it sounded as if they were all screaming.

"Of course I remember the fight," I was saying now, "and, as I said, you were lucky that night. When you had him on the ropes and he didn't go down, you reached out with your left, put your glove behind his head and tried to pull him forward. There were only eight seconds left in the round, so if you had pulled him off the ropes and he had gone down, the count would have killed the rest of the round. You had that cut and you were exhausted, and you would never have survived the next five rounds."

"You're right," he said.

"And I'll tell you a night," I said, "when you did out-smart yourself."

"What night was that?" he said.

"That night in the Yankee Stadium when you fought Maxim and it was 104 degrees in there. You were not only licking him, but you were licking him so easily that you made a show of it, dancing around in and out, throwing unnecessary punches. That's why, in that heat, you collapsed at the end of the thirteenth."

"You're right, old buddy," he said. "That was a mistake. I was incoherent all the next day. I never remembered when Goldstein fell out. I had a premonition the night before that fight too. I had a premonition that I would die."

He had finished the pastry and reclosed the package again, and he returned it to the desk drawer.

"There's this Sugar Ray Leonard," I said, "who won a gold medal in the Olympics. There was another one—Sugar Ray Seales. How do you feel about these kids calling themselves Sugar Ray?"

"Bill, you know," he said, sitting back and smiling, "it's a good feeling to think that the kids think that much of me."

It was different when he was a fighter. There was another welterweight at that time named George Costner, and in Chicago in 1945 Robinson knocked him out in two minutes and fifty-five seconds of the first round. Five years later they were matched again, this time for Philadelphia, and in the days leading up to the fight, the other, by then known as George ("Sugar") Costner, was quoted on the sports pages as disparaging Robinson.

"Listen, boy," Robinson said to him at the weigh-in, "I've been readin' what you've been sayin' in the papers about what you're gonna do to me."

"Why, there are no hard feelings, are there, Ray?" Costner said. "I just did that to boost the gate."

"That may be all right," Robinson said, "but when I boost the gate I do it by praisin' my opponent."

The logic of publicity, revolving as it does around the build-up of the underdog, was all on Costner's side, but this time Robinson knocked him out in two minutes and forty-nine seconds. While it was succinct, this was, in its scientific precision, one of Robinson's finest performances.

"There's only one 'Sugar,'" Robinson was quoted as saying right after the fight, but I remember another aftermath. It involved still another welterweight who was asked by his manager if he would fight Sugar Costner.

"No thanks," the fighter said.

"But you can lick Costner," the manager said. "Robinson flattened him twice inside of one round."

"I don't want to fight anybody named Sugar," the fighter said.

"I've been remembering," I said to Robinson now, "the first time I ever met you. It was in Pete Vaccare's office in the Brill Building, and we heard you singing out in the hall, and you and June Clark came in wearing road clothes and harmonizing 'The Very Thought of You.' You two did it very well."

"Yeah," Robinson said, smiling. "June Clark, he was a musician—Armstrong was in his band—and he, too, was a believer in God."

"That was a long time ago," I said. "It was in March of 1946."

"Are you sure?" Robinson said. "Didn't we meet before then?"

"I'm certain," I said, "because I didn't start to write sports until I came back from the war."

"You were in the war?" Robinson said.

"Yes," I said, "but only as a war correspondent."

"Where were you?" Robinson said.

"All through northern Europe," I said.

"In the ETO?" he said. "Then how come we didn't meet over there?"

"I don't know," I said. It was as if I had just been stunned by a sucker punch, one you never expect the other to throw, and I was sparring for time.

"We were over there," Robinson was saying now. "Joe Louis and I we had a troupe, and we boxed in the ETO and everything."

I still didn't know what to say. There were the others at their desks—Thelma Smith and Mel Zolkover and a secretary—who could have heard us, and I didn't want to challenge it there. I am quite sure that, if we had been alone, I would have, just to try again after so many years to understand him, but as I have thought about it since, I believe it was better that I let it ride. He is a man who has his own illusions about his life, as do we all, about the way he wishes it had been, and there is little if any harm, although some sadness, in that now. I shall send him a copy of this book, however, and when he reads this chapter I hope he understands that, as a reporter, my responsibility, as pompous as this may sound, is to draw as accurate and honest a portrait as I can.

"I want you to meet Mr. Fillmore," he was saying now. "Mr. Fillmore can tell you a lot about the foundation."

"I'd like to meet him," I said, and he led me into Fillmore's office and introduced us.

Fillmore, a slim, immaculate man, bald and wearing dark glasses, said that he would be seventy-eight in a couple of months. He had worked, he said, for the Southern Pacific Railroad for forty years, as a waiter and then as an instructor, and he had been retired for seven years when Robinson and he started the foundation in 1969.

"The first time I met Ray personally," he said, "was through his present wife. She was rooming with us, and he was going with her, and then he finally married. We got to talking and got to be buddies, and one day I got a telegram from London that he wanted to see me.

"I wondered, with all the people he knew, why he wanted to see me. I waited, and he and his wife flew in and, it being hot, we sat in the back yard. I asked him what was so important, and he said he'd always wanted to do something for youth. I said, 'What do you want me to do about it, Ray? With all the people you know, you want me to put together something for children? I'm retired.' He said, 'No. You have just started working.' I told him, 'We need money, and we need children. If you can get the money, I can get the children.'

"From the back step we moved to Millie's kitchen, then to the church, and when it got too big for there, we moved here. Since 1969 there's no black mark on this organization, and I challenge anybody to go to the IRS or wherever.

"The Southern Pacific," he said, "had given me a three-year course in human relations, and what we try to do here is make good citizens, not only a Sugar Ray Robinson or a Sandy Koufax. We had these fellas here, and they called themselves 'The Young Black Panthers.' They knew every way to do wrong. There was 'One-Legged Joe' and there was 'Bluefish,' and the one was fourteen and the other was fifteen, and we gained their confidence.

"The news came out one time that a hamburger stand had been held up, and it sounded to me like 'One-Legged Joe' and 'Bluefish,' so I called in Tony, one of the lesser lights. I said to him, 'Where were you on such-and-such a night?' He said, 'I know what you want, but I wasn't in it.' I said, 'I know, but if I could find out where it was and I could find the pistol, I could help out.

"He told me where it was, where to find the pistol, and it was a toy. 'One-Legged Joe' went to UCLA and stayed there three years and got a job. 'Bluefish' joined the Navy, and that was what Ray Robinson had in mind, and what we try to do."

When I came out of Fillmore's office, Robinson was at his desk, finishing another Danish, and he suggested that we go over to the foundation's annex. We walked up the sidewalk, then through the blacktopped parking area of a shopping center, and at the far side, into what had been a store and was now partitioned into several rooms. He led me into a conference room, and we sat down with Zolkover, and with Richard Jackman, a then thirty-two-year-old law graduate who is the program director, and his assistant, Scott Mc-Creary, then twenty-six and a graduate of the University of California at Santa Barbara.

"Tell Bill," Robinson said, at the head of the long table, "what we do here."

"Well, take our baseball program," Zolkover said. "We kind of take the place of the YMCA and the Little League for kids six to sixteen in the lower socio-economic areas where they can't afford those others. The children are not allowed to pay, and when you think of it, when Ray was a kid his mother couldn't afford it."

"We're not trying to build a Sugar Ray," Jackman said.

"That's right," Robinson said, "and the last thing, that we're just goin' to start now, is the boxing. I didn't want people to think we're a boxing organization."

"At the same time," Jackman said, "it's Mr. Robinson's charisma that makes it go. He has friends all over the world, and if we get the Junior Olympics started here it could include ten to fifteen cities, and we could expand to Europe, too."

"He can open any door," Zolkover said, nodding toward Robinson. "One day the question was, where could we get readership? I said, '*The Reader's Digest.*' I looked up the chairman of the board, and Ray called, and it was, 'Hey, Ray!'

"You see," he said, "we're like a church. We pay no money, so we have to have people with dedication like Ray."

"When he was boxing," Scott said, "they called him the greatest fighter, pound-for-pound. We say that, pound-for-pound, we get the greatest distance out of our money."

When Robinson and I left them a few minutes later, we stood for a moment on the sidewalk edging the parking area, looking out over the quadrangle of parked cars. The California climate, unlike that of the Northeast where I abide, is conducive to keeping cars clean, and I was struck by how they glistened, older models as well as new, in the sunlight.

"Are you still on the Cadillac kick?" I said to him.

"No," he said. "No more."

"I remember you turned that chartreuse one in for the fuschia one."

"The car I drive now," he said, and then pointing, "is that little red Pinto over there."

"That's your car?"

"Yeah," he said, and then, smiling, "but I've been there."

"I'll say you have," I said.

We walked slowly across the parking area. We were dawdling in the warm sunlight.

"While you were fighting," I said, "did you take out any annuities?"

"Nope," he said.

"Did you buy any stocks?"

"A few, and I sold those."

"When you had all those investments in Harlem," I said, "I was always afraid you were going to get clipped."

"That's right," he said.

"So how do you get along now?"

"I've got friends," he said. "I borrow five grand, and I pay back three. I borrow three, and pay two. Then something drops in, and I pay everybody. People say to me about this foundation, 'What are you gettin'?' They can't understand doing something for kids. I've always been a Christian believer in God. I was gifted with a talent that helped introduce me to people, and all that was in preparation for what I'm doin' now."

"And I celebrate it," I said.

When we got back to the office I called for a cab. While I was waiting for it, he said he thought he would take his five-mile walk, and we shook hands and wished each other well. He went out the door and, through the wide front window, I saw him start up the sidewalk, the greatest fighter I ever saw, the one I wanted so much to know.

So Long, Jack

from *Once They Heard the Cheers*

> There are two honest managers in boxing. The one is Jack Hurley, and
> I can't remember the name of the other.
>
> **—Damon Runyon**

It was while we were still driving West, heading for Medora and then Jim
Tescher's. We were crossing the Red River on the wide, many-laned bridge
between Moorhead, Minnesota, and Fargo, North Dakota, and it was mid-
morning.

"Are we going to stop in Fargo?" my wife said.

"Maybe on the way back," I said. "I'm not sure."

I have a friend named Walter Wellesley Smith, whose mother called him
Wells, and who is known as Red. He was born and grew up in Green Bay,
Wisconsin, and while he was running an elevator in the Northland Hotel
summers and going to Notre Dame the rest of the year, he used to dream
about sometime seeing a World Series, a heavyweight championship fight,
and a Kentucky Derby. He writes a sports column for the New York *Times*,
and in close to a half century he has attended forty-four World Series, fifty-
four heavyweight championship fights, and thirty-three Kentucky Derbies.

"When we drive out to Jim Tescher's," I was telling him several months
before, "we'll be going through Fargo. I'm thinking of stopping there and
seeing if anybody remembers Jack."

"Oh, sure," he said. "You've got to do that."

"I'll go to the sports department of the paper," I said, "and ask somebody,
'Can you tell me where Jack Hurley is buried?'"

"Of course," he said, "and you'll get some young noodnik who'll say, 'Jack
who?'"

"I'm not much for visiting graves," I said.

"Oh, but you've got to do that," he said. "You've got to get Jack in the book."

About ninety miles west of Fargo I turned off the Interstate where we saw several of those gas station signs on their high-legged towers, and got gas and drove into the adjacent restaurant for lunch. The waitress led us between two rows of booths, and in one of them a young man in his late teens, blond, blue-eyed and sturdy, was sitting, looking at the menu. He had on a freshly laundered, blue football jersey with the white numerals 54 and, in orange block letters, the name WASHBURN across the chest, and he was leaning back at ease the way in high school my football heroes used to loll in class.

"Oh, you're from Washburn?" I heard a woman say in a reedy, treble voice. She was one of three, all of them white-haired, that the waitress had started to lead between the booths and, while the others had gone on, she had stopped at the young man's.

"Yes, ma'am," the young man said.

"I used to live in Washburn," she said. "What's your name?"

"Tracy," he said.

"Tracy?" the white-haired woman said. "Tracy? Well, you're a younger generation. I don't remember a Tracy."

"But I'm from Washburn High in Minneapolis," he said, indicating the name on the jersey.

"Tracy?" she said. "It's been such a long time since I lived in Washburn. Tracy?"

The young man started to say something but then, embarrassed, he shrugged and looked away. The woman, still repeating the name, walked on and joined the others in the booth. I looked at my wife and shook my head, and when I glanced over at the other booth again the young man had left.

"She scared him right out of the booth," I said. "Jack Hurley should be here, and it would get him started on the creatures again."

It was Jack Hurley's contention that more fighters are ruined by women, whom he called creatures, than by opponents' punches, alcohol, or whatever. The affliction, as Hurley saw it, was epidemic, affecting not only fighters but all married men, whom he called mules, in all callings, and nothing reaffirmed this for him more convincingly than the sight of women of advanced years enjoying a meal in a public place after, he was certain, they had driven their husbands into early graves.

"On the way back," Betty said, "we'd better stop in Fargo. After all, Jack Hurley meant so much to your life."

Of all those I came to know in sports nobody else ever fascinated me as did Jack Hurley. He seemed to me to be a literary character, as if he had stepped out of the pages of a novel, and I put him in one about a prize fighter and his manager. A novel, of course, should be larger than life but there was no way I could make my Doc Carroll bigger than Jack.

There were the last days I spent with him in Seattle and Boise in September of 1966, and all week I kept telling myself that I had written the book ten years too soon. He was moving his last fighter then, a heavyweight name Boone Kirkman, and when I got off the plane he was at the airport. I hadn't seen him in eight years, but there he was at the edge of the crowd, tall and bony, craning his neck and then waving. He looked a lot older and thinner and paler, and there was dark green glass over the right lens of his bifocals.

"How are you?" I said, as we shook hands.

With Jack I always knew what the answer to that one would be. The moment I would ask the question, I would get the feeling that I was the straight man in an act.

"No good," he said.

That had to be the truth. He was sixty-nine then, and wracked with the rheumatism he said he picked up in France in World War I. In addition to that, the surgical profession had been whittling away at him for years. They had taken his tonsils and his appendix for starters, and then, after he retired Billy Petrolle—his one great fighter—in 1934, they took two thirds of his stomach because of ulcers. While they were still trying to cure sinusitis with surgery, he had twenty-three operations, and recently I had read in *The Ring* that he had had a cataract removed from his right eye.

"Who hit you in the eye?" I said.

"Ah," he said. "Cataracts, so I decided to go for the operation."

"Good," I said. "That's one they've become very proficient at."

"Don't I know that?" he said. "So what happens? When it's over, I say to the doctor, 'Now, Doc, I understand that after ninety per cent of these operations, the patient's sight can be corrected with glasses to 20–20. Is that right?' So he says, 'Well, that's about right.' So I say, 'But, Doc, I'm not gonna have 20–20, am I?' He says, 'Well, no.' So I say, 'All right. How good is my sight gonna be?' He says, 'Well, pretty good.'

"Now wouldn't you know that?" Jack said, that pinched look of disgust coming over his face. "Ninety per cent are successful, but I have to be in the other ten per cent. Why?"

"I don't know," I said.

"Now tell me something else," he said. "What does he mean by 'pretty good'? Just how good is 'pretty good'?"

"I don't know that, either," I said.

"I can't see a damn thing," he said. "Oh, hell. I can see some, but at the hotel I've already fallen down the stairs twice, and now I've gotta have the other eye done. How about that 'pretty good' though?"

Jack had been living in room 679 of the Olympic Hotel since he had left Chicago seventeen years before to manage a light-heavy-weight named Harry "Kid" Matthews. He had also left his wife.

"So I'm hustling to make a living in Seattle," he told me once, "when one day these two detectives from Chicago show up. They've got a paper charging me with desertion, and they drag me back. Now I'm in Chicago again, and late one afternoon I come into the lobby of the hotel where we're living. All the creatures are sittin' around there—they've got nothing else to do—and as soon as I walk in I see them start lookin' at one another and their heads start going. One of them says to me, 'Oh, Mr. Hurley. When you get upstairs you won't find your wife there.' I say, 'Is that so?' She says, 'Yes, she's left you.'

"You see?" Jack said. "She can't wait to let me find it out for myself. So I say, 'Is that so?' She says, 'Yes, she's gone to Miami.' I say, 'Thank you.' I turn right around and I go over to the station house. I walk up to the desk sergeant, and I say, 'I want to report that my wife has just left me.' So the desk sergeant says, 'So what?' I say, 'So what? I'll tell you what. You know those two donkeys you sent out to Seattle to bring me back? Now I want you to send them down to Miami to bring my wife back.' You know what he said?"

"No," I said.

"He said, 'Listen, Hurley. You get out of here before I lock you up.' Now, isn't that terrible? What kind of justice is that?"

It was Hurley the teacher and ring strategist, however, who captured me. In boxing I knew three great teachers. Ray Arcel worked with seventeen world champions and, as one of the most gentle, kind, and refined of men, was concerned about the fighter as a person more than anyone else I ever knew. To him I would have entrusted a son. Charley Goldman worked on a fighter like a sculptor working on a block of marble, always trying to bring out all the truth within, and always afraid that if he did not go deep enough, he would leave some of it hidden, but also afraid that if he cut too deep, he would destroy some of it forever. Over a period of several years I watched him as, without destroying the fighters' gifts, he made a great heavyweight champion out of the awkward Rocky Marciano. Jack Hurley, the great ring strategist and perfectionist, as he crouched at ringside, squinting through those thin-rimmed glasses, saw a fight as a contest of the mind in which he was always moving his fighter a move or two ahead.

"I don't know why it is," Jack was telling me once, "but I can look at a fighter and know that he must do this or he must do that to lick the other guy. There are a lot of things I can't do. You can sit me down at a piano and I couldn't play 'Home Sweet Home' if you gave me the rest of my life, but I can just look at fighters and know what's right.

"Some people are just like that. Some years ago out in the Dakotas there was a kid playing third base for the Jamestown club in the Dakota League. Behind first base there was this high fence, and this kid playing third used to field the ball—and he had a terrific arm, and he'd not only throw the ball over the first-baseman's reach, but he'd throw it over the fence.

"So one day," Jack said, "the word got around that a scout for the Yankees was in town to look at the kid. Everybody laughed. They said, 'What is this? He's wasting his time with a kid who can't throw any better that that.'

"The scout knew something, though. He had the ability to see something that no one else could. He took that kid and put him in at shortstop. He put him at deep shortstop, where the kid could cover a lot of ground and where he could make the throw. He played shortstop for the Yankees for a number of years. His name was Mark Koenig. I still don't know why it is that some-body can see something when everybody else can't."

Over the years, though, I came to know why Jack could see things in fight-ers and fights that others couldn't. I never saw his one great fighter, Billy Petrolle, in the ring, but fifteen years after Petrolle retired, Wilbur Wood was still telling me about his fights, Joe Williams, the Scripps-Howard sports editor and columnist, once wrote that, in twenty-five years of watching fights in Madison Square Garden, the greatest he ever saw there was the first Petrolle-Jimmy McLarnin fight. As I watched Jack work with other fighters, and listened to him for hours while he talked about Petrolle's fights, it was obvious that he could see what no one else could because he had analyzed and broken down the science that precedes the art.

Jack was born and grew up in Fargo, and he was thirteen when his father, who was a switchman on the Canadian-Northern, was killed pulling a cou-pling between boxcars. As the oldest of five children Jack had to go to work, and he started selling newspapers on Broadway and Northern Pacific Avenue where, to protect his corner, he had to fight. There was a gym in the base-ment of Saumweber's Barbershop across the river in Moorhead, and he started to hang around there, learning what he could by watching the other fighters. When he was fifteen he weighed 120 pounds, and he began boxing at smokers at night.

"I liked the boxing business," he told me once, "but I figured there must be an easier way. Then I got the idea of using the talents of others. I figured that if I could get a half-dozen kids and get them each a fight a month I could make more money than if I was fighting myself."

He was eighteen when he started managing fighters. He would go down to St. Paul and corner Mike and Tom Gibbons. They called Mike "The St. Paul Phantom," and Tom went fifteen rounds with Dempsey, and Jack would ask them questions, and as he watched fights, he would lift a move here and a move there, starting to build up his own library of moves and punches.

When World War I started, Jack got into it. He was in D Company of the 18th Infantry of the First Division that, a generation later, I would come to know in Normandy and the Huertgen and in Germany on both sides of the Rhine. For a while they were in Heudicourt in the St. Mihiel sector, and the British sent in a Sergeant Major named Cassidy, to teach the Yanks the bayonet manual.

"He was a miserable s.o.b.," Jack used to say, "but he knew his business. He would stand there unarmed with his hands down at his sides, and he'd say, 'Stick me!' You'd have your rifle with the bayonet fixed, and you'd make a lunge at him and you'd miss. Maybe the next time your rifle would go up in the air, or you'd get the butt of it under your chin. He did it all with feinting and footwork. He'd draw you into a lead, and that would be the last you'd have to do with it. You'd have the bayonet, but this Cassidy, without even touching the bayonet, would be controlling it.

"I used to go and see this guy at night," Jack said. "His stuff fascinated me, so one night I said to him, 'This puts me in mind of boxing.' He said, 'The bayonet manual was taken from boxing. If you're standing in the on-guard position, and I take the rifle out of your hands, you're standing like a boxer. Now I put the rifle back in your hands, and at the command of 'long point' you make a left jab. Now you move the opponent out of position, and you come up to hit him with the butt. Isn't that the right uppercut?'"

It was the footwork that impressed Jack, though. As Jack told it, this Cassidy would stand right there with his feet spread, and he wouldn't move them more than a couple of inches and still they couldn't reach him with the bayonet.

"If a boxer would master this style," Cassidy told Jack, "he'd save thousands of steps. He'd be just as safe as I am, and he'd save all those fancy steps."

"And can't you see it now?" Jack would say. "As you look back on Billy Petrolle, can't you see where I got that famous shuffle step?"

Jack would forget, of course, that I had never seen Petrolle fight, that I was a high school kid at the time, but I had built up such a book on him, listening to Jack and others talk about him, that it was as if I had been at all those fights. Even now, after watching thousands of fights, I can "see" those Petrolle fights, punch by punch, as I have seen few fights.

There was the first McLarnin fight, that Joe Williams cited as the greatest he ever saw in the Garden. One of the moves that Jack had taught Petrolle was the knack of turning away from a right hand and throwing a right hand back, and just before the fight he sat down with Petrolle to map it out.

"Now remember," he said, "you can't turn away from McLarnin's right because he punches too long and too sharp. You'd be too far away from him to hit him. With this guy you have to resort to an amateur move. He won't expect it from you because he knows you're a good fighter, and he thinks you know too much. What you've got to do is drop the left hand. He'll throw the right, and you lean down under it and counter with the left instead of the right. He won't be looking for it, and you can't miss him with it."

Petrolle started drawing the right and countering with the left, and McLarnin didn't know where those punches were coming from. He knew they weren't coming from Petrolle, because Petrolle wouldn't do a thing like that and, as Joe Williams wrote later, at one point he looked at Patsy Haley, the referee, as if to ask, "Are you hitting me?"

"But McLarnin was some fighter," Jack said and, of course, McLarnin went on to win the welterweight title, "and after a while he figured it out. Then I had Petrolle switch. He walked out there and started jabbing and missing, jabbing and missing. McLarnin thought he had him all figured out again, and he tried to anticipate Petrolle and moved in. He came in, right into a right that Petrolle had been building up all the time, and down he went."

Petrolle won that decision, but Jack always said his greatest fight was with Justo Suarez in the Garden seven months after McLarnin. Suarez was out of the Argentine, a bull of a light-weight, and they called him "The Little Firpo." After he came to this country and licked three of the best light-weights around, no one wanted to fight him, but Jack took him for Petrolle.

"After the match was made," Jack used to say, telling about it, "I went up to the gym to get a line on Suarez. He used to box sixteen or eighteen rounds a day without more than breaking a light sweat. The day I was watching him, he fell out of the ring and landed on his head and got up and went right back in. I said, 'Oh-oh, this is going to be it!'

"Well, Petrolle was some hooker, you know, and in the first round he had Suarez down three times. At the end of the round Suarez had Petrolle back on his heels, and when Billy came back to the corner, I said, 'Now don't hit him on the chin again. When you leave this corner you bend over and you punch with both hands to the body.' Petrolle used to follow orders to the letter, and for six rounds it was the most scientific exhibition of body punching anybody ever saw. At the end of the seventh round Petrolle said to me, 'Jack, I think he's ready.' I said, 'Not yet. Stay right down there and punch up.'

"At the end of the eighth round I said, 'All right, now is the time. Start this round the same way, and after three or four punches to the body, raise up and hit him a right hand on the chin. If he don't go, get down again and then raise up and hit him a left hand on the chin. If he don't go, you stay down.'

"Petrolle went out, belted that Suarez three shots in the body and then came up. He landed the right hand flush on the chin and he shook Suarez. Now, another fighter would have been tempted to throw another right, but Petrolle went back to the body, and the second time he rose it was with the hook, and Suarez went over on his head. Hell, it was easy, if they'll only do what you tell them. The other fella doesn't know what he's doing. He's just guessing, but you know, because you've got it figured."

What Jack meant was that Jack had it figured. Crouched there below the corner he wouldn't be watching his own fighter, because he knew what his own fighter could do. He would be watching the other fighter, and not slipping or ducking any punches, he would be studying the other fighter's moves and analyzing his errors.

"So tell him about the Eddie Ran fight," Wilbur Wood said to him one day. We were in one of the dressing rooms at Stillman's Gym when Jack had Vince Foster, who looked like another Petrolle until Jack lost his grip on him to whiskey and women, and at the age of twenty-one, he died one night in a highway crash near Pipestone, Minnesota.

"Yeah," Jack said, "but the thing about Petrolle was that people never knew how good he was. They thought he was a lucky fighter, but what he did he did because it was planned that way. It wasn't any accident when he won a fight.

"Petrolle, you know, wasn't easy to hit. He gave the impression that he was easy to hit. Sure he did. He invited you to hit him. Do you know why? Because then he could hit you back. Petrolle would go in there and put it up there where you could hit it. He'd take two or three jabs, and then slip under and let go with the heavy artillery. That's a good trade any time you can take three light punches to let go with the heavy stuff. What gave people the impression that Petrolle was easy to hit was that he was always on the edge of danger. That's the place to be. Be in there close where you can work, where you take advantage of it when the other guy makes a mistake, and . . . "

"And don't pull back," Wilbur said. "That's where they get hurt."

"Certainly," Jack said. "For fifteen years I've been schooling myself. If I ever get into a theater fire I'm not gonna get up and rush for the exit. What chance have I got? Like the others, I'm gonna be trampled to death. Do you know what I'm going to do? I'm gonna sit right in my seat for thirty seconds and figure it out. Then I'm going to get up and walk over the others and pick my exit."

"But tell him about the Ran fight," Wilbur said.

"Sure," Jack said, "but, you see, it's like that when you fight. You're safest when you're closest to danger. You're inside where you may get your block knocked off if you don't know what you're doing, but if you know what you're doing it's a cinch. You look so easy that the other guy has to try to hit you. Don't you see? He can't help himself, and then when you've got him coming, you work your stuff, you let the heavy stuff drop. Why, Petrolle used to just sit there in that rocking chair and belt them when they came in."

"The Ran fight," Wilbur said.

"Yeah," Jack said. "In the first round he had Ran down a couple of times with hooks. When he came back to the corner I said, "You're not going to drop him with a hook again. You've got to get him to throw the right. You've got to slip it like this . . . ""

He had his hands out in front of himself, and he moved his head as if he were slipping a punch.

"Do you know," he said, "that we had to wait until the sixth round for that chance for Petrolle to get that opening for his own right? He went out there, jabbing and jabbing and hooking light and sticking it right out there, and Ran wouldn't do anything. All of a sudden, though, Ran fired that right, and Petrolle slipped it and let his own go. It was really a hook with the right, and Ran went down—like this—like he'd been cut down at the knees with a scythe.

"After the fight, though," Jack said, that pinched look of disgust coming into his face again, "do you know what they said? They said Petrolle was lucky. They said, 'My, what a lucky punch. What a lucky fighter.' It wasn't luck. It was the work of an artist, and after Petrolle got dressed he went into Ran's dressing room. Ran said to him, 'Billy, I'm embarrassed.' Petrolle said, 'Why?' Ran said, 'I'm embarrassed of Eddie Ran. I knew you were gonna do that to me, but I couldn't help myself. You made it look so easy I just had to throw that right.'

"Then when he came out," Jack said, "Petrolle says to me, 'Jack, we'd better not fight them again. They're hep.'"

I wrote that for the next day's paper, the conversation in the dressing room with Jack talking and making the moves and Wilbur Wood cueing him. A couple of days later the old, white-haired receptionist at the paper who, it seemed to me, must have been there when they ran the headline that Lincoln had been shot, came shuffling into the sports department, and he had the name on the slip of paper and he said, "There's a Mr. Eddie Ran here to see you."

"Oh?" I said. "Send him in."

Seventeen years had gone by since the fight. How many times Eddie Ran had refought that one I had no idea, and how does a man react when, suddenly in a newspaper, he reads a description that brings back a night when he was knocked out?

"Mr. Heinz?" he said, walking up to me and putting out his hand. "I'm Eddie Ran."

He had on heavy work clothes, brown pants and a brown windbreaker and heavy work shoes. He was slim, and his face was tanned.

"I'm glad to meet you," I said, shaking his hand and waiting.

"I'm glad to meet *you*," he said, and then he smiled. "Gee, that was some column you had in the paper yesterday. I'm working on the docks over at the river, so I just had to come in and tell you."

"All I did was write what Jack Hurley said."

"Hurley told you the truth," he said. "That was some fight, and like Hurley said, I knew Petrolle wanted me to throw that right, but I just couldn't help myself."

Jack named Petrolle "The Fargo Express," and gave him one of the great trade names of boxing. Petrolle was of Italian descent, but he had high cheekbones to go with his black hair and dark eyes, so Jack gave him one of the great trademarks—an Indian blanket—to wear into the ring. When Petrolle retired after 255 fights and built a home in Duluth, he wanted to hang that blanket on the wall of his den.

"But it has blood on it," his wife said.

"Only some of it is mine," Petrolle said.

All Petrolle and Jack ever had for a contract was a handshake, but after thirteen years Petrolle retired during the Depression with $200,000 and an iron foundry in Duluth. When I met him years later, he owned a religious goods and gift shop in Duluth, and he was the chairman of the board of directors of the Pioneer National Bank.

After Petrolle retired, after his hook was gone and after his legs had left him, Jack announced in Duluth that he was looking for somebody to take the place of "The Fargo Express." The story went out over the Associated Press wire, and within the next week six hundred candidates showed up in Duluth.

"I forgot what it cost me to get them out of town," Jack used to say. "The Police Department came to me and said, 'Look, you got Michigan Street loaded with guys stranded here.' I had to pay the fare home for half of them, and there wasn't a fighter in the lot. Most of them should have been arrested for even entertaining the thought that they could be taught to fight."

There were very few people in the fight business then who wouldn't have found a way to make some money out of those six hundred, but not Jack. To Jack a fighter was a tool, and he was always looking for the tool that, when he finished shaping it and honing it over the years, would be the perfect tool to do the perfect work. He put all of himself into it, and when a Hurley fighter went into the ring Jack took every step with him. That fighter was what Jack would have been if he had had the body for it, and that is why it took so much out of Jack when, under pressure, the tool broke.

The best Jack had after Petrolle was Harry "Kid" Matthews, who had had seventy fights in twelve years but was getting no-where when Jack took him on. Before he was done with him, Jack actually started a Congressional investigation into why the International Boxing Club wouldn't give Matthews a fight in the Garden. When they did, they put him with Irish Bob Murphy, who was belting everybody out, and they gave Murphy to Jack because nobody else would take him.

"Well, you're in," somebody said to Jack. "All you have to do is lick this guy and you're in."

A half a dozen of us were sitting around in the boxing office on the second floor of the Garden. We had just been making small talk when Jack had come in. He was fifty-three then, and Royal Brougham had written in the Seattle *Post Intelligencer* that he looked like a stern-faced deacon passing the collection plate at the First Methodist Church.

"Sure, we're in," Jack said, those ice-blue eyes narrowing behind those glasses, and a hurt look coming over his face. "We're in with a murderer. This guy never lets up. He rips you and slashes you and tears you apart inside. He's rough and strong, and you can't hurt him."

Jack turned and started to leave. He got as far as the door, and then he turned back and his eyes were big now behind the glasses and he had fear all over his face.

"That's the kind of guy you have to fight to get in here," he said. "Why, we're liable to get killed."

He left then. Pete Reilly was sitting there, and he had been around for so many years and worked so many a deal that they called him "The Fox."

"Listen to Hurley," Pete said, smiling and shaking his head. "When Jack talks like that you know he's got it figured. You know he's ready to slip one over. You can bet your bundle on that."

The smart money bet the bundle on Murphy, and it was some licking that he and they took. Matthews would draw a lead, and then he would slide with that shuffle step into one of those Hurley moves and he would belt Murphy so that the cops with the duty out on Eighth Avenue must have felt it. It was the greatest exhibition of body punching I have ever seen, and all the time that it was happening to Murphy there wasn't any way that Murphy could avoid it without turning his back and walking out.

The next day, up in the Garden, everybody was crowding Jack. They were slapping him on the back and telling him it had been years since they had seen anyone who could punch like that, and that it had been some fight.

"When I got home last night and went to bed," Irving Rudd was telling Jack, "it was like I had just finished a great book. I kept seeing it over and over, and I couldn't get to sleep."

"Why, in the ninth round," Jesse Abramson said to Jack, and Jesse was writing for the *New York Herald-Tribune* then, "your guy hit Murphy seven solid hooks without a return. I counted seven terrific hooks to the body, and Murphy couldn't help himself. It was wonderful."

"Yes, wasn't that wonderful?" Jack said, and now that pained look came into his face again. "Why, that was stupid. After he'd hit that Murphy with three of those solid hooks and turned him around, if he'd just thrown one right-hand uppercut he'd have knocked that stiff out."

"But it was a still a great fight," somebody said.

"And he'll do the same with that Marciano," Jack said, "if I can get him the fight."

That was one I never wanted for Jack, and I tried to talk him out of it. Putting Matthews against Marciano was like sending an armored jeep against a tank, but by the time Jack had sold the press and the public on Matthews he had also sold himself.

"I've been watching Charley Goldman working with Marciano," I told Jack. Jack had come into New York and we were having lunch in one of the booths in Muller's across Fiftieth Street from the Garden.

"Oh?" he said.

"Charley's really making a fighter out of him," I said.

"He is, is he?" Jack said.

"That's right," I said. "He's got him moving inside now and punching to the body, and you know he can sock."

"Ah," Jack said. "You know what you do with those body-punchers? You belt them right back in the body, and that puts an end to that."

"But this guy is too strong for your guy," I said. "You can't hurt him."

"Ah," Jack said, and there came that look, as if he had just bitten into another lemon. "Matthews will do to that Marciano just what he did to that Murphy. It'll be the same kind of fight."

Jack really believed it, and he had $10,000 bet on Matthews when they climbed into the ring in Yankee Stadium that night. I had to give Matthews the first round, because there he was, drawing Marciano's leads, moving off them and countering in that Hurley style, but all the time that it was going on, Marciano was backing him up. Matthews was winning the round, but losing the fight, and then, just as the bell sounded, Marciano hit him a right hand under the heart and Matthews bent under it, straightened up and started for Marciano's corner. Jack hollered at him, and he turned and walked to his own corner and I knew it was over. Early in the next round, and with a left hook, Marciano knocked him out.

"So are we going to stop in Fargo?" my wife was saying now. "We'll be there well before noon."

Driving back now from Jim Tescher's, we had got as far as Bismark, and had spent the night in a motel on the outskirts. We were having breakfast, and I was looking at the front page of *The Forum*, the Fargo-Moorhead paper. There was a two-column picture of a farmer standing thigh-deep in a fissure in his alfalfa field near Durbin, North Dakota. The farmer's name was Richard Hillborn, and it said in the caption under the picture, that he couldn't recall conditions ever being so dry, even in the drought of the 1930s.

"I guess so," I said, "but as it's a Saturday, there may not be anybody in the sports department of the paper. They may all be out covering football games for the Sunday paper."

"But I'm sure there'll be someone there in some department," she said. "You'll probably find someone to ask."

"I'd like to find somebody in sports, though," I said. "I doubt that anybody on the city side will remember Jack, but I'll find out."

When we passed the turnoff to Jamestown, and I saw the high-towered gas station signs on the left now, it reminded me of the white-haired woman who had flushed the high school football player out of his booth. The last we had seen of him he had been having a sandwich across from the cashier's counter when I had stopped to pay the check. The last we had heard of her she was still rasping, as she had been throughout our lunch, about ailments, not only her own but those of what must have been a whole battalion of invalided friends or acquaintances, none of whom, as walking wounded, could compare with Jack.

"Now isn't this something?" Jack was saying outside the Olympic when we got out of the cab that time he met me at the Seattle airport. "I checked in here for a week to manage that Matthews, and I've been here seventeen years. You have to remember, too, that I've got the two worst things in the world for this climate—rheumatism and sinus."

He waited while I checked in, and then we followed the bellhop up to the room. The bellhop went through all the business with the window shades and the closet doors and the bathroom light, and Jack beat me to the tip.

"All right," he said, when the bellhop had left. "Let's go down and get something to eat."

"Eat?" I said. "It's the middle of the afternoon."

"You know me," Jack said. "You know I have to eat every three hours."

Jack hated to eat alone, and that was how Ray Arcel came to call him "The Life-Taker." Jack was still around Chicago at the time, and it was just after they had taken two thirds of his stomach and he had to eat six times a day.

"It was during the Depression," Ray told me once, "and Jack had just retired Petrolle and had money, so he'd take these poor guys who were half-starving to eat with him. Jack would have a bowl of soup, or milk and crackers, but they'd order big steaks. One guy ate so much that Jack had to buy him a new suit of clothes, and another one actually ate himself to death."

They used to say around Seattle that while Jack had Matthews he would spend $1,000 a month feeding sportswriters and cops and press agents and hangers-on. Whenever he had it, he spread it around.

"When Petrolle was fighting," he told me once, "I loaned out $60,000. I had it all in a little book. Then, when I had the ulcers and I went into the Mayo Clinic, I sent out eight letters and six telegrams to guys who owed me $500 and up. I never got one reply, and I've got $75,000 more standing out since."

That first afternoon I walked Jack down Fourth Avenue to his favorite cafeteria, and watched him have a bowl of soup and a sandwich and a cup of tea. Then we walked over to the Eagles Temple at Seventh and Union, where the fighter trained, and all along the way people recognized Jack.

"How are you, Jack?" they'd say.

"No good," he'd say.

"Why, Jack!" they'd say. "How are you feeling?"

"No good," he'd say.

One noon we sat down in the restaurant in the Olympic Hotel. He had been living in that hotel for so long by then that just about everyone on the staff knew him, and when the waitress came over she was smiling.

"Why, Mr. Hurley!" she said.

"Hello, Hilda," Jack said.

"Mr. Hurley," she said, "you won't like what I'm going to say."

"What's that?" Jack said, squinting up at her.

"You're looking much better than the last time I saw you."

"Isn't that terrible?" Jack said to me. "You know I set the world's record for those sinus operations. They found out with me that there's no sense in operating. I was a guinea pig for medical science, just a living sacrifice to make the world safe for guys with bad noses."

That first afternoon at the Eagles Temple, I could see why Jack was high on the fighter. He was a dark-haired, dark-eyed kid who looked right at you, and you could tell that he was not going to be cowed by anybody or anything. He had a good pair of legs, but the best of him was up in the arms, chest, and shoulders, and he was just the right height to carry 195 pounds and still get under tall jabbers who stick out a left hand and think that they're boxing.

"So he was the 1965 National A.A.U. heavyweight champion," Jack was saying while the fighter was getting into the ring, "but he was like all amateurs—awkward and over-anxious, and just a wild right-hand swinger. For six months, every day, we worked on the footwork. His stance was too wide, so I had to tie his feet together with shoe laces and a piece of inner tube that would give about six inches. He'd walk with it, shadow-box with it, and this is a long tedious thing. You get sick and tired of it, but it's balance and leverage that make punching power.

"All right," he said to the fighter. "Move around. Let's see how fast you can move. Now slow it down. Good.

"You see?" he said to me. "He slows the action down to where he wants it—to one punch. I've taught him that speed is detrimental, because if you're moving fast you're also moving your opponent fast. If you're out hunting, would you rather shoot at a slow-moving or a fast-moving target? It's the same thing. He's been taught how to put two thirds of the ring behind him. He doesn't want it, but those jabbers and runners do, and he deprives them of it."

Jack had the fighter box three rounds then, but there was the same shortage of fighters in Seattle as everywhere else, and the light-heavyweight he was in with had been around Jack and the fighter too long. As soon as the fighter would start to build up a move the light-heavyweight would know what was doing, but you could see one thing. You could see that this was another Hurley fighter, and if you knew anything about boxing you could tell a Hurley fighter from the others as easily as an art expert can tell a Rembrandt from a Harry Grunt. There was that shuffle step, that came out of Heudicourt and the bayonet drill that Jack perfected with Petrolle, and there were those moves, with the hands low and in punching position, inviting you to lead and have your block knocked off with the counter.

"But don't you see?" Jack was saying to the fighter when it was over. "You were jumping in instead of sneaking that right foot up. You gotta sneak it up so they don't know it's coming. They think you're just jabbin', but that's only the camouflage so you can move the artillery up behind the jab. I don't even care if the jab misses."

With Jack eating every three hours and not going to bed until two or three in the morning because he had trouble sleeping, we spent a lot of time sitting around restaurants and cafeterias and the lobby of the Olympic with Jack's cronies, talking about the way things used to be and what the world was coming to. That was Jack's hobby.

"Isn't it terrible, the condition the fight game is in today?" Jack would say. "You wouldn't believe it, would you? A lot of Johnny-come-lately booking agents who call themselves managers and don't know the first thing about it. Amateurs! Why, amateurs just clutter up the world. They louse up everything they put their hands to.

"Look at what that television did, too," he'd say, "and it'll do it to pro football next. Why, you can't give your product away free and have people still respect it. That TV cheapens everything it touches. It would even cheapen the Second Coming."

Late every afternoon, of course, we would be over at the Eagles Temple, with Jack hounding the fighter. No matter what the fighter would be do-ing—boxing, shadow-boxing, punching the bag, or skipping rope—Jack would be after him.

"No, no," Jack would say, the fighter shadow-boxing around the ring. "Don't set your feet. Just walk. Now the left hook to the head. You're too tense. Just turn with it. All right. Now you jab, and the guy is a runner, so you're too far away. Now you gotta step again. Now the guy is pulling away, so you gotta throw three punches, but only one is gonna land. Now you're with a guy throws an uppercut. Now turn away so it misses, and throw the right hand up into the body. Good.

"You see?" Jack said to me. "He's like a pool player, practicing those draw shots. He's gotta get that ball back there, so he practices hour after hour un-til it becomes instinct. Like a pool player, he's also playing position at all times, and you know how long this practice lasts? His entire career. He'll still be practicing it when he quits, and you know something? If he's having trou-ble hitting a left hook to the body, it's nothing for me to sentence him to two weeks of doing nothing else. He wants to learn it to get rid of me.

"All right now," he'd say to the fighter. "You're in there with one of those runners, so you don't want to scare him or he'll start running again. Easy now. Left hook to the body. No, no! Let him see it. Start it back farther so he'll be sure to see it, because you want him to drop his hands. Good. Do that again.

"You see?" Jack said to me. "Other guys breed fear, but it's like cornering a frightened pig. This guy has been taught to encourage them, to make them feel safe. He'll sometimes miss a jab to give 'em courage, and Petrolle even had the facial expressions to go with it. The first thing you knew, he'd catch those suckers moving in."

The last afternoon, though, Jack was discouraged. We had to be in Boise the next day so Jack could go on TV and radio and talk up the fight. The fighter was going to come in two days later, just in time for the weigh-in, with Marino Guaing, the little Filipino who was training amateur fighters around Seattle and helped Jack.

"No, no," Jack was saying to the fighter, watching him hit the big bag. "The left hook is too tight. It's got to be looser. Just throw it up there. No good. Your feet were off the floor. No. Bend those knees a little. It's like you're on stilts.

"Isn't that terrible?" Jack said to me, turning away from the fighter and shaking his head. "He never did that before. You gotta watch 'em every damn minute of the day.

"Now start soft," he said to the fighter. "Easy. Now increase the power a little. Now your stiff-legged again. Start over."

The sweat was dripping off the fighter's chin. The floor under the bag was speckled with it, but Jack was still unhappy walking back to the hotel.

"Now where would he have picked that up?" he said. "You see what I mean? He picks up a bad habit, or he goes on the road and he steps on a pebble and he turns his ankle. He's liable to sleep with the window wide open and catch a cold. He comes to the gym and he may get his eye cut or hurt his hand. That's why, when you manage a fighter, you end up with cancer, heart trouble, or ulcers. I took the least."

"But look at the rewards," I said, hoping to kid Jack out of it. "How about all that fame and fortune?"

"Yeah," Jack said. "You raise him like a baby. That ring is a terrible place to be in if you don't know what you're doing in there, but you teach him how to survive. You teach him how to make his first steps, and you bring him along until he becomes a good fighter and starts to make money.

"Now, when you come into the ring with him you don't do nothin'. He's a professional fighter. He doesn't need people pawing at him and dousing him with water and tiring him out. He needs a little quiet advice, but no one sees that. So they see me up there, and they say to the fighter, 'What's *he* do for you?' Twenty guys say it, and it means nothin'. By the time eighty guys say it, though, the fighter forgets. This one will too.

"I'll tell you," Jack said. "Regardless of the outcome, this is my last fighter."

At 7:30 the next morning I met Jack in the lobby, and a bellhop named Harry carried our bags out and wished Jack luck. In the cab on the way to the airport Jack was looking at the heavy traffic heading into town.

"Look at the mules," he said. "Isn't that terrible? At 4:30 they'll all be heading the other way to take those paychecks back to the creatures. When I started out, my mother wanted me to get a steady job. I said, 'Mom, a steady job is a jail. I see these fellas I grew up with here, and they're in prison ten hours a day. I want to see something, go somewhere, and I can make a living doing it.' You care where you sit on the plane?"

"No," I said.

"I like to sit over the wing," Jack said. "It kinda gives you the feeling you've got something under you. Besides, I couldn't sleep last night. I think I slept an hour, so I want to grab a little nap."

We were the first in line and the first on the plane, and I had Jack take the window seat where he wouldn't be bothered by the traffic in the aisle. I reached up and got him a pillow, and he had just settled his head back and closed his eyes when I heard the small voice right behind us.

"Eeee choo-choo, Mommy?" the voice was saying, "Eeee choo-choo?"

"No," the woman's voice said. "Not choo-choo, dear. Airplane."

"Eeee choo-choo?"

Jack opened his eyes. He had that pinched look on his face again, and he sat up.

"Isn't that something?" he said, shaking his head. "With the whole plane to pick from I gotta draw a creature and her kid. Wouldn't you know it? Ninety per cent of those eye operations are successful, too, but I gotta be in the other ten per cent."

It didn't make any difference, because Jack wasn't going to sleep anyway. We weren't off the ground more than twenty minutes when Jack's rheumatism started to act up, and he had to stand in the aisle, holding onto the arm of my seat, almost all the way to Boise.

"Isn't that terrible?" Jack said, as we were getting off. "A whole plane, and that creature and the kid have to sit behind us."

"But he was a cute kid," I said.

"Yeah, you're right," Jack said. "I took a look at him, and he was."

Then Jack really went to work. After we checked into the hotel we walked down Main Street, with Jack saying he couldn't see a thing in the bright, shimmering sunlight and with me helping him up and down the curbs, to Al Berro's. Al Berro was promoting the fight, but for a living he was running the Bouquet Sportsmen's Center. The Bouquet had one of those long Western bars down the right side, with the meal for the day chalked on a blackboard at the far end, and along the opposite wall a half dozen tables with faded green baize covers and the nine-card joker rummy games going.

"Am I glad you're here!" Berro said, shaking Jack's hand.

"How's it look?" Jack said.

"Pretty good," Berro said.

"There goes that 'pretty good' again," Jack said to me.

"I think we'll do all right," Berro said, "but I've got you lined up for the radio and TV. You ready to start?"

In the next eight hours, with Berro driving us around town, Jack was on two television and four radio stations, and at 9 o'clock that night he was over at the *Idaho Daily Statesman*.

"Now what brings you to Boise?" one of them, interviewing Jack on the TV or the radio, would say, as if he didn't know.

"Well, I've got Boone Kirkman boxing Archie Ray, from Phoenix, at the Fairgrounds arena on Thursday night," Jack would say. "My best friends in the boxing game tell me I may be making a mistake, though, because my fighter has had only four fights and Archie Ray has had twenty-three, with eighteen wins, ten by knockout."

"What's going to happen at the Fairgrounds arena on Thursday night?" another would say.

"Well, it's hard to tell," Jack would say. "All the people in the fight game tell me Archie Ray is gonna lick my fighter for sure, but of course I don't think so."

"Jack, is Boone going to shoot for a first-round KO," another would say, "or is he going to play with this fella?"

"He doesn't play with anybody," Jack would say. "You see, all my boxing friends tell me Archie Ray is gonna be too much for my guy, but we'll find out Thursday night at the Fairgrounds arena."

Jack did some job. Knowing how he felt, and that he hadn't slept much the night before, I was amazed that he got through the day.

"Ah, I don't have the enthusiasm for it anymore," he said when we got back to the hotel.

"You've got me beat," I said.

"I'm old and I'm sick and I'm tired," he said, "but you can't let the bastards know it. They'd kill you."

On the day of the fight, the fighter and Marino, the trainer, got in about twenty minutes before the one o'clock weigh-in at the State Capitol. The elevator operator who took us up was a middle-aged woman wearing a white uniform blouse and dark skirt. She was sitting on a stool in front of the panel of buttons and, open on her lap, was an instructional volume of the Famous Writers School.

"Do you subscribe to that course?" I asked her on the way down.

"Yes," she said, looking up at me and her face brightening. "Do you?"

"No," I said, "but I've heard about it."

"I think it's just wonderful," she said. "I'm really enjoying it."

"Good," I said.

"What was all that about?" Jack said to me when we got off.

"She's taking a correspondence course in how to be a writer," I said. "It costs over four hundred bucks, and I think that, for the ones like her, it's a lonely hearts club."

"That figures, don't it?" Jack said.

When we got back to the hotel, Jack had the fighter rest until 3:30. Then we took him to the restaurant across the street.

"You'd better bring him two of your top sirloins," Jack said to the waitress, "and a baked potato and hot tea."

"The baked potato doesn't come on the menu until five," the waitress said.

"In Idaho?" the fighter said.

"Isn't that terrible?" Jack said, looking at me. "They want you to eat what they want you to eat when they want you to eat it."

After the fighter finished eating he took a walk with Marino, and Jack and I went down to a cafe he liked on Main Street, and he had a ham sandwich on whole-wheat bread, sliced bananas, and a cup of tea. At 7:30 Jack was sitting in the hotel lobby when the fighter and Marino came down from their rooms with Marino carrying the fighter's black zipper bag.

"Listen," Jack said to the fighter, "when you finished eating across the street there, did you remember to tip the waitress?"

"Gee, no," the fighter said. "I forgot."

"Here," Jack said, handing him a bill. "Go over and do it now."

When the fighter came back we all got in a cab and went out to the Fairgrounds. In the dark the cabbie missed the main entrance, so we rode around between a lot of barns before we got to the arena with the sign SALES PAVILION over the door.

"You see?" Jack said when we got inside, the customers milling around us. "It's like the old Cambria in Philadelphia."

From where the ring was set up in the middle of the floor the solid planking of the wooden stands went back and up like steps on all four sides to where the walls and the ceiling rafters met. The stands were about half full, with more customers climbing up and sliding along the rows and sitting down.

"You gonna fill up?" Jack said to Al Berro.

"I don't know," Berro said. "I've got eleven hundred and fifty bucks in, and I've only collected at the Stagecoach, Hannifin's and a couple of others. I've got Homedale and Mountain Home coming in yet, so we'll do pretty good."

"There goes that 'pretty good' again," Jack said.

They had the fighter dressing under the stands in a small room with a wash basin and a toilet in it and a shower without a curtain. There was no rubbing table, only a green painted bench, and when the fighter stood up, he had to be careful not to hit his head on the naked light bulb sticking down from the low ceiling.

It was hot in the room, so the fighter had stripped down and was in his black trunks with white stripes. He had put on his white socks and was lacing his ring shoes. Through the wall you could hear the ring announcer bringing on the first preliminary.

"Marino," Jack said, "tell them I'm gonna start bandaging and to send somebody over here if they want to watch."

"But I just there," Marino said. "They don't come in yet."

"Then the hell with them," Jack said. "I'm gonna start anyway."

"Oh, excuse me," one of the customers said, looking in. "I thought this was the men's room."

"Next door," the fighter said.

"This will go on all night," Jack said. "They sell a lot of beer here."

With his bad eyes Jack had to squint to see what he was doing, but after bandaging fighters' hands for a half century, he could have done it with his eyes closed. While he was putting it on—the gauze around the wrist, and then across the palm and between the thumb and index finger, and then back around the wrist and around the hand and across the knuckles, and then the tape—we could hear the crowd hollering and then, over our heads, the stamping of feet.

"All right," Jack said to Marino when it was over. "Grease him up."

Marino rubbed the cocoa butter on the fighter's arms and shoulders and chest and neck and face. When he had finished, Jack sent him to watch the other people bandage and put the gloves on. The fighter was sitting on the bench, his bandaged hands in his lap, serious now.

"The hell with them," Jack said after a while. "We might as well get into the gloves. Then you'll have plenty of time to loosen up, because they take that intermission to sell more beer."

"Good," the fighter said.

Jack helped the fighter into the right glove first, the laces down the palm and then around the wrist, then tied the ends and put a strip of tape over it. When he had finished with the left glove, Marino was back.

"They all done now," he said.

"All right," Jack said to the fighter. "Loosen up, but be careful of that light. Now jab . . . hook . . . jab . . . move up behind it. All right, but don't stand there. You gotta move right up behind it. And another thing, if you start to miss punches just settle down and start over again."

"I know," the fighter said.

"We're ready to go Jack," Al Berro said, sticking his head through the doorway after the fighter had had about five minutes of it. "You ready?"

"Yeah," Jack said, and then to Marino, "You got the mouth-piece?"

They went out and down the aisle, Marino first, carrying the pail, and then the fighter and then Jack. The aisle was crowded, some of the customers still trying to get back to their seats with their containers of beer, and then the calls started from the stands.

"Hey, Jack! How many rounds?" . . . "Good luck, Jack!" . . . "Hey, Kirkman, how about our money's worth tonight?"

When the bell rang, Jack's fighter walked out in that Hurley style, hands low and in punching position, and he walked right to Archie Ray. Archie Ray was a straight-up fighter, with a pretty good jab and a straight right hand, and he started out to make a fight of it. He punched right with Jack's fighter, and I gave him that first round. Jack hadn't said a thing, but now he was up in the corner, bending over the fighter and lecturing him, and when he came down the steps at the start of the second round I could see he was still mad.

"Hey, Kirkman!" some loudmouth was hollering. "You're gonna get yours tonight!"

"His stance was too wide, and his feet are too flat," Jack said. "What's the matter with him?"

"He's tense," I said. "He'll fight out of it."

"Tense, hell," Jack said. "He's never been like this before."

He didn't fight out of it. In the second round you could see he was trying to settle down and put his moves together, but he was still too anxious. The young ones, if they're really fighters, are usually that way. They know what they're supposed to do, but then they are hit with a good punch, and they widen that stance and start swinging because they want to end it with one. Jack's fighter was still throwing punches from too far out, but he was hurting Ray with right hands. You had to give him that second round and the third, too, although he came out of a mix-up he should never have been in with his nose bleeding.

"Hey, Kirkman!" the loudmouth was hollering when he saw the blood. "How do you like it now?"

"Isn't this terrible?" Jack was saying. "All he's got to do is jab and move up before he lets those right hands go. What's the matter with him?"

"He's still trying too hard," I said.

"Hell," Jack said.

In the fourth round he had Ray against the ropes and then through them, but he couldn't finish him, and in the fifth round he dropped him with a nice inside right hand to the body and still couldn't put him away. Ray looked like he was in there just to stay now, and by the sixth round you could see Jack's fighter tiring, the way they all do until they learn pace. He would be all right for the first half of a round, but then he would flatten out and start to flounder. In the eighth round, though, he made one good Hurley move. He drew that right hand of Ray's and, when it came, he turned from it and turned back with his own. It was a little high—on the cheekbone—but it caught Ray following through and moving into it, and Ray's knees started to go as he backed off.

"He's got him now," I said to Jack.

"And everybody in the house knows it but him," Jack said over the roar, and by the time he said it, the chance was past. "Isn't that terrible?"

That was the last round, and it had been enough of a war so that the crowd liked it. Jack's fighter got the unanimous decision, but when we got to the dressing room he was still disgusted, and Jack was, too.

"I swear I can fight better than that," the fighter was saying to two of the local sportswriters. "That's the worst fight I've ever had."

"He was in a trance," Jack said. "He couldn't even follow orders, and he always follows orders to the letter."

"I didn't even feel like I was in a fight," the fighter said. "I can't understand that."

"The hell with it," Jack said finally. "Let's get out of here."

And hour later we were still sitting in the restaurant across the street from the hotel. The fighter had a milk shake, and Jack was nibbling on a ham and cheese sandwich on whole wheat and still going over the fight.

"He comes back at the end of the first round," he said to me, "and he says, 'I'm not sick, but something's the matter with me.'"

"That's right," the fighter said.

"So I said, 'It's too bad, but you're here. You're having a bad night, but you'll fight out of it. You're punchin' from too far back. Jab and move up and then wing those right hands.'

"So you've got him against the ropes," Jack said to the fighter now, "and he's lookin' for the punch, ready to duck it, and you give it to him, instead of the jab. Let him duck the jab and into the right."

"I know," the fighter said, shaking his head.

"Now you know what it takes to be a fighter," Jack said. "You've got to settle down and live it and sleep it and eat it."

"But I do," the fighter said.

"But you've got to do it more," Jack said. "You can't afford bad nights like this."

"I know," the fighter said.

The fighter left then to pick up a couple of the display cards with his picture on them that Al Berro had for him. That is how new he was, and Jack took another bite of the sandwich and then left the rest of it and we walked out onto the street.

"That's the worst I've seen him," Jack said. "He knows how to do those things. Why couldn't he do them? How could he possibly be that bad?"

"Don't get sore," I said. "When you figure it out, he's had six rounds of professional boxing before tonight. You know it takes time."

"But I haven't got too much time," Jack said. "Hell, I think I'll walk down to Berro's and find out how much they took in tonight. Maybe I'll finally find out how good that 'pretty good' is."

"I'll go along with you," I said.

"No," Jack said. "You've got that early plane to grab. You've got to get some sleep."

"I'd rather go with you."

"I can make it alone," Jack said. "Hell, the way the eyes are now, I can see better at night than I can in that damn sunlight."

"If you say so," I said, and we shook hands, "but take care of yourself."

"Yeah," Jack said, "but wasn't that terrible tonight?"

The last time I ever saw him I watched him then, old and half-blind and aching all over, start slowly down the empty Main Street of Boise, Idaho, at one o'clock in the morning, heading for the Bouquet Sportsmen's Center to find out how much money there had been in the house. Once, after that, I did see him in a way. Four-and-a-half years later, I sat in a theater and watched as George Foreman, too big and too strong for Boone Kirkman, took him apart in two rounds. It was the armored jeep against the tank again, and the old Hurley moves never got started. The old dreamer that was in the old pragmatist had dreamed too much too late, and Jack's forty-year search for another perfect tool like Billy Petrolle was over.

When we turned off the Interstate now, my wife had the *Rand McNally Road Atlas* in her lap. There was a two-page spread of the Dakotas, and a street map of Fargo, and the Saturday traffic was light. We found *The Forum*, and I parked in a black-paved lot across the street.

"I don't know how long I'll be," I said. "If there's no one in there who ever heard of Jack, that'll be the end of it, and I'll be right out."

"Take your time," she said. "I'll just wander around."

Off the lobby on the left there was a door identifying the classified advertising department, and I opened that. It was a large room, with a counter along the right and a lot of desks. Behind two of them, and facing the counter, two young women were sitting, and when I walked in they looked up.

"Excuse me," I said, "but can you tell me where your sports department is?"

"The sports department?" one of them said. "That's on the second floor?"

"And I go up these stairs out here?" I said. "And then it'll be on the left or right?"

"The left or the right?" the same young woman said, and then she stood up. While I watched, she turned her back to me and she pointed with one hand one way, and with the other hand she pointed the other, and then she turned around again. "It'll be on the left."

"Thank you," I said. "Thank you very much."

"You're welcome," she said.

Jack should have watched that, I was thinking, walking up the stairs. Out in Seattle that last time, before we flew down to Boise, we were sitting around the lobby of the Olympic with some of Jack's cronies one night, and Jack was expounding again on all the hazards and all the heartbreak in trying to make and move a fighter.

"And how about women?" I said to him, playing the straight man again. "Have you explained women to this fighter?"

"The creatures?" Jack said. "I've explained it all to him. I've told him, 'Look, marriage is for women and kids, and it's expensive. You've got to be able to afford it. Your best chance to make a lot of money is to become a good fighter, and then you'll be able to afford marriage.' He understands that point.

"Did I ever tell you," he said, "about the fighter I had who started looking at the creatures, and one day he went to the movies? When he came back, I said, 'How was the picture?' He said, 'It was good. It was a Western.' I said, 'Any dames in it?' He said, 'Yeah, one.' I said, 'How many guys were after the dame?' He said, 'Three.' I said, 'Anybody get killed?' He said, 'Yeah, two.' I said, 'The dame one of them?' He said, 'No. Just two of the guys.' I said, 'There! Doesn't it figure? Don't you see how the odds are stacked for those creatures?' It didn't do any good.

"Then I had another one." Jack said, "who was starting to think he was in love. You can tell when they don't have their minds on their work, so one day we're walking along the street and the light changes and I said, 'Wait a minute.' Next to us is this creature with a little creature, about three or four years old, and the little creature is all dolled up and has a little pocketbook. I nudge the fighter, and I said to the little one, 'Hello, little girl. That's a very nice pocketbook you have there. Do you have any money in it?' So she says, 'Yes, three pennies.'

"So the light changes again and they go on their way, but I say to the fighter, 'Don't move.' Here comes another creature now with a little boy, and the light changes again, and they stop. I nudge the fighter again, and I say to the little boy, 'Say, son, that's a nice new suit you're wearing. Do you have any money in your pocket?' The little kid looks up at me, and he shakes his head, and he says, 'Nope.'

"So I say to the fighter, 'You see that? That little creature with the pocketbook is being educated in how to handle money. This poor little mule here is being taught nothing. All he'll be taught when he grows up is to bring the paycheck home each week to the creature. Don't you see that?' You know what the fighter said to me?"

"No," I said.

"He said, 'But, Jack, my girl is different.' Now the light changes again, and this time I go *my* way. Isn't that terrible?"

At the top of the stairs now I turned left and walked into the city room, almost somnolent now on a Saturday morning. Across the room, at the far right, a young man, bearded and in a short-sleeved sports shirt, was typing. On the left two others, older, were sitting at their desks and talking, and from the right another was walking toward them.

"Excuse me," I said to him, "but I'm looking for your sports department."

"Over there," he said, pointing, "where you see that young fella."

"Thank you," I said, and I walked over between the desks. I waited until he stopped typing and looked up at me.

"I'm sorry to bother you," I said, "but can you tell me where Jack Hurley is buried?"

"Jack Hurley?" he said. "I don't know, but that man over there can probably tell you."

"The one in the white shirt?" I said, thinking that well, at least he had heard of Jack.

"Right."

"Thank you," I said.

"Okay," he said, and as I turned he went back to his typing.

The one in the white shirt was still talking with the other at the next desk when I walked up. He stopped and turned toward me.

"Excuse me," I said, "but can you tell me where Jack Hurley is buried?"

"Jack?" he said. "Gosh, I don't know. It's in one of the cemeteries around here, but I forget which one."

"There are several?"

"Three," he said, and he reached into a drawer of his desk and brought out a telephone directory. He started to turn through the yellow pages, and then he said, "Wait a minute. His brother Hank is still around town."

"He is?" I said.

I had known that Jack was the oldest of five children, but he had talked little about the others. It had been as if it would have detracted from his pose as an opponent of all domesticity.

"Sure," the one in the white shirt said now. "He's got a religious goods store. Here it is. It's at 622 Second Avenue, only a few blocks from here."

He gave me the directions and I thanked him and I went out and walked over. At the address he had given me, the store was vacant.

"Excuse me," I said, "but I'm looking for Hurley's religious goods store."

He was standing in a doorway. He needed a shave, and he looked as if he were coming off a bad night, or several of them.

"It ain't here any more," he said. "They moved around the corner there to Broadway, just up there."

"Thank you," I said.

"Yeah," he said.

The sign outside made clear that it was a gift shop and religious goods store, and the shelves and the counters displayed dishes and glassware and household ornaments. When I walked in, a woman, smiling, came forward to meet me.

"May I help you?" she said.

"Is Mr. Hank Hurley in?" I said.

"Hank Hurley?" she said. "No, he's not. He doesn't own this store any more. Mr. Donald McAllister owns it now."

"Oh?" I said. "Do you know where I might find Hank Hurley?"

"I don't," she said, "but maybe Mr. McAllister can help you. He's back there in the office."

He was coming out of the office as I walked toward it. I introduced myself, and told him I was trying to find Hank Hurley.

"Hank?" he said. "He lives in the hotel right around the corner here. The college has taken it over, but they're letting him keep his room for a while. Maybe I can get him on the phone."

He picked up the phone and he dialed and he asked for Hank Hurley. He waited, and then he put the phone down.

"He's not in his room," he said. "He's probably at the Elks Club, having his lunch. He always eats early, and we could try him there."

"That's all right," I said. "I can try him at the hotel later, but I'd like to know where his brother Jack is buried."

"Jack?" he said. "I think it's the Holy Cross Cemetery. It'll be right here in the book from the funeral."

From a drawer of the desk he took out the book with its light gray watered-silk cover. He opened it on the desk.

"This is Hank's desk," he said. "A year and a half ago he sold the business to me, but I've still got the desk and Jack's trunk down in the basement. It's full of scrap books and I don't know what."

"I can imagine," I said.

I remembered the trunk from room 679 at the Olympic Hotel. The room was just big enough to contain the bed, the steamer trunk, the footlocker for Jack's files and the desk where, on the thirty-year-old Corona portable, Jack pounded out the publicity. While he was making Harry "Kid" Matthews into a leading contender and starting that Congressional investigation, he was spending $10,000 a year for stationery, stamps, and the newspapers that carried stories about him and the fighter that he used to clip and send to sportswriters throughout this country.

"Don't write about me on Sundays," he used to tell his friends on the sports pages. "Sunday papers cost more, and you're running up my overhead."

"Here it is," McAllister said now, reading from the book, "'Holy Cross Cemetery, West one-half, lot 35, block 7, old section. Laid to rest, November 21, 1972, 12:15 P.M.' Say, you almost made it!"

"Made it?" I said. "Made what?"

"You almost made 12:15 P.M. It's 12:45 now."

"How about that?" I said.

"'Born December 9, 1897,'" he said, reading from the book again.

"'Died November 15, 1972.' Then here's all the relatives and friends who came and signed their names."

"May I look through those?" I said.

"Sure," he said. "I've looked at this before. These two sisters have died since, but here's Billy Petrolle's signature. He was here."

"Good," I said, "and I'm glad to see that so many came."

"Well," he said, "let's count the pages here. There are, let's see, nine pages of signatures. Now let's count how many signatures there are on a page. Eighteen. Just a second."

He reached over to the adding machine. He punched some numbers on it, and looked at the tape. He went back to punching numbers again.

"I'm not doing something right," he said, "but there must have been about 160–75 attended."

"I make it 162," I said.

"Right," he said. "You know, Hank goes out to the grave twice a week to water and put flowers on it. It's been so dry that he's been doing it every night. In case you don't find Hank, I'll draw you a map of how to get there."

On a page from a desk memo pad, he drew the map showing how we should go north to the airport and then turn left. The page bore the imprint of the Muench-Kreuzer Candle Co., Inc., of 4577 Buckely Road, Liverpool, N.Y., 13088.

"You've really been most kind," I said, as we shook hands, "and I thank you."

"Glad to do it," he said, smiling. "I guess Jack was quite a guy."

"Yes," I said. "He was."

I walked around the corner to the hotel and, when I had the college student at the desk ring the room, Hank Hurley answered. He said he was amazed, and he sounded it, that I should be right there in the lobby. He had been about to take a nap, he said, but he would be down as soon as he dressed. I told him I would walk back to *The Forum*, where my wife would be waiting in the car, and he said he would meet us in the parking space across from the hotel. When we got out of the car he walked up, shorter and with more weight on him than Jack, but with the same look in the eyes and the same mouth. He took us to lunch at the Elks Club, and while we ate, he talked about Jack.

"You know," he said, "Jack used to say to me, 'When the good Lord takes me, I hope he does a clean job.' I told my sister, 'He couldn't have done a cleaner job.' If he'd had all his marbles and been in one of those nursing homes, he would have been oh, so unhappy.'

"How did he go?" I said.

"At the Olympic," he said, "Jack was always there at the front desk when the four o'clock mail came in. When he wasn't there, and it got to be 4:45, somebody got the assistant manager and they found him dead at the foot of his bed in that room 679."

It was out of that room that, in 1957, Jack also promoted the Floyd Patterson-Pete Rademacher fight for the heavyweight championship of the world. Cus D'Amato was protecting Patterson then, and he accepted Rademacher, who was the Olympic heavyweight champion but had never had a professional fight, as a likely victim and Jack as the logical promoter. Jack forgot for a while that he had no use for amateurs and, out of his pockets and a box under the bed, he sold $74,000 worth of tickets out of the $243,000 they took in, and Rademacher, green as he was, had Patterson down in the second round before Patterson put him down six times and then, in the sixth round, knocked him out.

"Just think," Jack said, after it was over. "An amateur did this for me. I guess it just goes to show there's some good in everybody. Somebody told me that he went to a college, too, and took a course in how to be an animal husband. Now what kind of a college course is that?"

"At the Olympic," Hank Hurley was saying now, "they put a floral display on the door of the room. In the dining room, at the table where Jack always sat, they had a black ribbon and a single rose and a card that said, 'Reserved for Jack Hurley.' At a chair at the counter they had another single rose and another card, and they kept them there for a week."

"They thought a lot of him there," I said, "and I remember he used to tell me, 'You know I've got my plantin' suit. I've had it for years, and every now and then I try it on to see that it still fits.'"

"He had several plantin' suits," Hank Hurley said. "Every now and then he'd buy a new one."

"He said he had sent you an insurance policy and told you, 'When I check out, this is for the burial, but nothing fancy. Just have them sharpen my feet and drive me into the ground, and I hope it's not during the winter.'"

"That's right," Hank said, "he used to tell me, 'Don't make a production of it, and don't open the casket except for you and our sisters and a couple of friends. Nobody else knows me there.' We did open it for our sisters and Billy Petrolle."

After lunch he drove us out past the airport and then turned left onto a gravel road past two cemeteries on the left and then into the third. He stopped the car about 150 feet inside the gate, and we walked over the sun-baked sod, the dried yellow grass making a sound under our shoes. Backed by two spruce, there was the gray granite headstone with Jack's father's name on it and a cross on top and a red geranium at the base. To the left there two granite markers, one with Jack's mother's name on it and the other with his sister's. On the right was the marker that said "John C. Hurley." So severe was the drought that there were cracks about an inch wide in the black top-soil and they outlined in a rectangle the shape of the coffin.

"Jack hated that name John," Hank Hurley was saying. "Oh, how many fights he got into in school when somebody called him 'Johnny.' I guess I made the mistake. On the memorial card it said 'Jack C. Hurley,' and I sent it out to the stone-cutter. When I saw this I called him and he said, 'But you ran a line through it and wrote "John."' I guess it's my fault."

"Forget it," I said. "It was the name with which he was christened. That makes it right."

"I don't know," he said. "I don't remember doing that, but I guess it was my fault."

After he drove us back to our car and we thanked him and said good-by, I drove back through the city and out to the Interstate once more. I was seeing again that rectangle in the ground.

"I can just hear Jack," I said to my wife. "I can hear him saying, 'Wouldn't you know it, Ninety per cent of the people get planted and everything goes all right. They plant me, and they have this drought. Why, there's a farmer in Durbin, North Dakota, who says it's worse than it was in the '30s. Isn't that terrible? How can you explain that?'"

Stan Musial's Last Day

from *Life*

It was 10:29 A.M. when Stanley Frank Musial, called the finest baseball player of his generation, left home to play the last of his 3,026 major league games. He came out the back door, wearing a black suit, black shoes, a white shirt and a dark tie. Behind him walked his wife, Lillian, and their 4-year-old daughter Jean, youngest of their four children.

"Jeanie?" Musial said, squatting down in front of her. "Where are you going to be today?"

"On the field," she said.

"Good, honey," he said, hugging her.

He got into his blue Cadillac and Horace McMahon, the actor and a friend for many years, got into the front seat with him. He had been up at 8:30 and gone to 9 o'clock Mass at St. Raphael's church with his family and McMahon. Now he backed the car out onto the curved concrete roadway and started away from the nine-room, red brick house in the quiet, upper-middle-class section known as St. Louis Hills.

In the mill town of Donora, Pa., Stan Musial grew up in a small frame house on top of a hill.

"Stan drove me by it once," Bob Broeg, the St. Louis sports-writer and Musial's confidant once said, "but, to tell you the truth, he didn't give me much of a look. He's not ashamed of it, but I think he feels that talking about it would embarrass his family. I said: 'Stan, just remember that Abe Lincoln grew up in a log cabin.'"

"What do you say, Marge?" Musial was saying now to a neighbor. He had stopped the car and McMahon had rolled down the window. "You and Jim all relaxed?"

"Oh, yes." Marge said. "I'm going to pray for you."

"You pray hard," Musial said, laughing. "You know? Everything breaks for me. It started out to be cloudy and look at it now."

The air was so clean and cool that it seemed it might, at any moment, shatter with a tinkling sound like thin plate glass.

"It was really something," he had said a couple of days before, talking about the morning in Donora in mid-September of 1941 when he got the telegram telling him to report to the Cardinals. "Imagine a 20-year-old kid who starts the year pitching with a sore arm and can't tell if he's going to make it anywhere in organized ball and he ends up the year in the outfield for the Cards."

He played his first major league game on Sept. 17 and Jim Tobin was pitching for Boston. Stan Musial had never seen a knuckle ball before and he popped it up. The second time Tobin fluttered one up, Stan Musial hit a double to right and drove in two runs, and the Cards won, 3–2. In 12 games that September he hit .426.

He was at the corner of Clifton and Watson now, slowed by the traffic. He was in the outside lane, and in the car on the inside lane were a man and a small girl.

"Hey, Stan!" the man shouted to him. "I hope you go out with a homer."

"I'll settle for anything today," he said, laughing.

On Sept. 22, 1948, on a chilly, windy day in Boston he got five hits in a game for the fourth time in one season, tying Ty Cobb's record. Both of his wrists were so swollen and sore that Doc Weaver, the Cards' trainer, taped them, but, unable to snap his swing, Musial had peeled the tape off.

"The pain in my wrists was so bad," he said later, "that I made up my mind I wasn't going to waste any swings. The five hits I made that afternoon were the only swings I took. I swung five times and got five hits."

He turned off the expressway at Grand Boulevard, and when he passed St. Louis University he pointed it out to McMahon.

"I'm on the president's council there," he said, "and we have a meeting once in a while."

"You might take some courses now," McMahon said. "You'll have the time and you could take public speaking—rhetoric."

"I might," he said, "but if I do anything, it would have to be private—you know? I mean, somebody come to my house. I can't do anything like that in public."

Ahead on the left he could see Busch Stadium. When he turned off Grand, he drove slowly, and the people crossing the street in the bright sunlight recognized him. The waving and the calling started. He drove into the parking lot and pulled into his place behind the hot dog stand. He got out and hurried across the street, the people running at him now from all sides, slowing him.

"Stan! Stan!" . . . "Please, Stan!"

"Stan, remember me?" one man right in front of him was saying. "You came to the hospital to see my Tommy when he was shot."

"Sure," Musial said. "Sure."

"He's doin' real good," the man was shouting after him now. "He's here today, Stan!"

He was up to the red stadium door now, and inside. He climbed the stairs past the visitors' club-house and a couple of the Cincinnati Reds waved to him and he waved back. When he opened the door to the Cardinals' club-house, he could see the TV camera crew and the newspaper and magazine photographers waiting.

"How come you got all these guys following you all the time?" Curt Simmons, the pitcher, said.

"I don't know," he said, laughing again. "I can't figure it out."

The first day Stan Musial ever entered that clubhouse, the first Card regular he met was Terry Moore the star center fielder and one of his idols. They were to become good friends.

"You look familiar," Moore said

"I ought to," he said. "You hit a homer off me in an exhibition game this spring."

"Are you that humpty-dumpty bum-armed kid?" Moore had said "How'd you ever get way up here?

"Now, Stan," the TV director was saying to him, "what we want you to do is to go out again and make a second entrance. This time use that door over there."

"You know something?" Stan said, smiling. "You guys are wearing me out. All I'm trying to do is retire."

After he had gone out and come back in again for TV, he took off his jacket and hung it on a hanger in his dressing stall. He took off his tie and unbuttoned his collar. He sat down on the red stool and looked around at the cameramen and photographers and reporters forming a semicircle around him. Along the two long walls of the room the other Cardinals were getting into their uniforms or, already suited up, leaving for the field.

"I'll tell you what I'm gonna do for you guys," he said to those around him. "I'm gonna start getting into the uniform at 12 o'clock. Right?"

"What do you recall about your first Cardinal uniform?" the reporter had asked.

"I remember," he said, "that when you came up in the fall the uniform they gave you wasn't one of those measured jobs like they give you in the spring. It wasn't number 6, that fall. I think it was something like number 24, but somebody would have to look it up. I can't remember."

Sitting there, he autographed pictures, baseballs and a bat for Mike Shannon, the 24-year-old outfielder. Then someone suggested that he pose with Shannon and Gary Kolb, the 23-year-old outfielder-infielder. Musial will be 43 years old next month.

"Sure," he said, putting an arm around each of them. "These are my young protégés. Four hundred outfielders are glad I'm retiring."

"Shannon," Horace McMahon said to a couple of the reporters "played football in high school with Stan's son Dick. That'll give you an idea, a perspective."

"Who would ever think," Kolb was saying, standing in front of his dressing stall and looking at the Musial bat, "that a guy could make so much money with a little piece of wood."

"Every time I go up to bat," Stan Musial said once, "I figure this is a base hit. Hitting is like swimming. Once you learn the stroke, you never forget it. What I do is learn to identify every pitcher's fast ball—the speed of it. Then I set up a zone about eight feet from the plate, and I follow the ball until it comes into that zone. If it keeps coming, I get the fast-ball flash. If it hesitates, I think: 'Curve.'

"It's the concentration that's the hardest," he said. "You have to give the pitcher your attention every second, and at the end of the game I'm beat. You have a lot on your mind, but you try to get rid of it before you go up to bat, and when you're really concentrating and following that ball, you can actually see the bat meet it."

"All right, you guys," he said to the two dozen of them in the semicircle in front of him. "It's 12 o'clock. You guys ready?"

"We're ready any time you are," one of them said, and they turned on their floodlights and in the bright, yellow-white glow he started to undress. He stripped to his shorts and reached into the stall for one of the sweatshirts with the red sleeves. He put it on over his head, leaving the buttons at the neck open. With the long tails of it covering him almost to his knees, he took off his shorts and got into his playing shorts.

"You characters notice how I did that?" he said, grinning. "Like they do in the movies."

He sat down and pulled on the white stockings and rolled them just below the knees. Over them he put on the red Cardinal stockings with the white and dark blue bands around them, rolling the tops. Then he stood up and got into the pants.

"Now put the shirt on slowly," the TV director said.

"But I've got to put the shoes on first," he said.

In the almost-silence, with just the whirr of the TV film camera and the clicking of the still cameras, he put on the shoes. Then he reached into the stall and took out the shirt with the number 6 and MUSIAL on the back and, slowly, got into it and buttoned it.

"Stan? Stan, could you turn this way?" . . . "Stan, could you just look over your shoulder?" . . . "Right over here, Stan."

Sad Sam Jones, the pitcher, was walking back and forth behind the semicircle. Out of a small plastic squeeze bottle he was spraying sneezing powder into the air and onto the shoulders of the photographers and reporters. Unaware of the cause, some of them started to blow their noses and to rub their eyes and then to sneeze. Sam Jones, the tears forming in his own eyes, had to turn away.

Musial sneezed.

"Some people are catching cold around here," Sam Jones said, his back to them and talking into his dressing stall and rocking with laughter.

"Okay, you guys," Musial said. "What say we go?"

He put on his cap and took his glove off the shelf. When he went out the door and crossed the cat-walk, the crowd waiting for him below called up to him. He looked down at the faces, all turned up toward him, the mouths open and shouting, and the hands waving. He waved back and went down the steps and under the stands. He came out through the dugout and into the sunlight where, when he emerged, the shouts and the applause rolled down to him.

Only once did they ever boo him in St. Louis. On Aug. 22, 1956, against Brooklyn, he made two errors and wound up hitless for the second straight night. They booed him when he stepped to the plate in the eighth inning, but the boos were gradually drowned out by the cheers.

"It was the worst game I ever played," he said later.

The next day 10 fans bought space in the St. Louis press and apologized.

In the batting cage, and with the six-piece Dixieland band on the grass behind home plate playing "Chicago," he lined four pitches between first and second, put one against the right-field screen and two into the right-field stands. Each time he hit the ball the applause came out of the stands. On his second turn he hit three to right field. When he left the cage, he signed baseballs for four of the Cincinnati players who were waiting for him. He ran out into center field and did squats and touched his toes. He signed baseballs for three more Reds and the grounds-keepers. He ran back into the dugout and walked back into the clubhouse, where he locked himself in the office of Johnny Keane, the Cardinal manager, to make notes on small cards about what he would say in his farewell speech.

"I'm not a speaker," he had said, "so you have nervous tension."

"When you were a kid back in school," the reporter said to him, "were you always scared when you were called on to recite in class?"

"I was a bashful guy in school," he said. "We had to learn one thing—what is it?—about Shakespeare."

"'Friends, Romans, Countrymen . . . '?" the reporter said.

"That's right," he said. "Something like that. I found out then that if you talk it out loud while you're memorizing it, it helps."

For the ceremonies in front of home plate, the Cardinals lined up along the third-base line and the Reds along the first-base line. In the first row of folding chairs in the infield, Musial sat with his wife and 4-year-old Jean. In the row behind them sat their son Dick, 23, who is a Notre Dame graduate, a lieutenant in the Army and the father of a month-old son; and their daughters Geraldine, 18, and Janet, 14.

Lillian Labash, daughter of a grocer in Donora, first saw Stan Musial on the pitcher's mound at Palmer Park. He was 14 and bat boy for the zinc works team managed by his neighbor, Joe Barbao. One day, having run out of pitchers, Barbao sent the kid in against the Monessen team. He struck out 13 in six innings.

"Look at that Polish kid pitch against those men," Lillian's father said to her. Five years later she and Stan Musial, a pitcher with the Williamson (W. Va.) team in Class D and making $65 a month, were married.

Sitting there in the sunlight and listening to them praise him, Musial was trying to keep from crying. He was biting his lips and blinking his eyes while the governor of Missouri, the mayor of St. Louis, the president of the National League and the commissioner of baseball extolled him. Two Cub Scouts gave him a neckerchief, the Chamber of Commerce gave him an equestrian statuette of Louis IX of France, the city's patron saint; the president of the American League awarded him a plaque; and Ken Boyer, the Cardinal third baseman and captain, gave him a ring from his teammates with the number 6 set in diamonds.

He made his speech after they had given him a four-by-six-foot framed drawing, in color, of the $40,000 statue of Stan Musial they will erect when they have built the new riverfront ballpark. By now he had conquered his tears and, referring to his cards, he could speak his thanks easily. He climbed into a salmon-colored open convertible and sat down for the long, slow tour around the borders of the field. His wife and their two younger daughters rode in a white convertible behind him. In a gray convertible his oldest daughter and his son held up the drawing. The statue will depict him leaning against a bat and signing an autograph for a small boy. Exclusive of its pedestal, it will be nine feet tall.

"I don't know how I'll feel when I first see the statue," he had said. "Down in Florida, at St. Petersburg Beach, there's this museum—a wax museum—and that was the first time I saw a statue of myself. It was kind of funny, looking at myself. I took a picture—you know, being there and taking a picture of yourself—it gives you a strange feeling."

Jim Maloney, the young fast-ball pitcher who won 23 games this year, was pitching for the Reds, and when Musial, batting third, came up in the first inning, there were two outs. While the applause flooded down around him, he stood far back in the batter's box, holding the bat down and swinging it loosely. As Maloney started his windup. Musial went into that stance, feet close together, his crouching body twisted to the left, the bat back and up. He wiggled his hips once and Maloney threw the fast ball.

It was over the outside corner and when Al Barlick, who 22 years before had umpired behind the plate in Musial's first game, called it a strike, the crowd booed. They stopped the game and gave the ball to Musial. He ran over to a box near the Cards' dugout and, posing for photographers, presented the ball to Sid Keener, director of the Baseball Hall of Fame. When he came back, he fouled the second pitch into the stands behind third base. Then he watched Maloney's curve ball catch the outside corner for the third strike and the crowd booed Barlick again.

When he came up to bat in the fourth, there was one out. Maloney's first pitch was a ball, outside. Musial took an inside curve for a called strike, and then he hit the fast ball to the right of second base and into right field for the

Cardinals' first hit. Now, with the big crowd standing, applauding and cheering, he received the ball and gave it to Joe Schultz, the first-base coach, to save for him.

During his first swing around the National League, that September of 1941, Stan Musial got six hits in 10 times at bat in a doubleheader at Chicago. Jimmy Wilson was managing the Cubs then.

"Nobody," Wilson said, "can be that good."

Casey Stengel was managing the Boston Braves. After the Cardinals left Boston, the Brooklyn Dodgers moved in and Stengel had news for the Brooklyn sportswriters.

"Your fellas will win it," he said, "but those Cardinals got a young kid in left field you guys are gonna be writin' about for 20 years."

In the sixth inning, with the game still scoreless but Curt Flood on second base and one out. Musial fouled back a high fast ball. Maloney's curve was into the dirt and then his fast ball was wide. Now Musial waited and the crowd waited and Maloney's arm came down. It was a curve, breaking over the inside of the plate as Musial uncoiled from that crouch, and the ball was through the hole between first and second and into right field for Musial's 3,630th major league hit. The crowd was standing, roaring, Flood was across the plate and Musial was standing on first base.

In 1948 Eddie Sawyer was the new manager of the Phillies. One day the sportswriters asked him his opinion of the league.

"Of all the teams I've seen so far," he said, "Musial is the best."

Gary Kolb was coming out of the Cardinals' dugout to run for Musial and, for the last time as a player, Musial was running off the field. The crowd's cheers turned to groans and then to boos. In the dugout Musial posed for photographers, and after the end of the sixth inning he was back in front of his dressing stall, the floodlights on him, the semicircle of photographers and reporters in front of him again.

"You know, that's the way I came in, he was saying, "two base hits—and that's the way I leave."

They took pictures of him getting out of his uniform for the last time, the uniform that will go to the Baseball Hall of Fame, and they asked him what kind of pitches he hit.

He was in his street clothes, lying on his back on a rubbing table in the trainer's room, the door locked, when the Cardinals came up in the last of the 14th inning, the score tied 2–2. Overhead he could hear the fans stamping their feet, and on the radio he could hear Harry Caray describing the game. Then, suddenly, the roar of the crowd came to him, down through the ceiling.

"AndtheCardinalswinit," Harry Caray was saying, "3 to 2!"

"That's something, too," Musial said. "That first game I played in, we won 3 to 2."

Two hours later there were 300 people at the farewell party in the banquet rooms of the St. Louis restaurant that is one of Musial's many investments. Most of the men were in dinner jackets and the women in cocktail dresses. At one table Frank Pizzica, an auto dealer in Monongahela, Pa., and Dr. Michael Duda, president of California State College, in California, Pa., were sitting together. Dr. Duda was Musial's basketball and baseball coach at Donora High School, and they both go back almost 30 years with Musial.

"I had this basketball team," Pizzica was saying. "It was called the Frank A. Pizzica Monongahela Team, and Stan was a forward. He was 18 and a hungry, lean boy with the craziest left-handed hook shot you've ever seen. He could feint those people onto their faces. His teammates carried him on a pedestal."

"It was always that way," Dr. Duda said. "In the first game he pitched for me he struck out 18 of the 21 batters he faced in the seven-inning game.

"I don't wear dark glasses, but I have them today, because tears came to my eyes."

"We just sat there," Pizzica said "and thought of being associated with someone who's ranked with Ruth and Cobb, I cried today and I tell you that unashamedly."

So Long, Rock

from *Sport*

We were sitting in the living room of a hotel suite in Chicago, and it was about nine o'clock at night. Rocky Graziano was sitting in an easy chair, with his legs over one of the arms. He had on slacks and a T-shirt, and he was sucking on a dry pipe and trying to spit small, almost-dry spit into a wastebasket over by the near wall.

There were a couple of sparring partners on the sofa, and Whitey Bimstein and Irving Cohen were sitting with a card table between them and Irving was counting through a batch of tickets. There was a small radio on the windowsill and the Cubs' game was on. The only noise in the room was the noise of the announcer.

I was watching the Rock. I was watching him sit there, sucking on the pipe and spitting and then staring straight ahead, and I had it all figured out for myself.

This is a guy, I was thinking to myself, who is not listening to a ball game. This is a guy who is twenty-five hours away, a guy in a ring fighting Tony Zale for the middleweight title for the second time and remembering the first time in Yankee Stadium when he had Zale down and beaten and Zale came out the next round, his legs wobbling, and pumped that right hand into the body so it brought this guy's right knee up and then followed it with the hook to the chin that knocked this guy out.

"It's a single over short going into left center field," the announcer said, his voice rising. "The runners on third and second will score, and here they come . . . "

"You see?" the Rock said suddenly, swinging his feet around onto the floor and taking the pipe out of his mouth and pointing it at us. "If they make that double play they get out of the inning and no runs score. You see?"

I am thinking of this now because on February 20 the Rock is going back into that same ring in Chicago, this time against Sugar Ray Robinson for that same middleweight title. This is just a guy out for the big paynight now, but when he had it he was the most exciting fighter of our time. Now they say this is where he gets off and that this will probably be the last magazine piece anybody will write about him for a long time.

"All right," Whitey said after a while. "You better get up to bed now, Rock. It's time you were in."

He got up from the chair and he stretched and he started out the door. Whitey motioned over his shoulder with his head and I followed them out.

We went down the hall and took the stairway up to the next floor. It was a two-room suite with three cots in one room for the sparring partners and two beds in the other room, one for Whitey and the other for the Rock.

"You better try those trunks on," Whitey said.

The Rock got undressed. He had been training for months and he was in great shape, and he tried on the two pairs of trunks, black with the red stripes, squatting down and standing up.

"The first ones are too tight," he said. "These are best."

He got, naked, into one of the beds then and he pulled the covers up. He put two pillows under his head, so he was half sitting up, and Whitey walked into the other room.

"So, I'll go now, Rock," I said.

"Okay," he said.

"You have to lick this guy, Rock," I said suddenly, bending over the bed. "If you ever had to win a fight, you have to win this one."

He knew what I meant. In New York they had revoked his license for failing to report the offer of a bribe he had never accepted for a fight that had never been fought. There were those of us who had gone day after day to the hearings, who had been able to see through this to the politics behind it, and we had been appalled that such a thing could happen in this country.

"I despise them for what they did to you," I said, "and you hate them, and there's only one way you can get even. If you lose tomorrow night, you're done, not only in New York but everywhere. You have to win, Rock."

"I know," he said.

"You have to stick it," I said. "You have to win the title, because when you win the title it's yours and they can't take it away from you outside the ring. You win it and they need it and they'll come crawling back, begging you on their hands and knees."

"I know," he said, lying there in the bed and looking right at me. "If I have to, I'll die in there, tryin'."

We shook hands and he snapped off the light over the bed and I left. I felt bad for having made a speech like that, because they make few better guys than Tony Zale and they make them no tougher inside the ropes, and where do you get off telling another guy he has to take those Sunday shots in the belly and on the chin while you sit at ringside feeling a lot but taking nothing and just looking up?

It was 120 degrees at ringside inside the Chicago Stadium that July night. They drew $422,918 for a new indoor record and had them hanging from the rafters. Suddenly the hot, wet, sweat-smelling air was still and the organ started "East Side, West Side" and a roar went up in the back and down the aisle came the Rock. He had the white satin robe with the green trim over his shoulders and Whitey and Irving and Frank Percoco were behind him. The noise was all over the place now and Whitey was rubbing his back under the white robe as they came and then, two steps from the stairs, he broke from Whitey and took the three stairs in one step and vaulted through the ropes, throwing his arms so the robe slid off.

"Yes," I said to myself, "he'll stick it all right."

He stuck it, and there were times when it looked like he'd have to die doing it. Over his right eye the brow swelled and came down and shut the eye, and when Zale cut the left eye the blood flowed into it so he was stumbling around blind or seeing only through a red haze. Zale pitched all his big stuff at him and he took it all. There were times in the third round when I said to myself that if this were just a fight, and not bigger than a fight, he would go down. I said to myself that he couldn't win it but at least he showed them he had guts. Then a funny thing happened.

Between the fourth and fifth rounds, Frank Percoco took the hard edge of a quarter and, pressing with it between his fingers, broke the skin of the swelling over the right eye. When the blood came out the swelling came down enough for the lid to pull up, and the Rock could see. For two bits they won the middleweight title and made maybe $250,000 and it was the beginning of all that would follow.

He had Zale helpless on the ropes now in the sixth round. Zale, collapsing, had his back to him and, in that frenzy that made him what only he and Dempsey were, the Rock climbed all over him, hitting him wherever he could find a place to hit him. Then the referee stopped it. And now he was standing in the shower stall, the right eye shut again, a clip holding the other cut closed, only a fireman in uniform with us, standing guard.

"Well," I said to him, "the world is a big place, and how does it feel to be the middleweight champion of it?"

"I don't know," he said, hurt and leaning back and resting one arm on the shower handles, trying to think and to talk. "I don't know. I mean . . . I mean as a kid I . . . I mean I was no good . . . I mean nobody ever . . . You know what I mean?"

He was standing, naked and cut and swollen, in this basement and holding his hands out to us. It was quiet but for the drip of the shut-off shower.

"I know what you mean, Rocky," the fireman said, out of nowhere. "You're giving a talk on democracy."

"I mean I never . . ." The Rock said, and then he turned to the fireman and he said, "You're a good guy. You're all right. You know what I mean?"

They came through the door then, a half-dozen newspapermen from the mob in the dressing room. They got him in a corner, all of them with their pencils and paper out.

"But how did you feel in there?" one of them shouted at him.

"I wanted to kill him," he said. "I got nothing against him. He's a nice guy. I like him, but I wanted to kill him."

That is the kind of a fighter he was, a special kind. I remember the night he fought Marty Servo in the Garden. Marty had just knocked out Red Cochrane for the welterweight title, and now Graziano had him against the ropes, holding Marty's head up with his open left glove, clubbing him with his right. He'd have killed Marty if he had had a knife in there that night, and he would have been guilty of only one thing. He would have been guilty of giving himself over completely to that which they send two men out to do when they face each other in a ring.

Don't you know, too, that the Rock liked Marty and Marty liked the Rock? Marty was never a fighter again after that beating. He had to give up his welterweight title without ever defending it, and by that beating he lost the money he had counted on to give him security the rest of his life. I remember a night a couple of years later. The Rock was walking ahead of us and we were going out to eat.

"Where are we going?" I said.

"We're going to that place where Marty Servo tends bar," Irving Cohen said. "Rocky likes him and he always tries to bring business into the place."

We went into the place and Marty, in a white jacket, was standing behind the bar, leaning against the rack that holds the glasses in front of the mirror. When he saw us his face brightened and he leaned over the bar and shook hands. When he shook hands with the Rock, he smiled and faked as if to hook with his left. The Rock, leaning over the bar, stuck his left under Marty's chin as he had that night and faked to throw the right, and then the two of them dropped their hands and laughed.

"I'll be glad when that Graziano stops fighting," a guy said once in Still-man's. "It's gettin' so you can't even move in here."

When the Rock trained, they would stand packed, all the way back to the wall. They would be packed on the stairs and they would be packed in the balcony, too. In his dressing room, there was always a mob. There was one little guy there named Barney who always wore a dirty cap and who played the harmonica. He didn't play it by blowing on it with his mouth. He played it by blowing on it through his nostrils.

"Ain't he a good musician?" the Rock would say, sitting back in his robe and listening. "Did you ever see anybody do that before? I'd like to get this poor guy a job."

The guy would smile and then he'd play some more. He had three num-bers. He'd play "Beer Barrel Polka," "The Darktown Strutters' Ball," and "Bugle Call Rag." All the time he was playing "Bugle Call Rag," blowing on the harmonica through his nostrils, he'd salute with his left hand.

"Ain't that great?" the Rock would say, and he would mean it. "Why can't I get this guy a job?"

The guy was satisfied. The Rock staked him. He staked a lot of them. One day I saw him give a guy the shirt he was wearing. The Christmas of the first year he made any money he bought a second-hand 1940 Cadillac and filled it with $1,500 worth of toys. He drove it down to his old neighborhood on the East Side and unloaded the toys on the kids and another $1,500 on their par-ents. He never mentioned it. It came out because a trainer from the gym who lives in the neighborhood saw it.

"Look, Rocky," Irving Cohen said to him. "It's nice to do things like that, but you haven't got that kind of money and you've got to save money. You won't be fighting forever."

"Sure, Irving," the Rock said, "but those are poor people. They're good people. They never done no wrong. They never hurt nobody. They just never got a break."

One day in Stillman's, the Rock walked up to Irving. He asked him for a touch.

"I've got fifty bucks," Irving said.

"Give it to me," the Rock said, "and hustle up another fifty for me."

Irving circulated and borrowed fifty and gave that to the Rock. The Rock walked away and Irving, who is a little, round guy, sidled after him.

As you come into Stillman's there are rows of chairs facing the ring. In one of the chairs there was a former fighter sitting. This one is still a young man, but he is blind. The Rock sat down next to him and talked with him for a while. Irving sidled up behind them, and then the Rock leaned over and slipped the rolled-up bills into the lapel pocket of the fighter's jacket.

"There's something in your pocket," he said, and he got up.

It is a shame we lied to a guy like this when we told him that, if he won the title that night in Chicago, he would be all right because they could never take it away from him outside the ring. We didn't tell it as a lie. It just came out a lie. It came out a lie because when he won the title he became big in people's minds. He was a name, and now they got it out of Washington that he had gone AWOL in the Army, had put in seven months in Leavenworth, and had a dishonorable discharge. They wanted to bar him from the ring.

I remember the night after he ran out on a fight in California. His disappearance made headlines, and finally he walked through the door into a suite at the Capitol-Hotel across Eighth Avenue from the Garden. He had on a beautiful camel's hair polo coat, but there was the growth of several days' beard on his face, and under the coat he wore an old woolen shirt and dirty slacks and there were heavy running shoes on his feet.

"I'm with my friends," he said, and he held his hands out.

They were New York sportswriters called there on the promise that he would show up. Only some of them were his friends, but they all stood up when he came in and when he said that you could hear every breath.

"It's like I got a scar on my face," he said, staring through them and bringing his right hand up slowly to his right cheek. "Why don't they leave me alone or put me in jail?"

Of course, they took his title away outside the ring. They let him defend it against Zale in Newark on June 10, 1948, and they paid him for it, but he was no fighter then. The things they had done to him had taken out of him that which had made him the fighter he had been. He walked toward Zale as he was to walk toward those others in that hotel room another time, and Zale measured him and for two rounds gave him a terrible beating and in the third round knocked him out.

It is an odd thing, but once Rocky Graziano would have fought Ray Robinson for the fun of it. That would be four or five years ago, and he made Irving Cohen's life miserable with it.

"Get me Robinson, will you, Irving?" he would say, over and over again. "Believe me, Irving, I'll knock him out."

"Sure, Rocky," Irving would say. "Sure you will. But wait."

There were just those two things, you see, that the Rock had that made him what he was. He could take your head off your shoulders with that right-hand punch, and he fought with that animal fury that is the pure, primitive expression of the essence of combat.

He has not put those two things together in a ring since the night he won the title from Zale in Chicago and they pulled the Army on him. There is no evidence that they are any longer a part of him, and if that is so then this is the end of the road, the last big paynight, the final chapter of a memorable book—and I can't find the one big sentence with which to end it.

Against Ray Robinson, in the third round that night in Chicago, he still put enough of that fury into one right-hand punch to drop Robinson. Then Robinson got up and, with that barrage that was typical of him, knocked him out.

Now the fighter and his wife live in a high-rise apartment in what is known as New York's fashionable Upper East Side, three miles north of where he was born and grew up. He is sixty-one years old, and they are grandparents.

"I just made The Big One," he told me fifteen years ago.

"The Big One?" I said. "What's that?"

"A million bucks."

"You're worth a million?" I said.

"Yeah," he said. "My accountant just told me. How about that?"

It started with his ring earnings, and it came from his autobiography, *Somebody Up There Likes Me*, from the movie they made from it, from his television and personal appearances, and from radio and television commercials. He visits schools and talks on juvenile delinquency, and when he told me that he had lectured at Fordham University I asked him what he had said.

"I spoke to all the kids who were graduatin'," he said, "and a lot of elderly people, like professors and priests."

"But what did you tell them?" I said.

"You know what it is," he said. "I start out, whether I'm talkin' about criminology or juvenile delinquency, and I say, 'You know, I'm so glad my father took the boat, because this is the best country in the world, and if there was another country like this one, I'd be jealous.'"

The Shy One

from *Once They Heard the Cheers*

Floyd is a kind of a stranger.
—**Cus D'Amato, 1954**

On the telephone two nights before, he had told me to turn off the New York Thruway at the New Paltz exit and then left on Route 299. He has said that I should follow that through the town, across a railroad track and over a bridge and then take the first road on the right.

"What's the name of the road?" I had asked.

"Springtown Road," he had said. "You go half a mile to a fork and then take the right. Two-tenths of a mile after that it's the first house on the left."

"And what time do you want me to show up?"

"Three o'clock," he had said. "I'm looking at my schedule. I may have an appointment, something to do, for a half hour at 3:30, but 3 o'clock is all right."

It was just after two when I turned off the Thruway. There was a motel off to the left, but I decided to drive into the town and, perhaps, find one that would be closer and more a part of the town.

The terrain there, west of the Hudson and just south of the Catskill Mountains, is hilly, and the town, with Route 299 as its main street, spreads down over the western slope of a ridge. The stores, restaurants, and other places of business are close-packed on both sides of the steeply slanting street that was congested now with traffic, and off to the south and on the crest of the ridge there is a multistoried highrise, an architectural aberration erected without regard for the still rural nature of the countryside. Seeing it towering alone there on the ridge like the beginning in New Paltz of a new

153

Bronx, I surmised that it would turn out to be a part of the college, a branch of the State University of New York.

Coming down off the ridge, the road crosses the railroad tracks with the old wooden station on the right, and there was a sign on the station offering it for rent. Beyond the tracks I drove over the bridge and out onto the flat of a valley with farming lands on both sides of the blacktop road. Ahead I could see another blacktop to the right, and when I reached it and saw the Spring-town Road sign I backed around and drove the way I had come and back up the hill through the town.

There was a small motel on the left, and when I got to the top of the hill I pulled off and into a gas station. The attendant came out, a young man with red hair and wiping his hands on a rag.

"Fill it up?" he said.

"Please," I said, "and maybe you can tell me something. Do you know where Floyd Patterson lives?"

I wanted to get an idea of how well a former heavyweight champion of the world, this former heavyweight champion of the world, might be known in his adopted town. He had always run from renown, and even as champion had sought seclusion. The fame that came with his title seemed to embarrass him, as if he could never forget that he was a refugee from the black ghetto of the Bedford-Stuyvesant section of Brooklyn. As a child, he had been so shy that he could never look others in the eye and so maladjusted that only special schooling saved him. I liked him very much because, although he was always so serious—even appearing troubled—that I never heard him laugh, his observations were perceptive and reflected a supreme sensitivity, and his answers were honest. He always seemed to me, though, to be the most mis-cast of fighters, for while he had the physical attributes to be a great fighter—always excepting his inability to absorb a heavy-weight's big punch—he also had the compassion of a priest, and I never knew anyone else in sports whose antennae were so attuned to the suffering of others.

"Are you bothered by the sight of blood?" I asked him once.

"How do you mean?" Patterson said.

"Have you ever been scared, as a child or since, when you've been cut?"

I asked this question because a fighter must regard lightly the changes his profession makes upon his physical person. He must also be relatively unaf-fected by the hurt he inflicts upon others.

"No," he said. "I've seen my blood flow from me when I was younger. One time I got a nail stuck in my foot, and I kept it there for three hours, un-til my mother came home from work. You see, there was this lady baby-sit-ting for us, and I was scared to tell her about the nail because she was very mean and she would beat you. So when I got this nail in my foot I kept it there and stayed in the front room for three hours until my mother came home and I told her about it."

"What about seeing blood on others?" I said.

"On somebody else?" he said. "Well, this hasn't happened lately, but in the wintertime, when it's cold and my nose feels cold, I'd sometimes see two people fighting in the street. I'd actually see a guy with a big fist hit another guy square on the nose or face. You know?"

"Yes."

"Well," he had said, "when I'd see that, I'd feel it myself. It really seemed that I could actually feel it, and I would rather be fighting the one guy and taking the punishment than to see the other guy taking it, because I could just imagine how it feels to get hit when you're cold like that."

He was that way in the ring, staying away from a cut when he opened one on an opponent. The day of his second fight with Ingemar Johansson they weighed in at noon at the Commodore Hotel. The big room was crowded with sportswriters and photographers and members of the fight mob, and I was talking with Johnny Attell, who had been matchmaker around New York for many years, when Billy Conn, who had been one of the best of the all-time light-heavyweights and enough of a heavyweight to give Joe Louis one of his toughest fights, walked over.

"Who do you like tonight, Bill?" Attell said to him.

"Me?" Conn said. "I like the Swede for his punch."

"I don't know," Attell said, shrugging. "Patterson's got the equipment to take him if he fights him right."

"You hear what somebody had Patterson say?" Conn said.

"What?" Attell said.

"Patterson said that when he gets a guy cut he lays off the eye and hits him in the belly," Conn said. "You know somebody told him to say that, because he'd pour salt in a cut if he could."

"No he wouldn't," Attell said.

"Are you kidding?" Conn said.

"No," Attell said. "This guy Patterson is really that way."

"Then he's got no business being a fighter," Conn said.

But he was a fighter, an Olympic champion, and then the youngest ever to win the heavyweight championship of the world and the first even to regain it. I hadn't seen him to talk to since 1963, before the second of his two fights with Sonny Liston in which he never got by the first round. Liston, I knew beforehand, would out-body and bully him, and I had given Patterson no chance, and then on television I had watched Muhammad Ali humiliate him twice. Howard Cosell, who knew him well and had seen much of him while Patterson's career was running down, had written in his own autobiography that Patterson had come to live off martyrization and sympathy. Then I had heard that he had been appointed to the New York State Athletic Commission and was living in New Paltz, and I wondered how he was totalling the wins and losses of his life.

"Floyd Patterson?" the attendant said now. "Sure."

"You know where he lives?"

"Sure," he said, pointing. "You go down through town here and across the steel bridge and you take the first right. That's Spring-town Road. At the fork you take a right, and I think it's the second house on the left."

I was thinking that no, Floyd said it was the first house on the left, and the young man's earnestness and sincerity made me a little ashamed of my deceit.

"Fine," I said, "and tell me something else. Is that motel beyond the top of the hill the best around here?"

"Right," he said. "That's a good one."

I checked into the "good one" that would have been better if someone had washed the woodwork in recent time. When I turned the thermostat on the air conditioner-heater the sound that came from behind the bent vanes of the grill low on the wall was of a spin-dry washer gurging a load of nuts, bolts and aluminum pie pans. The bathroom had been scrubbed clean, however, and over all, it was an improvement over some of the places where I had known Patterson while he was a fighter.

First there was the Gramercy Gym, on East Fourteenth Street in Manhattan, with the two flights of stairs that groaned and gave underfoot and led up between the mustard-colored walls that were dusty with soot and stained with grime. At the top of the stairs, and low in the door into the gym, there was a jagged hole covered with heavy wire mesh, and behind the door and snarling through the mesh there was a German shepherd that Patterson or Cus D'Amato, who managed him, would chain in a back room before they would let a visitor in. D'Amato reasoned that this approach would weed out the faint-hearted who just thought they might like to be fighters.

Then there was La Ronda, in the woods outside of Newtown, Connecticut, where Patterson lived and where he trained almost as a recluse most of the time, for nine months through the autumn of 1959 and the following winter and spring, to get his title back from Ingemar Johansson. It was an otherwise abandoned road-house that was owned and had been operated by Enrique Madriguera, who had finished second to Xavier Cugat in the battle of the big Latin dance bands. Set into the wall beneath the stairway to the second floor there was a cracked ornamental tile of a young boy playing a violin, and that had been Madriguera when he had been a child prodigy, and once, scattered amid the debris in the back yard, I had found pages of sheet music, blowing in the wind. The place was infested with rats that Patterson shot with a .22. While Johansson lived in a private cottage at Grossinger's, the luxury resort in the Catskills, and had his meals served in style, Patterson and Dan Florio, his trainer, cooked for themselves and the sparring partners in the vast kitchen and on the big ranges and in the oversized pots and pans that had been intended to hold the Iberian edibles for the multitudes of music lovers and conga dancers who never came.

When I turned onto Springtown Road now for the second time, I went to the fork and took the road to the right. I watched the odometer, and after two-tenths of a mile, as Patterson had said, on the left on a rise beyond a field of golden-brown stubble, I saw the two-storied, white-shingled house. The blacktop driveway rises for almost a hundred yards between tall pines, and as I drove up it I saw the two gray metal boxes, one on either side of the driveway amid the trees. At the top I turned left and parked by a stone wall in front of the garage doors under the house, and got out. There was an off-white dog of good size and indefinite breeding confronting me and barking at me as I got out of the car, and I could hear a male voice calling.

"Cotton! Cotton! C'mere, Cotton!"

It was Patterson's voice, and as the dog turned from me and started up the steps toward the back of the house, I followed it. Patterson was holding an aluminum combination storm and screen door open, and when the dog disappeared inside, he came out and we shook hands. He was wearing freshly laundered blue jeans and an immaculate white T-shirt, and he didn't look much heavier at age forty-one than he had at age twenty-five when, that night in the Polo Grounds, he landed that wide left hook on Johansson's jaw and became the first fighter ever to regain the heavyweight title.

"Nobody can sneak up on you here," I said.

"That's right," he said.

"I mean with the dog and those boxes down on the driveway. Is that a warning device?"

"It rings a bell in our bedroom," he said. "It's mostly for at night."

He was the third oldest of eleven children, born into poverty and an overcrowded world that he found frightening and from which, from his earliest years on, he tried to escape. Once he told me that when he was six he used to hide all day in the basement of P.S. 25, the school he was supposed to be attending. As he became older, and when he had the eighteen cents for admission, he hid in the Regent and Apollo and Banko movie theaters, and some nights he slept in Prospect Park and others in subway stations.

"You have a lovely home here," I said.

He had led me through the kitchen and the dining room and, off the entry hall, into a family room. There was a twenty-foot field-stone, mahogany-topped bar curving in front of the far wall, the mounted heads of two mountain goats above it, the windows behind it looking out onto the driveway. Across the entry hall I could see the living room, with a baby grand piano, and I was impressed by the orderliness of everything, the furniture precisely placed and none of the incidental leavings of daily living lying about.

"It's nice," he said.

"How many rooms are there?" I said.

"Well," he said, "there's four bedrooms, one play room, the living room, the kitchen, the dining room, the bar room and four baths."

"Does your wife have help?"

"Help?" he said.

"Someone who comes in to clean?" I said, and his own mother, whom I remember as a serene, soft-spoken and sensitive woman, had been a domestic before she found a job in a Brooklyn bottling factory.

"Nope," Patterson said. "I help her."

"How much land do you have?"

"Forty acres," he said, and he walked to a window and pointed down at the field between the house and the road, the grass stubble in it that golden brown in the sunlight. "You see that field? I did it with a hand scythe and with a hand saw, all summer long."

"That's good," I said, "but what's that monstrosity over there on the ridge?"

"The what?" he said.

"That tower," I said.

"Oh, that's the college."

"That figures," I said. "We're trying to teach people to live with the environment and not abuse it, and a college does that."

A yellow school bus had stopped at the foot of the driveway. Two small girls had got out and were starting to walk up the drive.

"That's my daughters," he said. "They go to the Duzine school. That's the public school, what they call the Duzine school, but next year they'll go to the Catholic school in Rosendale, and I'll have to drive them over."

"You don't like the public school?"

We had walked back from the window. He was sitting on one of the bar stools, and I was sitting on another.

"The public school's all right here," he said, "but New Paltz was number two in the nation for drugs. Los Angeles was number one."

"Can that be correct?" I said.

"That's right," he said. "Three or four years ago I read it in the *Daily News*. That's why I started my boxing club. The Huguenot Boxing Club."

I had read somewhere that he was training young amateur fighters. As a fighter himself he was prone to errors, as the naturally gifted in anything often are. In most of his fights, however, his great hand speed and mobility covered his mistakes and let him get away with them although, of course, they were still there.

"There's this Father Daniel O'Hare," he said, "and he's the founder. It's called AMEN—Americans Mobilized to End Narcotics—and he founded it. He used to be in the rectory here, and about three years ago I got to know him. He's now in the rectory in Newburgh, and he's a very down-to-earth priest. I've gotten to know him so close that sometimes I say a word you don't say to a priest."

"I know what you mean."

"I joined up two years ago, and he takes care of the educational parts, and I take the physical."

"About this drug problem," I said. "I keep reading that it's been with us always. Were there drugs around when you were growing up?"

"No," he said, "the only thing was cigarettes."

"Not even in Bedford-Stuyvesant?"

"Nope," he said. "There were no drugs around in the fifties, but I remember as a youngster I was always getting in trouble, stealing fruit, and from the five-and-ten small stuff. Who knows what I'd be now if it wasn't for boxing."

"You're not the only one," I said.

"So I opened the boxing club," he said. "If you give a youngster something to do that he enjoys, he won't hang around on corners."

"That's right."

"About a year and a half ago," he said, "I opened the gym in this building right out here. It was a barn and a chicken hatchery, and I took young and old. Then I said I was going to close it because they were abusing the equipment, but my wife told me things I didn't know."

In 1956 Patterson had married Sandra Hicks, when he was twenty-one and she was eighteen, and they had three children. I had heard that they had been divorced, and that Patterson had married a white woman, and that they had two daughters, the two girls I had seen starting up the driveway.

"My wife is very personable," he was saying now. "She talks to all, and they tell her things they wouldn't tell me. She told me about this Thruway attendant who had a couple of kids, and every night he used to stop at a bar on the way home. Since he got into the boxing here, he hadn't done that, and I kept the gym open."

"How old are these fighters?"

"The one I told you about is twenty-one. He was about nineteen then, and I have several fifteen-year-olds. I have one—Andrew Schott—who feels as I did. It's like a religion. The kid is here every day. He has had twenty-five fights, and he can recall every fight he's had. There's no chance of him ever getting involved in drugs."

"How many of them," I said, "do you take to tournaments and get fights for?"

"There are fifteen actual fighters," he said. "Then there are two firemen from Poughkeepsie and a councilman from Rosendale that work out and spar to keep in shape. The councilman lost forty-five pounds, and he's been coming here a year and a half, and the gym is open seven days a week, except when we have fights."

"I would think that the town would appreciate what you're doing," I said.

"I like the town," he said, "and I like the people. I have no trouble whatsoever with the people in general, the old as well as the young, as long as I keep away from politics."

"You have a right to be interested in politics," I said.

"It would cause a lot of flak," he said. "Everybody knows me as just plain Floyd. I'm liked by most people, but not by all. No one has done anything to harm me, but I know, given the opportunity, the ones who don't like me would hurt me. I don't know how to say it, and I don't want to say it."

"But you went down to Alabama with Jackie Robinson at the time of all the trouble in Birmingham and Selma," I said.

"Jackie asked me," he said. "A lot of name people went, and I remember landing at the airport and for the first time in my life I saw different rest rooms for blacks and whites. I took movie pictures of the signs—actually there was no film in the camera—so the people would know it was unusual to me, and I was taking it back."

His two daughters were standing in the doorway, and he called them in and introduced them—Janene, who was nine, and Jennifer, seven. We shook hands, the older one looking right at me, and the younger, her head down, examining me out of the tops of her eyes.

"How is school?" I said.

"Fine," the older one said.

"Excuse us a minute," Patterson said. "I have to ask my wife something."

He left, with the girls following him, and I walked around the room, looking at his two championship belts, the plaques and trophies he had been awarded, and the framed photographs. There were pictures of him with Eartha Kitt, Jimmy Durante, Harry Bellafonte, Jack Palance, Bob Hope, Jackie Gleason, Lauren Bacall, one with James Cagney and Roland Winters, that I remembered being taken at Newtown, and another, taken in the White House, with Patterson, his wife and their two girls standing with Richard Nixon. There was, also framed, the gate-fold I had put together for *The Fireside Book of Boxing* in 1961 of pictures of all the heavyweight champions in succession from John L. Sullivan through Patterson. I had discovered three photographs that, when placed together, showed the crowd of 80,000 crammed into Boyle's Thirty Acres in Jersey City on July 2, 1921, for the Dempsey-Carpentier fight, the first million-dollar gate. I needed something for the other side of the fold, and lined up photographs of all the twenty champions in their fighting poses, Patterson twice and on either side of Johansson.

On a shelf at the right of the bar were record albums of Percy Faith, Johnny Mathis, Roger Williams, Jackie Gleason, André Kostelanetz, Hank Williams, and Jo Stafford, the music I remember Patterson listening to in his training camps. Behind the bar the glasses were neatly aligned, the only bottles being two fifths of Seagram's Crown Royal, the tax seals on them unbroken.

"Do you do much business at this bar," I asked, when Patterson came back.

"It was here when we bought the house," he said. "Like those animal heads up there. My wife takes a drink now and then, but I can't stand the smell of the stuff."

"Don't fight it," I said.

"I was going to have an appointment, like at 3:30," he said, "but the man didn't come. He's the piano teacher, and I told him, 'I'll call you if I'm not going to be here today.' I just called him now to see where he was, and he assumed I would call if I wanted him to come."

"Who's taking the lessons?"

"My daughters and I. I take them because Jennifer is a perfectionist, and she hates to make a mistake and she won't play in front of the teacher. She has taken one lesson and Janene has taken three and I've taken three, and Jennifer plays better than both of us. She's the only one who doesn't have to look at the keys, so I reasoned I should take lessons with her and maybe that would help her.

"She's a natural athlete, too," he said. "She has tremendous coordination, but she hates to be the center of attraction. I remember when she was small and her birthday came and we got her a cake. My wife and I and my older daughter started to sing and she was crying, 'Don't! Don't!'

"In the school she'll play all the games with team participation, but when it comes to her doing it alone, she won't do it. She took ballet. The teacher, he told me she was fantastic, the best of all, and he had about fifty between the ages of six and twelve, but we took her out because she wouldn't do it alone in front of the others."

"I think I can understand that," I said.

"It's understandable to a certain degree," he said.

"I mean," I said, "that I remember a fella who was very shy."

"Yes," he said. "I know."

It was only three weeks after he had knocked out Archie Moore to win the heavyweight championship and it was just before Christmas, but he was back in training at the Long Pond Inn at Greenwood Lake, New York. The inn burned to the ground some years ago, but there used to be a bar and restaurant on the first floor with the living quarters and the gymnasium over it. When I checked with Ollie Cromwell, who was one of the owners and tended bar, he said that Patterson was up in his room, and I went up there where he was lying on the bed and listening to that music, and we shook hands.

"What time is it?" he said.

"One o'clock," I said.

"I'll be down in the dining room in a half hour," he said.

I waited in the dining room for three and a half hours. As I sat there, the place came alive with teen-agers who had been ice skating on the lake, and who had come in to play the juke box and dance. Finally, at 4:30, one of Patterson's sparring partners came in and walked over to the table where I was sitting.

"Floyd says he'll meet you in the gym in five minutes," the sparring partner said. "He apologizes."

"That's fine," I said, annoyed. "Where has he been?"

"Up in the room," the sparring partner said. "He came down a couple of times, but when he saw all these kids here, he went back. He was embarrassed to come in."

I said nothing about it when I met him in the gym, but two nights later we were standing and talking by the pool table beyond the bar. A couple of sparring partners were shooting pool, and I was working Patterson around slowly when I mentioned it, trying to get him to elaborate on the feelings he had had when he saw the dining room jumping with those kids.

"You're heavyweight champion of the world now," I said, "Doesn't that give you the security to walk through a room of teen-agers?"

"No," he said. "I still don't like to be stared at."

I thought of John L. Sullivan, this country's first sports hero, who used to stride into saloons and announce, "I can lick any man in the world!" The next morning we were standing in front of the Long Pond Inn, waiting for one of the sparring partners who had been sent to town to buy the morning newspapers, when I came back to it.

"But you're going to be stared at a lot," I said.

"I know," Patterson said.

"When did you first realize that this was going to be a problem?"

"The day after I won the title," he said. "Just before the fight my wife gave birth to our daughter, so right after the fight, these friends and I, we got in the car to drive back from Chicago. The next day we stopped at one of those roadside restaurants and went in. By then the fight was all over the pages of the newspapers, pictures and all, and I could see the people around the place recognizing me and starting to whisper. I figured we better get out of there quick, so we didn't even finish our meal."

Just before he won the title, Patterson had bought a ten-room house in Mount Vernon, New York, for his mother and the eight youngest of her eleven children. After Patterson beat Moore, the mayor of the city, who was an ex-fighter, staged a torch-light parade for him, and I asked Patterson what that was like.

"I was ashamed," he said.

"Why?" I said.

"Me sitting in an open car and waving to people," he said. "Those are things you only see kings and Presidents doing."

A heavyweight champion has to spend some of his time banquet-hopping, and Cus D'Amato made Patterson buy a tuxedo. He said it embarrassed him to wear it because, in his view, formal clothes were for those who had been born and raised to them, and he was not. When he was not in camp he lived with his wife and daughter in St. Albans, on Long Island, and he would do roadwork in a park there a couple of days a week.

"What time do you run?" I asked him once.

"I get up at 5:30, so I finish before the people start to work and see me," he said.

"Doesn't anybody ever see you?" I said.

"Usually I run on Saturday and Sunday when everybody don't get up so early," he said, "but one day I ran during the week. It was a Thursday, and after I finished in the park the fella who was supposed to pick me up was late. About an hour passed before he came, and there I was sitting on the park bench with my heavy clothes on and all sweaty and a towel around my neck. All these people were going to work by then, and they were looking at me like I was crazy."

"Didn't anyone recognize you?" I said.

"No," he said. "I was the champion, so I hid my face."

"Shyness is so deeply ingrained in you," I said to him another night at the Long Pond, "that I suppose one of your earliest memories is of being embarrassed in public."

"I guess that's right," he said. "I remember when I was just a little kid. I used to have long hair and my father would comb it. Then he'd send me around the corner for cigarettes, and I remember one day a lady stopping me and running her fingers through my hair. I was so embarrassed that I wanted to cry, and I ran."

He thought about it. It was after dinner and we were still sitting at the table.

"I had to be just a tiny kid for a lady to do that," he said, "but I never forgot it."

So all of that was twenty years before, and now he was supplying a gym and running a boxing club to provide a port for the young of the area who need it. At forty-one he was starting to take piano lessons to help a daughter in whom he saw himself.

"I hope she can come out of it by herself," he said now. "The first time somebody asked me for my autograph there were like twenty people waiting, and the guy gave me the piece of paper and I forgot how to spell my own name. I got a mental block."

"I remember you saying how long it took you to be able to look people in the eye."

"It took years," he said, "and I don't want her to have to go through what I went through. When I came back from the Olympics—and I won the Olympics when I was seventeen—I went to a dinner and they handed me a microphone. I panicked. Fortunately the gentleman before me had said something, and I stopped to think about that and I commented. Thousands of microphones have been handed to me since then, and it's easier, but it's never easy."

"I recall," I said, "how you used to say that some day you wanted to own a place in the country and have horses. Do you own horses?"

"No," he said. "We've got three dogs and a cat and we travel. I take the family wherever I go, to England, to Sweden, to Portugal, to Spain, and to get somebody to take care of horses, too, would be too difficult. Even for me it would be difficult, because I devote so much time to my family. I get up with the kids, and I put them to bed at night. I try to do as much with them as I can, because in my first marriage that was lacking. I was in camp all the time."

"How are your other children?"

"My son spent three weeks with me this summer, and he's thirteen now. The two daughters I see occasionally, but they live in Springfield, Massachusetts, and I don't see them as much as I'd like."

"How did you meet your present wife?" I asked.

"Janet?" he said. "It's strange how I met her. After I had rewon the title—not right then but in 1962—the secretary I had got married. I used to get thousands of letters, and I needed someone to answer the mail. I have this friend, Mickey Allen . . . "

"I remember him. He wanted to be a singer, and once you arranged for him to sing the National Anthem at one of your fights."

I remember how pleased and excited about it Allen was. He reasoned that the exposure on national television would launch him on his vocal career.

"That's right," Patterson said. "He owns a discothèque and a catering service now, and he said, 'My wife's sister can type. She was secretary to the vice-president of the New York Stock Exchange.' So she worked for me once a week, and that's how I met her. She was born in Rosedale, New York, but her parents moved to Greenwood Lake. I have a house right here for her parents when they come here, and they may stay a week or a month."

"I'd like to meet your wife," I said, "and I'm wondering if I might take you both to dinner tonight?"

"That would be nice," he said, "but I'm not sure. There's this seventy-five-year-old woman my wife got to know, and she just lost her husband. She's lonely, and I know it's on the calendar that we're supposed to visit her tonight. Maybe she can change it to tomorrow night, and I'll ask her."

He went out and I walked around the room again reading the inscriptions on the plaques, and there was a framed hand-lettered quotation from Vince Lombardi that had been presented to Patterson by the 501st Replacement Detachment of the First Armored Division. It was about making winning a habit, even as losing can be, and about doing things right not once in a while but all of the time.

"I'm sorry," Patterson said when he came back. "My wife says the lady is expecting us, and she's very lonely and she doesn't want to disappoint her. She's sorry."

"I understand," I said.

"It's time I went over to the gym," he said. "You want to come along?"

"Yes, indeed," I said.

We walked out through the entry hall and the dining room and into the kitchen. The two girls were in the kitchen.

"I'm going over to the gym now," Patterson said to them, "and you lock the storm door after us. All right?"

Outside he turned and waited while one of them locked the door. We walked across the parking area at the top of the driveway to the white-painted two-story barn. The ring is on the first floor, with stairs leading up to the loft, like a balcony, overhanging the first floor. In the loft were a couple of heavy punching bags and one light bag and two full-length mirrors. At the back of the loft is the dressing room with steel lockers, and there was a hand-printed notice on the wall:

TO ALL CLUB MEMBERS
    Do Not Invite Anyone To The Gym Without
    First Telling Me—I Do Not Want Strangers
    Wandering Around My House—Casing the Place
    —Should Anyone Violate This I Will Have
    To Ask Them To Leave.

There were four young fighters, who seemed to be in their teens, undressing in front of the lockers and getting into their ring trunks and boxing shoes. It had been chilly all day and it was cold in the locker room and, after he had stripped, Patterson put on thermal underwear and a sweat suit.

"You see," he was saying, sitting and lacing one of his ring shoes and looking up at one of the young fighters, "if anybody quits, they can't came back. I take the time. I take the punches, so they can't come back."

"I know," the fighter was saying, nodding. "I know."

Two more young fighters came in, and when Patterson finished lacing his shoes and got up, the ones who were ready followed him down the stairs to the gym. It was 5:15, and it was 7:15 when Patterson called it quits. Others came in, the two firemen from Poughkeepsie among them, and Patterson took them on one after the other; moving around on the worn canvas patched with green plastic tape, blocking and picking off their punches, occasionally countering and the sweat beading on his neck and face so that between rounds he had to towel. For two unbroken hours there was the thwack sound of gloves against gloves and the thup sound of gloves landing to the body, the shuffle sound of the shoes on canvas, the rhythmic sound of heavy breathing, and over it, Patterson's comments.

"You're not bringing your second jab back. Bring it all the way back," he was telling one. To another, "The moment you get close you tend to rear back. Keep your distance. That's it, but don't pull your shoulder back. Keep it relaxed, and when you throw the right hand, throw it from there. If you hold the shoulder up you force the right hand down." To another, "When are you gonna get your hair cut? Every time you lower your head your hair covers your eyes and you have to raise your head." To another, "Why move in? You're smothering your own punches. You have to keep your distance, and you know why you're missing so much? I know what punches you're gonna throw before you throw them. You have to mix them up." To another, "Keep your head down. Every now and then touch your chin to your shoulder." To another, "Throw the right. No good. You're just putting it there. Throw it. That's better. Again. Good."

When we judge professional performers we tend to take for granted, and forget, some of the things that they do well. During the years when I had watched Patterson fight I had fastened on his flaws, and I was impressed now by his boxing knowledge and his ability to spot the errors of the others, even though they were just beginners.

"You see," he was saying to one of them, after I had followed him and the others back upstairs, "as much as I know about boxing, if I was going to fight again I'd need a trainer, because I can't see what I'm doing wrong. I don't know. That's why I tell you these things, because I can see."

He started to undress, then, to take his shower, and I told him that I thought the boxing lessons had gone very well. I said I wanted to see him again the next morning.

"That's all right," he said. "How about 10:30?"

"Fine," I said.

At 10:30 the next morning, when I drove into the parking area at the top of the driveway, Patterson was washing a car. It was a golden-tan Lincoln Continental with the New York license plate FP 1, and Patterson was in the jeans and T-shirt. He turned off the hose and we shook hands.

"Here's something that might interest you," I said.

I had brought along a copy of the February 28, 1959, issue of *The Saturday Evening Post*. In those days the magazine ran long interview pieces they called "visits" with celebrities, and they used to give me the fighters. I did Patterson and Johansson and Jack Dempsey, always with Jacob Lofman photographing it and with my friend Jim Cleary taping it because, although I had been taking accurate notes for twenty years by then, the magazine insisted that everything be recorded and then transcribed onto some sixty pages of typescript from which I had to work.

The Patterson piece led the issue, and on the opening page there was a picture of him in the ring after he had knocked out Hurricane Jackson. At the bottom of the page, was a shot of the two of us sitting and talking by the ring in the Gramercy Gym. Patterson, gesticulating, was wearing a sand-colored, medium-weight cardigan.

"You haven't changed much," I said, showing him the picture, "but I have."

"Look at the sweater," Patterson said. "I still have that sweater."

"I remember it as a particularly fine one."

"Is it all right if I show this to my wife?" he said. "My wife would be interested to read it."

"Of course," I said.

He took the magazine, and I followed him around the front of the house and into the entry hall. He motioned me into the bar room and then excused himself and disappeared with the magazine.

"I'm always interested," I said when he came back, "in the relationships, years later, between fighters who fought each other. In your travels do you ever see Johansson?"

"I've been to Sweden a few times," he said, "but I and Johansson never showed any friendship until lately. He said so many derogatory things. In 1964, when I beat Eddie Machen in Stockholm, he said that Machen would knock me out and that Floyd was over the hill. It was an afternoon fight, and just as I walked out to get in the ring, Ingemar was in the first row. Our eyes met and I went over and shook hands and everybody booed. I don't know why."

"Probably," I said, "because he'd taken himself and his money to Switzerland."

"Then in 1974, after I hadn't fought in two years, I was in a restaurant in Stockholm, and who walked over but Ingemar Johansson. He was very nice then, and I've seen him a few times since."

"What about some of the other fighters you fought?"

"There were some of the guys, coming up in my career, like Hurricane Jackson and Jimmy Slade who were in the same camp until we fought. In camp, Jimmy Slade and I would play cards, and he'd get angry when I won. He'd throw the cards in my face, and in camp he'd be in charge.

"Then one day Cus asked me would I fight Jimmy Slade. I said, 'Of course not. We're friends.' Cus said, 'There comes a time in a fighter's career when he has to forget friendship.' I said, 'Ask Jimmy.' Jimmy said, 'Sure.' I was hurt, it came so easy to him.

"The guys I fought I don't dislike," he said, "and I'd like to stay in communication with them. I tried to call Jimmy Slade for days and days after I beat him, but I never got an answer. Dick Wagner, though, my first fight with him was difficult, and in the second I stopped him, but I made it known to the press that I respected him. He's out in Portland, Oregon, where he works on the railroad, and he's married to a school teacher. I had dinner at his house and his family met my family and I sent him cards from Sweden.

"A lot of guys I fought, though, have nothing but derogatory things to say. I saw Roy Harris when Joe Frazier fought Bob Foster. I met him in the lobby of the hotel and we talked a while, and the following day there was an article in the press where he said some derogatory things. Brian London said derogatory things. Why do they do this?"

"I guess they're still trying to win fights they lost to you years ago."

"It tends to bring them down," Patterson said. "They should carry themselves like Joe Louis."

When Patterson was small Louis was his idol. He kept scrap books filled with clippings and pictures of Joe, and after Patterson won the title the two met for the first time at a dinner.

"What was it like finally meeting him?" I asked Patterson, shortly after that.

"Well," Patterson had said, "I said to myself, 'Is this really Joe Louis? Am I finally meeting the man who is my idol?' I almost couldn't believe it."

"But you were the heavyweight champion of the world," I had said. "You have his old title."

"It seemed to me," Patterson had said, "like Joe Louis was still the champion, and I wasn't."

"Do you ever see Joe?" I asked him now.

"I see Joe often," he said, "and I'll still flash back to when I was nine, ten, and eleven and how I admired him, the way he carried himself. Here it is thirty years later, and I try to carry myself so that they might say the same thing about me."

"You picked a good model," I said.

"I know who I am," he said, "and what I believe in, but today you must be militant—down with Whitey—to be accepted. If that's what it takes, then I'll be the white man's black man, because I won't accept it the other way. I'd leave the country first. In my gym there are whites and colored and Puerto Ricans. I believe in an equal society. I see no colors. Everybody is the same like in my gym—but the militants don't like me."

"You know that?"

"I go over to the college here," he said. "This black group—the black something—asked me to give a speech. I knew they'd harass me. This one guy said, 'How come you call him Cassius Clay. Why not Muhammad Ali?' I said, 'First of all, I think Cassius is a beautiful name, and I can't pronounce Muhammad. My tongue won't pronounce it. Then you give him rights you don't give me. I believe Clay believes in a separate society. You believe the same, or you wouldn't be all blacks here. He called Liston 'The Ugly Bear.' He called George Forman 'The Mummy.' He called me 'The Rabbit.' You must give me the right to call him 'Clay.'"

"But what did you say in your speech?" I said.

"I'll get it," he said. "I'll be right back."

What I had really wanted to say was that he should be done with the name-calling, that the beauty he ascribes to the name Cassius and his problem in pronouncing Muhammad are pretexts and have nothing to do with it. Louis would have pronounced it as best he could. When he came back now he handed me the typewritten speech and I read:

"To all you young people, I would like to see you go out in the world and have all your dreams come true, and they can if you work hard at your God-given talents. Our people have come a long way, and we have had to struggle to get where we are today.

"You young people are our hopes and pride. It is you who must continue to struggle. This world is not all black, and we can't make it so. We must live with all people. The sooner we realize that, the happier we'll be. You're young and you're beautiful and have a whole lifetime of living to do. Be conscious of your dreams and pride. Leave color at the end of the list—not the beginning.

"Black power is not a true power. White power is not a true power. What I ask you to look for is the power of right, not the power of might. My career has shaped my life, and I have learned much. I have met people from all over the world, the highest to the most humble. The finest of these people accept a man for what he is. Be men, and other men will know you at a glance. Remember Jesus said; 'Love.' Racists say: 'Hate.' One of most renowned Americans who died for what he believed preached love. He was a black man. Some of our people did not agree with him, but in the annals of history his name will be at the top. I speak of Martin Luther King."

At the age of ten Patterson was unable to read, and he refused to talk. His family had moved seven times, and he had attended irregularly seven schools before they sent him to Wiltwyck, a school for emotionally disturbed boys, at Esopus, New York, and later to P.S. 614, one of New York City's five schools for maladjusted children.

"That's a good speech," I said now.

"My wife helped me with it," he said. "She helps me with all my speeches."

"What kind of a reception did it get? Did they applaud?"

"Yes," he said. "About two thirds did. One third, I guess they couldn't be broke. If I reach one, though, I think it's fine."

"If I may say so," I said, "you should shut your mind to Ali. To begin with, you were in no shape to fight him the first time, and . . . "

"I had a slipped disc," Patterson said. "It started in 1956, before the fight with Archie Moore, and I took three or four days off. Before the fight with Clay it went out. I took some days off, and it was all right. Then in the first round it went out, and there was a knot in my back as big as a fist. The pain was so bad that it was the first time in a fight I was begging to be knocked out."

Between rounds, as I had watched on television, Al Silvani, who trained Patterson for the fight, would stand behind Patterson and put his arms around him, under the armpits and across the chest. He would lift Patterson, Patterson's feet dangling above the canvas as Silvani tried to slip the disc back in. Then, during the rounds, until they stopped it in the twelfth, Ali would taunt and torture him.

"In the eighth and ninth rounds," Patterson was saying now, "I was saying to myself, 'The first good punch he catches me with I'm going to go down.' He hit me good punches. I was down. I was dizzy, but when I opened my eyes I was up again. I could not take a dive."

"I believe that," I said, "and you should be proud of it."

"There are things I like about myself," he said. "I could not stay down. In boxing you learn about yourself. The feeling of shame I will never lose, because I let people down, but I will never again feel ashamed of being ashamed."

"And you shouldn't," I said.

"It's me," he said. "I can't change it."

"I was impressed yesterday," I said, "watching you teach those kids. When it was over you were telling one of them that, if you were to fight again, you'd need a trainer because you wouldn't be able to see what you were doing wrong."

"That's right," he said.

"I know," I said, "and I remember something you used to do wrong, and I begged you not to do it against Johansson in that second fight."

"You did?" he said.

In their first fight, Johansson, firing the big right hand, had had him down seven times in the third round before they had stopped it. Before the second fight, Alvin Boretz, the television writer, and I wrote a half-hour special that was to be aired on the ABC network the night before the fight. With Manny Spiro, the producer, and a camera crew, I had gone to both camps, first to interview Johansson late one afternoon in the octagonal ski hut at Grossinger's, and then Patterson early the next afternoon in the main dining room of the dilapidated roadhouse in Newton.

We shot them both the same way, from the waist up and full face to the camera and, off camera myself, I asked both of them the same questions, about how they started as fighters, about their previous fights, in particular about what feelings they had had about the men they had fought, before and after those fights. Johansson was excellent, confident and even haughty—the way, if you are handling a fighter, you want him to be.

"After you had knocked Patterson down seven times and were now heavyweight champion of the world," I said, "did you have any feeling, looking across the ring at him, of sympathy for him?"

"No," Johansson said, "I did not. He'd gladly like to have me in the same situation."

"How about in the days after the fight when you thought about him?"

"I know my sister," he said, "she walk over when Patterson went from ring. My sister walked to him and raised her hand, and did like this on his chin. She feel sorry for him. But not me."

"This guy was great," Leonard Anderson, the director, said, as we walked back to the main building at Grossinger's.

"Terrific," Manny Spiro said, and he was obviously excited. "Just terrific, but what is poor Patterson going to do compared to that?"

"Just wait," I said.

The next morning we drove down to Newtown and, coming right out of Grossinger's, the others were appalled by the place. When Patterson came out to greet us he was in his road clothes, and he shook hands humbly, in that small-boy manner, and then he went back inside while they set up.

"This is unbelievable," Leonard Anderson said. "Looking at the two camps and the two fighters, I can't give this guy a chance."

"I feel sorry for him," Manny Spiro said, and then to me, "After Johansson, what can this poor nebbish say?"

"Relax," I said. "In fact, I'll guarantee you one thing right now. I don't know how he'll do in the fight, but I'll bet you he boxes rings around Johansson and flattens him in the interview segment."

I went inside then, and I found Patterson. I explained to him how we were going to film him, just sitting on a stool and facing the camera.

"But I don't know what you want me to say," he said.

"It's going to be easy," I said. "I'll just ask you questions I've asked you before, about your first fight on the street, and about your feelings for other fighters. I'll ask you about how you felt about Archie Moore after you won the title, and then I'll ask you about how you went into seclusion after the Johansson fight, and then about the little girl in the hospital in Atlantic City. All you have to do is tell me what you've told me before."

"All right," he said.

Sitting there on that stool and looking right at the camera, he told it as he had told it to me before, the voice low level and neither rising nor falling, but the answers direct and explicit. He told about knocking out Moore, and then looking across the ring and, realizing that Moore had wanted the heavyweight championship as much as he and was now so old that he would never get another chance, feeling sorry for him. Then I asked him about the month he had spent in seclusion at home after Johansson had knocked him out, and he explained how he had felt that he had let all of his friends and the United States down, and that late one night he was sitting in the game room in the basement, still feeling sorry for himself.

"I was just sitting there, thinking," he said. "You know, when your mind just wanders. I was thinking about some things that had happened in some of the places that I had been to, and I thought about being in Atlantic City one time and going through a hospital for leukemia and blood diseases and cancer, and I specifically remember a girl in the hospital.

"She had leukemia," he said, and he gave a pause that you would celebrate a professional actor for timing. "Cancer. The doctor was showing me through the wards, and he brought me into this little girl's room and she had a tube running through her arms and whatnot, and said she was about four and she was small for a four-year-old girl and you'd think she was just born. She was just nothing but bones, and as I walked out of the room and upon viewing this, I remember the doctor saying to me it would be a miracle if she should live past tonight or tomorrow.

"So," he said, "after thinking about this, I thought, 'Who am I to feel sorry for myself?' I should get down on my knees and thank God for the things I do have, and actually all I did was lose a fight, and I got paid for the fight and I have a beautiful home, and all the things the average man would want and even more. So, why should I feel sorry for myself?' I began to come out of it then, and I started going out the very next day, and that night was the first night that I think I got a good night's sleep."

"Cut!" Leonard Anderson said. "Great!"

"Thank you, Floyd," I said.

"You're welcome," he said.

"Floyd, you were terrific," Manny Spiro was saying. "That was absolutely terrific."

The whole thing had taken no more than fifteen minutes, but I was spent. I walked out into the sunlight and onto the terrace, with the weeds starting to grow between the cracked and uneven slates. Bill Mason, the sound engineer, had set up his recording equipment out there, with the cord to the microphone running through an open window, and he was still sitting there in front of his gear on a wooden folding chair.

"Wow!" he said. "What an interview!"

"It was all right," I said.

"All right?" he said. "Let me tell you something. I've been in this business for twenty years, and I've recorded everybody, including Presidents in the White House. I never recorded anything like that."

"That's Patterson," I said.

"When he told that story about the little girl dying in the hospital," Mason said, "I couldn't see him, but just sitting here with the headset on and listening—I'm telling you—the tears were running down my cheeks."

They had signed up James Cagney to host the program, and I could remember him dying on the church steps in *The Roaring Twenties*, his body riddled with the sub-machine gun bullets that had spewed out of the black limousine as it came around the corner, sliding and careening across the screen, while I sat, a teenager, in the Proctor's theater, gripped and hollow-sad. I could remember him, dead and bound like a mummy and propped against his mother's front door, falling forward onto the floor in *Public Enemy*, and now the teen-ager still in me found it almost absurd that he should be reading lines I had written.

"Patterson's great in the interview," he had said, after we had shown him and Robert Montgomery in a screening room on Broadway the rushes of what we had shot in the camps, "but can he lick the other guy?"

Between reels, while we waited for the projectionist to change over, we had talked about fights and fighters he remembered, and I had found that he has what I call the ability to read fights. It is like the ability to read writing, when the writing is worthy of it—not just what a writer says, but what he doesn't say and what he implies. Reading fights is not just reading the punches, which are obvious, but it is reading between the punches, the styles and the thinking, or what each fighter should be thinking, to set up what he has to say while silencing the other.

"He can lick him if he fights him right," I had said. "All he has to worry about is that one punch, the right hand."

"It's some right hand," Cagney had said, "and the way Patterson comes up out of his crouch he bobs right up into it."

Alvin Boretz had shown me how, filming Cagney in the studio, we could interpolate him into the interviews, and then I had had to convince Jack Dempsey to give Patterson a chance. For the last segment of the program I had wanted Dempsey and Joe Louis, the dream match, with Dempsey picking Johansson and Louis explaining how Patterson could beat him. Someone at the advertising agency, or perhaps the sponsor, had discovered, however, that Louis was associated with an advertising firm that represented an account in Castro's Cuba, and so they had turned down Joe, who had defended his title without pay for Army and Navy relief and is one of the noblest of men any of us has known in sports, and they picked Gene Tunney.

"I like Johansson," Dempsey had said, when I had gone to see him in his Broadway restaurant about the segment on the show. We were sitting in one of the booths.

"I know," I said, "but Tunney picks Johansson. Let me tell you what I'd like you to say."

It was another absurdity. A small boy, his hair freshly shampooed and his mother insisting that he not go to bed before it had thoroughly dried, would come down the stairs to listen on the radio to "The Cliquot Club Eskimos," "The A & P Gypsies," or Billy Jones and Ernie Hare, who called themselves "The Happiness Boys" when they broadcast from the Happiness Restaurant in New York, and later "The Interwoven Pair" when they advertised men's hose. The small boy, out-punched in the playground and scared in the street scrambles, would be wearing a heavy flannel bathrobe with an Indian blanket design on it, as he walked into the living room.

"Here he comes now!" his father would inevitably announce, and the boy would inevitably cringe inside. "Jack Dempsey!"

So I told Dempsey how I thought Patterson should fight it. If he worked inside Johansson's left jab, which in the first fight had set him up for Johansson's right, and if he kept firing left hooks while he turned it into a street fight and backed Johansson up, he could win it.

"That's right," Dempsey said. "If he does that, he could lick the Swede. I can say that."

After we had filmed Cagney in the studio, leading into the interviews and then with Dempsey and Tunney, someone had asked him to visit the two camps for some publicity still photos with the fighters. The next day, he and his friend Roland Winters drove into Patterson's camp where a half dozen of us were waiting.

"You have a picture over there on the wall," I said to Patterson now, sixteen years later, "of you with James Cagney and Roland Winters. That was taken for that TV program before the second Johansson fight when I interviewed you and Ingemar."

"That's right," he said. "I remember."

"After the picture-taking," I said, "the rest of us went to lunch at the inn in Newtown. You weren't having your meal then, but you came along and sat with us. You were at the end of the table, with Cagney on your right and me on your left. We talked awhile, and you were about to leave to work out, and that's when I asked you not to make the same mistake again."

"You did?" Patterson said.

"Sure," I said, thinking that he should remember this. "I said, 'Floyd, do yourself and me a favor. This guy has only one punch, the right hand. His jab isn't much, but it's just heavy enough to keep you in range for the right, so you've got to slip the jab, work on the inside, back him up and turn it into a street fight. None of these fellas from Europe, who have that stand-up continental style, can handle it when it's a street fight.'

"Then," I was saying now, and I was up and demonstrating again as I had in that dining room at the inn, "I told you to finish every one of your combinations, every sequence of punches, with the left hook. I said, 'This is the most important point of all. When you finish with a right hand, and if you hurt him with it or back him up, it still leaves you over here on your left, and in line for his right. You've got to finish with the hook, every time, and I don't care if you don't even hit him with it. Even if you miss it, it will carry you over to your right and out of line of his right.'"

"That's correct," Patterson said now, sitting there and nodding. "That's right."

"So you said, 'But I'm not sure I can learn that, to always finish with the left.' I said, 'Of course you can. When you're shadowboxing, when you're sparring in the ring, finish with the hook. When you're running on the road, throw half-punches and finish with the hook. Keep telling yourself, 'Left hook. Left hook.' You've got to do that, because you'll be taking away his only punch and throwing your best one. You can learn it.' Then you said, 'I'll try.'"

He had shaken hands with us then, to go back to camp. I didn't tell him now what Cagney had said as soon as he had left.

"Tell me something," Cagney said to me. "Who's been teaching this guy?"

"I remember," Patterson said now, "somebody telling me that about the left hook, but I forgot that it was you. Then I remember I also got a letter from a man—I don't know who he was—and he told me to always double-jab."

"That was good advice," I said, "because Johansson liked to throw the right hand over your single jab. That was very good advice."

"And that was some hook I hit him with," Patterson said, a small smile of satisfaction crossing his face.

That night at the Polo Grounds, left hooks and the only anger he ever carried into a ring won the fight for Patterson. He had backed Johansson up from the start, working inside the jab, but he had been in and out of trouble a half dozen times when he had forgotten to finish his combinations with a hook. Only Johansson's inability to spot this and time him had saved Patterson, and then in the fifth round, with Johansson backing up again, he had let go a wide hook, that was more a leaping swing. Johansson's back was to his own corner, and when he went down he landed on his rump and then his head hit the canvas and he lay there, his right leg twitching and the blood coming out of his mouth, for what seemed like ten minutes, while I feared for him, and before, they dared move him back to his corner and prop him up on the stool.

When I next saw Patterson he was going into training for the third Johansson fight the following March in Miami. I asked him how he had felt after he had won the title back.

"When I left the Polo Grounds," he said, "the promoters had a car and chauffeur waiting for me. I was sitting in the back seat alone, and when we drove through Harlen and I saw all the people celebrating in the streets, I felt good."

"You should have," I said. "There'd been nothing like it since Louis knocked out Billy Conn."

I meant there had been nothing like it for the Negro race in this country, and this will show you how far we have come. In the summer of 1936 I worked with a mixed gang on the railroad tracks that run through the Bronx and into Manhattan, and the day after Max Schmeling knocked out Joe Louis, Joe's people, so expectant and exuberant the day before, worked all day in saddened silence. Then, after Louis had knocked out Schmeling in 2 minutes and 4 seconds in their second fight, I had read about the all-night celebration in Harlem, and I had seen some of it after the second Conn fight and after Patterson had knocked out Johansson, and we have all come so far that there has been nothing like it since.

"Then I thought about Johansson," Patterson had said, describing that ride through Harlem. "I thought how he would have to drive through here, too, and then he would have to go through what I went through after the first fight. I thought that he would be even more ashamed than I was, because he'd knocked me out the first time. Then I felt sorry for him."

"Do you think," I had asked him, "that you can call up the same kind of anger and viciousness the next time you fight Johansson?"

"Why should I?" he had said. "In all my other fights I was never vicious, and I won out in almost all of them."

"But you had to be vicious against this guy," I had said. "You had to turn a boxing contest into a kind of street fight to destroy this guy's classic style. When you did that, he came apart. This was your greatest fight, because for the first time you expressed emotion. A fight, a piece of writing, a painting, or a passage of music is nothing without emotion."

"I just hope," Patterson had said, "that I'll never be as vicious again."

He never was, in his third fight with Johansson, when he was on the floor himself before he knocked Johansson out, or in the two each with Liston and Ali, when anger translated into viciousness might have given him the only chance he had. In what is the most totally expressive of the arts, for it permits man to vent and divest himself of his hatred and his anger, deplorable though they may be, he had delivered his finest performance when he held himself to be out of character, or at least the character he has tried always to assume.

"You earned a good deal of money," I said now. "Did you get good advice as to how to handle it? Did you have good investment help?"

"I helped myself," he said, "after experiencing losing tremendous amounts of money through people who were handling my finances. I supposedly made $9,000,000 in the ring. I don't know who got most of it, Uncle Sam or the persons handling it. All the money went to the office. Like $100,000 at one time would go to the office, and I would call and say, 'Send me $1,000 to run the camp.' Then I would go back and look at the account and there would be $12,000 in it. I'd say, 'Where's the rest?'"

"But you'd had no training in investments," I said.

"I started learning about various things," he said. "I had some stocks that were very successful. With stocks, if it was not too much of a gamble, I would chance it."

"So you won't ever have to work again?"

"I hope not," he said. "I sure hope not. When you retire and leave the limelight, you do what you really want to do. The days go slower. It's healthier, and you live longer. I think all the time. I do most of my thinking while

I'm working, and before I realize it, it will be four or five hours later. It's the same thing when I go to sleep. I think a lot."

"And what are the thoughts that go through your mind?"

"I think about life now, as opposed to the way it used to be, and about my peace of mind."

"And the life you have now," I said, "is it what you wanted, and hoped that someday it might be?"

"Let me put it this way," he said. "Being raised in Brooklyn and coming up through the slums, life is very different. I don't think anyone knows what they want in life. They know what they don't want. It's a process of elimination. I knew what I didn't want. I didn't want the slums.

"Living here," he said, "married, with a couple of kids—I didn't know I wanted this, but I am perfectly contented. I have to remember, though, and that makes me appreciate more what I have today. I wouldn't change one thing in the past because it helped me to this."

"That's the proper way to look at it," I said. "If we could all look at our lives that way, realizing that there's nothing we can do about the past, we'd all be the better for it. I'm happy for you."

"Thank you," he said.

We talked for a few minutes more, about other fighters I would be seeing for the book and about the decline of boxing. Then I stood up to leave.

"If your wife has read that piece," I said, "I'd like the magazine back. It's the only copy I have."

"Oh, yes," he said, and then, after he had come back with the magazine, "My wife enjoyed it."

"I'm glad," I said.

He walked me out to the car and we shook hands. I backed out and drove out to Route 299 and back up the hill through the center of the town. I had checked out of the motel, so I turned onto the Thruway, and I was sorry that, for whatever reasons, I had not met his wife. Perhaps, if they had gone to dinner with me, and if she had trusted me, I could have led them to tell me what it is like, a mixed marriage, an island in the sea of our still social segregation. Perhaps they would have told me, if they had known that I have believed for a long time that fifty or a hundred years from now, if this planet survives that long, it will be accepted that the ultimate and only rational solution will be miscegenation.

MASH AND
OTHER FICTION

Excerpt from MASH

Colonel Henry Blake was busier than he had been since The Deluge, and happier than he had been since his arrival in Korea. The first thing he did on the morning after his new neurosurgeon Oliver Wendell (Spearchucker) Jones reported was call General Hammond in Seoul and, still chuckling to himself, wonder if, by any chance, the football team of the 325th Evacuation Hospital would care to meet an eleven representing the 4077th MASH.

General Hammond was delighted. The previous year his team had administered such thorough hosings to the only two pickup elevens in Korea foolish enough to challenge his powerhouse that both of those aggregations had abandoned the game. This had left him with a winning streak of two straight, visions of some day joining the company of Pop Warner, Amos Alonzo Stagg and Knute Rockne—and no one to play. The date was set for Thanksgiving Day, five weeks away, on the home field of the champions at Yong-Dong-Po.

The next thing Colonel Blake did was write Special Services in Tokyo and arrange for the use of two dozen football uniforms, helmets, shoes and pads, all to be airlifted as soon as possible. Then he dictated a notice, calling for candidates to report at two o'clock the next afternoon, and copies were posted in the messhall, the latrines, the showers and in the Painless Polish Poker and Dental Clinic. After that he showed up at The Swamp.

"Now," he said, after he had finished his report, "when do we start getting our dough down?"

"Why don't we wait a while, Coach," Trapper John suggested, "until we see what we've got for talent?"

"It doesn't matter what we've got," Henry responded. "That Hammond doesn't know anything about football."

"But if we seem too eager, Coach," Hawkeye said, "we may tip our hand."

"I guess you're right," Henry agreed.

The following afternoon, at the appointed hour, fifteen candidates appeared on the ball field. The equipment would not arrive for several days, so Henry, a whistle suspended from a cord around his neck, and as previously advised by his neurosurgeon, ran the rag-tag agglomeration twice around the perimeter of the field and then put them through some calisthenics. After that he just let them fool around, kicking and passing the three available footballs, while he and the Swampmen sized them up.

"Well," Henry said, at cocktail hour that afternoon in The Swamp, "what do you think?"

"Can we still get out of the game?" the Duke said.

"Yeah," Hawkeye said. "Whose idea was this anyway?"

"Yours, dammit," Trapper said.

"God, they looked awful," Hawkeye said.

"They'll look fine," Henry said, "once the uniforms get here."

"Never," the Duke said.

"Listen," Spearchucker said. "The coach is right. I don't mean particularly about the uniforms, but no team ever looks good the first few days. I noticed a few boys out there who have played the game."

"Besides," Henry said, "what does that Hammond know about football? It's like having another man on our side."

"The first thing we've got to do," Spearchucker said, "is decide on an offense."

"That's right," Henry said. "That's the first thing we've got to do. What'll it be? The Notre Dame Box?"

Trapper had been a T quarterback at Dartmouth, and Duke had run out of the T as a fullback at Georgia. Androscoggin, where Hawkeye had played end, had still used the single wing, but Spearchucker had played in the T in college and, of course, with the pros. Hawkeye was outvoted, 3 to 1, with Henry abstaining but agreeing.

"Now we've got to think up some plays," Henry said. "Why don't you fellas handle that while I look after some of the other details?"

Spearchucker diagrammed six basic running plays and four stock pass plays, and that evening presented them to Henry, with explanations. Henry studied these, established a training table at one end of the mess hall and ordered his athletes to cut down on the consumption of liquor and cigarettes. The Swampmen settled for two drinks before dinner and none after, and reduced their inhalation of nicotine and tobacco tars by one half.

For the next two days, Henry, with surreptitious suggestions from Spearchucker, had the squad first walk through and then run through the plays. When the uniforms arrived they turned out, to the dismay of the

Duke, who had worn the red for Georgia, to consist of cardinal jerseys, white helmets and white pants. As the personnel sorted through the equipment and found sizes that approximated their own, Henry fretted. He could hardly wait to see them suited up.

"Great! Great!" Henry exulted, as they lined up in front of him on the field. "You men look great!"

"We look like a lotta goddamn cherry parfaits," Trapper said.

"Great!" Henry went on. "Wait'll that Hammond sees you. He's in for the surprise of his life."

"It'll be the last surprise he'll ever have," the Duke said. "He'll die laughin'."

Things were not as desperate, however, as the Swampmen seemed to believe. To the practiced eye of their newest member, in fact, it was apparent that his colleagues possessed at least some of the skills needed to play the game. Trapper John, after he took the snap from center, hustled back and stood poised to throw, looked like a scarecrow, but he had a whip for an arm and began to regain his control. Hawkeye, when he went down for passes, exhibited good moves and good hands. The Duke had the short, powerful stride a fullback needs, ran hard, blocked well and, during the few semi-scrimmages, showed himself to be imbued with an abundance of competitive fire. Sergeant Pete Rizzo, the ex-Three I League infielder, was a natural athlete and a half-back. Of the others, the sergeant from Supply named Vollmer, who had played center for Nebraska, was the best. Ugly John made a guard of sorts and Captain Walter Koskiusko Waldowski, the Painless Pole, a survivor of high school and sandlot football in Hamtramek, was big enough, strong enough and angry enough to be a tackle. The rest of the line was filled out by enlisted men, with the exception of one of the end spots to which, over the objections of Trapper John, Dr. R. C. (Jeeter) Carroll was assigned.

The Spearchucker, of course, was kept under cover, except to jog around and catch a few passes. When anyone was watching he dropped them. No one guessed his identity, so scouts from the Evac Hospital could report to General Hammond only that the big colored boy was a clown, that whatever the Swampmen might have been once and were trying to be again, they had partaken of far too much whiskey and tobacco to go more than a quarter. Moreover, there were only four substitutes.

Hawkeye scouted the 325th. He went down one afternoon and tried to look like he was bound on various errands between the Quonsets that surrounded the athletic field, while he eyed the opposition.

"They got nothing," he reported on his return. "Three boys in the backfield looked like they played some college ball, but they probably aren't any better than Trapper, the Duke and me. They got a lousy passer, but their line is heavier than ours, and they got us in depth. I think that without the Spearchucker we could play them about even. With the Spearchucker they can't touch us."

"Good," Trapper said. "Then I suggest we do this: We hide the Spearchucker until the second half, and we hold back half our bets. We go into the half maybe ten points or two touchdowns behind, and then we bet the rest of our bundle at real odds."

"Great!" Henry said. "Everybody get his dough up!"

By the time everyone had kicked in—doctors, nurses, lab technicians, corpsmen, Supply and mess hall personnel—Henry had $6,000. The next morning—five days before the game—he called General Hammond, and when he came off the phone and reported to The Swamp it was apparent that he was disturbed.

"What happened?" Trapper asked. "Couldn't you get the dough down?"

"Yeah," Henry said. "I got $3,000 down."

"No odds?" Duke asked.

"Yeah," Henry said. "He gave me 7 to 5. He snapped it up."

"Oh-oh," Trapper John said. "I think I smell something."

"Me, too," Henry said. "That Hammond is tighter than a bull's ass in fly time. Whatever he's trying to pull, I don't like it."

"Tell you what we'd better do," Hawkeye said. "When I scouted those clowns they didn't look any better than we do but with them just as anxious to get their money down as we are, maybe I missed something. Spearchucker better go down tomorrow and nose around. He'll know a ringer if he sees one."

"Maybe I'd better go at that," Spearchucker said.

The next night Captain Jones returned from his scouting trip to Yong-Dong-Po. He didn't look any happier than Henry had the day before.

"What's the word?" asked Trapper John.

"They got two tackles from the Browns, and a halfback played with the Rams."

"That's not fair!" Henry said, jumping up. "Why, this game is supposed to be . . . "

"Wait a minute," Hawkeye said. "Are these guys any good?"

"Anybody ever ask you to play pro football, boy?" Spear-chucker said.

"I get your point," Hawkeye said.

"My arm is sore," declared Trapper. "I don't think I can play."

"What do we do?" asked Henry.

"Y'all are the coach," Duke said. "How about it, Coach?"

"I guess we have to play," Henry said, his dreams of gold and glory gone.

"The bastards outconned us," Hawkeye said.

"Maybe not," Spearchucker said. "We'll think of something."

"Like what?" Duke said.

"Like getting that halfback out of there as soon as we can," Spearchucker said.

"You know him?" Duke said.

"No," Spearchucker said, "but I've seen him. He played only one year second-string with the Rams before the Army got him. He's a colored boy who weighs only about 180, but he's a speed burner and one of those hot dogs."

"What does that mean?" Henry said.

"I mean," Spearchucker said, "that when he sees a little running room he likes to make a show—you know, stutter steps and cross-overs and all that jazz. He runs straight up and never learned to button up when he gets hit, so I think that, if you can get a good shot at him, you can get him out of there."

"Then let's kick off to them," the Duke said, "and get him right away."

"Good idea," Henry said.

"No," Spearchucker said. "He'll kill you in an open field. You've got to get him in a confined situation, where he hesitates and hangs up."

"Good idea," Henry said.

"Sure," Hawkeye said, "but how do we do that?"

"They'll run him off tackle a lot from strong right," Spearchucker said, "or send him wide. Hawkeye has to play him wide and turn him in, and when he makes his cut to the left he's gonna do that cross-over and Duke has to hit him high and Hawkeye low."

"Great idea!" Henry said. "That'll show that Hammond."

"Yeah," Duke said, "but can we do it?"

"It's the only way to do it," Spearchucker said. "If you don't get him the first time, he'll give you plenty of other chances."

"But when we unload him, if we can," Hawkeye said, "we'll have to break his leg to keep him from coming back in."

"Not necessarily," Trapper John said. "I got an idea."

"What is it?" Henry said.

"Tell you later," Trapper said, "if it works."

Trapper John excused himself, left The Swamp, walked over to Henry's tent and made a phone call. He talked for five minutes, and when he came back his teammates and their coach were dwelling on the problem presented by the two tackles from the Browns.

"We run nothing inside until I get into the game in the second half," Spearchucker was explaining. "These two big boys must be twenty or thirty pounds overweight. We run everything wide, except for maybe an occasional draw for Duke up the middle to take advantage of their rush on Trapper when he passes."

"God help me," Trapper said.

"And me, too," Duke said.

"In other words," Spearchucker said, "the idea is to run the legs off 'em that first half. I think that will be all the edge I will require, gentlemen."

"Right," Henry said. "Imagine that Hammond, trying to pull something like that."

On the day of Thanksgiving the kick-off was scheduled for 10:00 A.M., so shortly after the crack of dawn the 4077th MASH football team, the Red Raiders of the Imjin, all fifteen of them, plus their coach, their water boy and assorted rooters, took off in jeeps and truck. The Swampmen rode together in the same jeep and in silence. No bottle was passed and no cigarettes were smoked, and when they arrived in Yong-Dong-Po and headed for the Quonset assigned to the team as dressing quarters Trapper John excused himself and disappeared.

"Where the hell have you been?" Hawkeye asked him, when their quarterback finally returned just in time to suit up and loosen his arm.

"Yeah," the Duke said. "We thought y'all went over the hill."

"Had to see a man about a hot dog," Trapper said. "Good old Austin from Boston."

"Who?" Duke asked.

"About what?" Hawkeye said.

"Tell you about it if it works," Trapper said. "You two clods just take care of the halfback."

"All right, men," Henry was saying. "I want you to listen to me. Let's have some quiet in here. This game . . . "

He went into a Pat O'Brien-plays-Knute Rockne, stalking up and down and invoking their pride in themselves, their organization, the colors they wore and their bank accounts. When he finished, out of words and out of breath, his face was as red as their jerseys, and he turned them loose to meet the orange and black horde of Hammond.

"Look at the size of those two beasts," Trapper John said, spotting the two tackles from the Browns.

"We know," Duke said. "We were out here before. This is gonna take courage."

"I ain't got any," Trapper said.

"Me neither," Jeeter Carroll said.

"God help us," Trapper said.

Hawkeye, because it had been his idea to play the game in the first place, was sent out now, as captain, to face the two tackles for the coin toss. When he came back he reported that he had lost the toss and that they would have to kick off.

"Now keep it away from the speed-burner," Spearchucker instructed the Duke. "Kick it to anybody else but him."

"That's right," said Henry, regaining his breath. "Kick it to anybody else but him."

"I know," the Duke assured them. "Y'all think I'm crazy?"

"Let's go get 'em, men!" Henry said.

The Duke kicked it away from the halfback who had played a year of second-string with the Rams. He kicked it as far away from him as he could, but the enemy was of a different mind. The individual who caught the ball, by the simple maneuver of just running laterally and handing off, saw to it that the halfback who had played a year of second-string with the Rams got the ball. The next thing they knew, the Red Raiders of the Imjin saw an orange and black blur and they were lining up to try to prevent the point after touch-down, an effort which also failed.

"Stop him!" Henry was screaming on the sidelines. "Stop that man!"

"Yeah," the Duke was saying as they distributed themselves to receive the kick-off. "Y'all give me a rifle and I might stop him, if they blindfold him and tie him to a stake."

When the kick came, it came to the Duke on the ten and he ran it straight ahead to the thirty before they brought him down. On the first play from scrimmage Trapper sent Hawkeye, playing at left half until Spearchucker could get into the game, around right end. Hawkeye made two yards, and Pete Rizzo, at right half, picked up two more around the other flank.

"Third and six," Hawkeye said, as they came back to huddle. "I'll run a down and out."

"I'll run a down and in," Jeeter Carroll said, "but throw it to Hawkeye."

"My arm is sore," Trapper said.

"Y'all gotta throw," Duke said.

"God help us," Trapper said.

By the time he had taken the snap and hustled back, Trapper John knew that his blocking pocket had collapsed. He knew it because the two tackles from the Browns were descending upon him, and he ran. He ran to the right and turned and ran to the left.

"Good!" Spearchucker was calling from the sidelines. "Run the legs off those two big hogs!"

"Throw it!" Henry was shouting. "Throw it!"

Trapper threw it. Hawkeye caught it. When he caught it he lugged it to the enemy forty-nine. That was about as far as that drive went, and with fourth and five on the forty-four, Duke went back to punt.

"Don't try for distance," Hawkeye told him. "Kick it up there so we can get down and surround that sonofabitch."

"Yeah," Duke said, "if I can."

He kicked it high and, as it came down, the halfback who had played a year of second-string with the Rams, waiting for it on his twenty, saw red jerseys closing in. He called for a fair catch.

"A hot dog," Spearchucker said, on the sidelines. "A real hot dog."

"A hot dog," Hawkeye said to Duke as they lined up. "Spearchucker had him right."

"Yeah," Duke said. "Let's try to take him, like the Chucker said."

When the play evolved, it was also as Spearchucker had called it. The halfback who had played a year of second-string with the Rams went in motion from his left half position, took a pitch out, turned up through the line off tackle and tried to go wide. When he saw Hawkeye, untouched by blockers, closing in from the outside, he made his cut. He made that beautiful crossover, the right leg thrust across in front of the left, and just at the instant when he looked like he was posing for the picture for the cover of the game program, poised as he was on the ball of his left foot, the other leg in the air and one arm out, he was hit. From one side he was hit at the knees by 200 pounds of hurtling former Androscoggin College end, and from the other he was hit high by 195 pounds of former Georgia fullback.

"Time!" one of the former Brown tackles was calling. "Time!"

It took quite some time. In about five minutes they got the halfback who had played a year of second-string with the Rams on his feet, and they assisted him to the sidelines and sat him down on the bench.

"How many fingers am I holding up?" General Hammond, on his knees in front of his offensive star and extending the digits of one hand, was asking.

"Fifteen," his star replied.

"Take him in," the General said, sadly. "Try to get him ready for the second half."

So they took him across the field and into the 325th Evac. As the Swampmen watched him go, Trapper John was the first to speak.

"That," Trapper John said, "takes care of that. Scratch one hot dog."

"Y'all think he's hurt that bad?" the Duke asked.

"Hell, no," Trapper said, "but we won't see him again."

"I suspect something," Hawkeye said. "Explain."

"An old Dartmouth roomie of mine," Trapper explained, "is attached to this cruddy outfit. I called him the other night, after Spearchucker outlined the plot, and told him to put in for Officer of the Day today."

"I'm beginning to get it," Hawkeye said.

"This morning," Trapper went on, "I paid him a visit and cut him in for a piece of our bet. Right now Austin from Boston is going to place that hot dog under what is politely called heavy sedation, where he will dwell for the rest of the game and probably the rest of the day."

"Trapper," Hawkeye said, "you are a genius."

"Y'all know something?" the Duke said. "I think we can beat these Yankees now."

"Time!" the referee was screaming, between blasts on his whistle. "Do you people want to play football or talk all day?"

"If we have a choice," Hawkeye said, as they started to line up, "we prefer to talk."

"But you ain't got a choice," one of the tackles from the Browns said, "and you'll get yours now."

"What do y'all mean?" the Duke said. "It was clean."

"Yeah," Hawkeye said, "and you'll have to catch us first."

On that drive the enemy was stopped on the seven, and had to settle for the field goal that made it 10–0. For their part, the Red Raiders devoted most of their offensive efforts to pulling the corks of the two tackles, running them from one side of the field to the other. Midway in the second quarter they managed a score after Ugly John had fallen on a fumble on the enemy nineteen. Two plays later Hawkeye caught a wobbling pass lofted by a still fleeing Trapper John and fell into the end zone. Just before the end of the half the home forces rammed the ball over once more, so the score was 17–7 when both sides retired for rest and resuscitation.

"Very good, gentlemen," Spearchucker, who had been pacing the sideline helmeted and wrapped in a khaki blanket, told them as they filed in. "Very good, indeed."

"Yeah," Trapper John said, slumping to the floor, "but I gotta have a . . . "

". . . beer, sir?" said Radar O'Reilly, who had been serving during the time-outs as water boy.

"Right," Trapper said, taking the brew. "Thank you."

"Tell you what," Hawkeye said. "They got us now by ten, so we ought to be able to get two to one. Coach?"

"Yes, sir?" Henry said. "I mean, yes?"

"You better get over there quick," Hawkeye said, "and grab that Hammond and try to get the rest of that bundle down at two to one."

"Yes, sir," Henry said. "I mean, yes. What's the matter with me, anyway?"

"Nothin', Coach," Duke said. "Y'all are doing a real fine job."

Henry was back in less than five minutes. He reported that he had failed to get as far as the other team's dressing room. Halfway across the field he had been met by General Hammond who, having just checked on the health of his offensive star, had found him still under sedation. As Henry described him, the General was extremely irate.

"He was so mad," Henry said, "that he wanted to know if we'd like to get any more money down."

"Did you all tell him yes?" Duke wanted to know.

"He was so mad," Henry said, "that he said he'd give us three to one."

"And you took it?" Trapper said.

"I got four to one," a gleeful Henry said.

"Great, Coach!" they were shouting now. "How to go, Coach!"

"But," Henry said, the elation suddenly draining from his face, as he thought of something, "we still have to win."

"Relax, coach," Spearchucker assured him. "If these poor white trash will just give me the ball and then direct their attentions to the two gentlemen from Cleveland, Ohio, I promise you that I shall bring our crusade to a victorious conclusion."

Henry gave them then a re-take of his opening address. He paced the floor in front of them, waving his arms, exhorting, praising, pleading until, once more, his face and neck were of the same hue as their jerseys and once more, and for the last time, he sent them out to do or die.

As the Red Raiders of the Imjin distributed themselves to receive the kick-off, Captain Oliver Wendell Jones took a position on the goal line. The ball was not kicked to him, but the recipient, Captain Augustus Bedford Forrest, made certain that he got it. Without significant interference, Captain Jones proceeded to the opposite end zone. Captain Forrest then kicked the extra point, bringing the score up to 17–14, and while the teams dragged themselves back upfield, the two tackles from the Browns were seen loping over to their sideline. There they were observed in earnest conversation with General Hamilton Hartington Hammond who, as the two lumbered back onto the field, was seen shaking his fist in the direction of Lieutenant Colonel Henry Braymore Blake.

"Those two tackles, sir," Radar O'Reilly informed his colonel, "told General Hammond that they recognize Captain Jones, sir."

"Roll it up!" Henry, ignoring both his corporal and his general, was screaming. "Roll it up!"

"Keep it down," advised Hawkeye. "We may want to do this again."

"We may not have to worry about that," Spearchucker, still breathing heavily, informed them. "I guess I'm not in the shape I thought I was. This may still be a battle."

It was. It was primarily a battle between the two tackles and Spearchucker, with certain innocent parties, such as Ugly John and the Painless Pole and Vollmer, the sergeant from Supply and center from Nebraska, in the middle. When the Red Raiders got the ball again they went ahead for the moment, as Spearchucker scored once more on a forty yard burst, but then the enemy surged back to grind out another and, with three minutes to play the score was Hammond 24, Blake 21, first-and-ten for the home forces on the visitors' thirty-five-yard line.

"We gotta stop 'em here," Spearchucker said.

"We need a time-out," Trapper John said, "and some information."

"Time-out!" Hawkeye called to the referee.

"Radar," Trapper John said, when Radar O'Reilly came in with the water bucket and the towels, "do you think you can monitor that kaffee-clatch over there?"

He nodded toward the other team, gathered around their quarterback.

"I think I can, sir," Radar said. "I can try, sir."

"Well, goddammit, try."

"Yes, sir," Radar said, fixing his attention on the other huddle.

"What are they saying?"

"Well, sir," Radar said, "the quarterback is saying that they will run the old Statue of Liberty, sir. He's saying that their left end will come across and take the ball off his hand and try to get around their right end."

"Good," Spearchucker said. "What else are they saying?"

"Well, sir," Radar said, "now the quarterback is saying that, if that doesn't work, they'll go into the double wing."

"Good," the Duke said.

"Ssh!" Hawkeye said. "What are they gonna do out of the double wing?"

"Well, sir," Radar said, "they're having an argument now. Everybody is talking so it's confusing."

"Keep listening."

"Yes, sir. Now one of the tackles is telling them all to shut up. Now the quarterback is saying that, out of the double wing, the left halfback will come across and take the hand-off and start to the right. Then he'll hand off to the right halfback coming to the left."

"Radar," Hawkeye said, "you're absolutely the greatest since Marconi."

"Greater," Trapper John said.

"Thank you, sir," Radar said. "That's very kind of you, sir."

"Time!" the referee was calling. "Time!"

It was as Radar O'Reilly had heard it. On the first play the enemy quarterback went back, as if to pass. As he did, the left end started to his right, and the Red Raiders, all eleven of them, started to their left. The left end took the ball off the quarterback's hand, brought it down, made his cut and met a welcoming committee of ten men in red, only Ugly John, temporarily buried under 265 pounds of tackle, failing to make it on time.

"Double wing!" Spearchucker informed his associates as the enemy lined up for the next play. "Double wing!"

"Hut! Hut!" the enemy quarterback was calling. "Hut!"

This time the left halfback took the hand-off and started to his right. The eleven Red Raiders started to *their* right and, as the right halfback took the ball from the left halfback, ran to his left and tried to turn in he, too, was confronted by ten men wearing the wrong colors. This time it was the Painless Pole who, tripping over his own feet, kept the Red Raiders from attaining perfect attendance.

The first man to hit the halfback was Spearchucker Jones. He hit him so hard that he doubled him over and drove him back five yards, and as the wind came out of the halfback so did the ball. It took some time to find the ball, because it was at the bottom of a pile of six men, all wearing red jerseys.

"Time!" Spearchucker called, and he walked over and talked with the referee.

"What's the matter?" Trapper John asked him, when he came back. "Let's take it to them."

"Too far to go, and we're all bushed," Spearchucker said. "I just told the referee that we're gonna try something different. We're gonna make the center eligible by . . . "

"Who?" Vollmer, the sergeant from Supply and center from Nebraska said. "Me?"

"That's right," Spearchucker said. "Now everybody listen, and listen good. We line up unbalanced, with everybody to the right of center, except Hawkeye at left end. Just before the signal for the snap of the ball, Duke, you move up into the line to the right of the center and Hawkeye, you drop back a yard. That keeps the required seven men in the line, and makes the center eligible to receive a pass."

"Me?" Vollmer said. "I can't catch a pass."

"You don't have to," Spearchucker said. "Trapper takes the snap and hands the ball right back to you between your legs. You hide it in your belly, and stay there like you're blockin'. Trapper, you start back like you got the ball,

make a fake to me and keep going. One or both of those tackles will hit you
. . ."

"Oh, dear," Trapper said.

"Meanwhile," Spearchucker said to Vollmer, "when your man goes by
you, you straighten up, hidin' the ball with your arms, and you walk—don't
run—toward that other goal line."

"I don't know," Vollmer said.

"You got to," Hawkeye said. "Just think of all that dough."

"I suppose," Vollmer said.

"Everybody else keep busy," Spearchucker said. "Keep the other people
occupied, but don't hold, and Vollmer, you remember you walk, don't run."

"I'll try," Vollmer said.

"Oh, dear," Trapper John said.

"Time!" the referee was calling again. "Time!"

When they lined up, all of the linemen to the right of the center except
Hawkeye, they had some trouble finding their positions and the enemy had
some trouble adjusting. As Trapper John walked up and took his position behind the center and then Duke jumped up into the line and Hawkeye
dropped back, the enemy was even more confused.

"Hut!" Trapper John called. "Hut!"

He took the ball from the center, handed it right back to him, turned and
started back. He faked to Spearchucker, heading into the line, and then, his
back to the fray, he who had once so successfully posed as The Saviour now
posed as The Quarterback With the Ball. So successfully did he pose, in fact,
that both tackles from the Browns and two other linemen in orange and
black fell for the ruse, and on top of Trapper John.

Up at the line, meanwhile, the sergeant from Supply and center from Nebraska had started his lonely journey. Bent over, his arms crossed to further
hide the ball, and looking like he had caught a helmet or a shoulder pad in
the pit of the stomach and was now living with the discomfort, he had
walked right between the two enemy halfbacks whose attention was focused
on the trapping of Trapper John. Once past this checkpoint, about ten yards
from where he had started and now out in the open, the sergeant, however,
began to feel as conspicuous as a man who had forgotten his pants, so he decided to embellish the act. He veered toward his own sideline, as if he were
leaving the game.

"What's going on?" Henry was screaming as his center approached him.
"What's going on out there? What are you doing?"

"I got the ball," the center informed him, opening his arms enough for
Henry to see the pigskin cradled there.

"Then run!" Henry screamed. "Run!"

So the sergeant from Supply and center from Nebraska began to run. Back upfield, the two tackles from the Browns had picked up Trapper John. That is, each had picked up a leg, and now they were shaking him out like a scatter rug, still trying to find the ball, while their colleagues stood around waiting for it to appear, so they could pounce on it. Downfield, meanwhile, the safety man stood, shifting his weight from one foot to the other, scratching an armpit, peering upfield and waiting for something to evolve. He had noticed the center start toward the sidelines, apparently in pain, but he had ignored that. Now, however, as he saw the center break into a run, the light bulb lit, and he took off after him. They met, but they met on the two-yard line, and the sergeant from Supply and center from Nebraska carried the safety man, as well as the ball, into the end zone with him:

"What happened?" General Hammond, coach, was hollering on one sideline. "Illegal! Illegal!"

"It was legal," the referee informed him. "They made that center eligible."

"Crook!" General Hammond was hollering at Lieutenant Colonel Blake on the other sideline, shaking his fist at him. "Crook!"

"Run it up!" Henry was hollering. "Run it up!"

"Now we just gotta stop 'em," Spearchucker said, after Duke had kicked the point that made it MASH 28, Evac 24.

"Not me," Trapper John said, weaving for the sideline.

And stop them they did. The key defensive play was made, in fact, by Dr. R. C. (Jeeter) Carroll. Dr. Carroll, all five feet nine inches and 150 pounds of him, had spent the afternoon on the offense just running passroutes, waving his arms over his head and screaming at the top of his lungs. He had run button-hooks, turn-ins, turn-outs, zig-ins, zig-outs, posts and fly patterns. Trapper John had ignored him and, after the first few minutes, so had the enemy. Now, with less than a minute to play, with the enemy on the Red Raiders' forty, fourth and ten, Spearchucker had called for a prevent defense and sent for the agile Dr. Carroll to replace Trapper John.

"Let's pick on that idiot," Radar O'Reilly heard one of the enemy ends tell the enemy quarterback as Jeeter ran onto the field. "He's opposite me, so let's run that crossing pattern and I'll lose him."

They tried. They crossed their ends about fifteen yards deep but the end couldn't lose Jeeter. Jeeter stuck right with him but, with his back to play, he couldn't see the ball coming. It came with all the velocity the quarterback could still put on it, and it struck Jeeter on the back of the helmet. When it struck Jeeter it drove him to his knees, but it also rebounded into the arms of the Painless Pole who fell to the ground still clutching it.

"Great!" Henry was shouting from the sideline. "Great defensive play."

"That's using the old head, Jeeter," Hawkeye told Dr. Carroll, as he helped him to his feet.

"What?" Jeeter said.

"That's using the old noggin," Hawkeye said.

"What?" Jeeter said.

Then Spearchucker loafed the ball into the line twice, the referee fired off his Army .45 and they trooped off the field, into the waiting arms of Henry, who escorted them into their dressing quarters where they called for the beer and slumped to the floor.

"Great!" Henry, ecstatic, was saying, going around and shaking each man's hand. "It was a great team effort. You're heroes all!"

"Then give us our goddamn Purple Hearts," said Ugly John, who had spent most of the afternoon under one or the other of the two tackles from the Browns.

When General Hammond appeared, he was all grace. In the best R.A. stiff-upper-lip tradition he congratulated them, and then he took Henry aside.

"Men," Henry said, after the general had left, "he wants a rematch. Whadda you say?"

"I thought he was bein' awful nice," Spearchucker said.

"We might be able to do it to them again," Henry said, still glowing.

"Never again," Hawkeye said. "They're on to us now."

"Gentlemen," the Duke, slumped next to Hawkeye, said, "I got an announcement to make. Y'all have just seen me play my last game."

"You can retire my number, too," Trapper John said.

"Mine, too," Hawkeye said.

"Anyway, men," Henry said, "I told you so."

"What?" Hawkeye said.

"That Hammond," Henry said. "He doesn't know anything about football."

On December 17, 1933, 26,000 football fans in Chicago's Wrigley Field saw the Chicago Bears defeat the New York Giants 23–21 in the first National Football League Championship game. They also witnessed the first and last use of the center-eligible pass play when Steve Owen, coach of the Giants, had Mel Hein, his center, snap the ball between his legs to Harry Newman, the quarterback, who then handed it back by the same route to Hein who, cradling it against his body, rambled with it twenty yards downfield until Carl Brumbaugh, the Chicago safety, caught him from behind on the 5-yard line from where the Giants would ultimately score.

At the next league meeting, his protests having been unheard on the field, George Halas, the Bears' coach, had the scam banned. There it lay, buried in league history, until a quarter-century later I resurrected it with the amused approval of H. Richard Hornberger, M.D., the original Hawkeye Pierce and my co-author, for the good of the 4077th MASH.

w.c.h.
January 2001

Nicholas Braff

from *Emergency*

"Look, Nick," Whitey says. "Do me a favor, will ya? Why don't you wrap it up and go home?"

"Do you a favor?" I said. "I don't owe you anything, Whitey. I did you many a favor."

"All right," he says. "Then do yourself a favor, but knock it off and go home."

"Do myself a favor?" I said. "I don't even owe myself a favor. I don't owe anybody."

"Look," he says, "you're talkin' in circles. You have a couple more and you'll be walkin' in circles. Just go home."

"It's early," I said.

"I know," he says, "but you been here since three o'clock. For four hours you been soakin' it up."

"*Almost* four hours," I said. "I know what time it is. I learned to tell time."

Ain't that a laugh? *I learned to tell time.* That's ridiculous. Everything's ridiculous. Why, them reporters used to write that Nick Braff has a clock in his head. Like Arcaro, is what they wrote. Clock in his head. Why, when McGeady was breaking me in, and we were staying at them six-dollar-a-night-for-two motels with no rugs on the floor around them half-milers, he'd sit there every damn night with that stop watch in his hand. He'd start yakkin'—bitchin' about some racing secretary or the price of feed or the world in general—and then he'd punch that watch and keep talkin' and then he'd punch it again and say: "How much?"

How much? Hell, while he was yakkin' with that watch going, he'd ask me a question, to be sure I was really listening to him and not just clockin' in my head, and then he'd say: "How much?"

"It ain't hard," he'd say, while I was learning. "People who don't know think you're some kind of a smart genius if you can come within 2/5ths of a second, but it's 2/5ths either side of the second, and that's 4/5ths and damn near a whole second."

Then in the mornings it was something, too. We'd go out there together, me on one of his animals and old McGeady sittin' on that old stable pony and spittin' tobacco juice, and if he told me to work a mile in 1:41 he didn't want me coming down in :42. If I did you could be sure he'd be right alongside me, bouncing along on that pony while I'd be bringing his animal back, yakkin' at me, and all of a sudden—splat!—there'd be a hit from that tobacco juice right on the toe of my boot.

"And clean your goddam boot, too!" he'd say.

It was a funny thing about that tobacco chewin', because he was the neatest man I ever knew. Even with that he was neat, because he could hit a dime at five paces, and in them third-rate motel rooms he was always sittin' around with one of them paper cups they have in them dispensers on the wall. When I first came around him, and the way I grew up, I was a slob, but the boots had to be polished every night and the jodhpurs and all the clothing, including underwear, clean and the tack rubbed down until it used to shine. We stabled in some awful dumps on those half-milers, but the way we took care of those animals and those stalls you'd have thought we were Greentree or Calumet.

"McGreedy," they used to call him, but hell, he wasn't greedy. He was just the best at training cheap claimin' horses and schoolin' a jock I ever come across, but he fought with everybody—trainers, racing secretaries, stewards, patrol judges, owners—always trying to get the best for anything he dropped into a race.

"You gotta remember this," he used to tell me. "There are no Cadillacs in my stable, so I gotta fight for anything I can get and you gotta save everything you can save on any horse I ever run."

Then he'd watch me. Damn, how he'd watch me, from the time he'd boost me up until the time I'd get back. Them other jocks would be laughing and kidding going to the gate, but I would be one serious citizen. McGeady had better not see me laughing on one of his, and I never rode a race for him that he didn't tell me everything I did—whether I took a long enough hold coming out of the gate, and whether I pulled him up too short or sawed on his mouth or whatever, and especially if I went around a bunch when he thought there was room to come through on the rail.

"Damn, I've told you this a hundred times!" he'd scream. "I can't run a horse that much the best, and you gotta save ground. You can't take the married man's route on one of mine. Goin' wide is for those blue-blood stables with all the silverware in their trophy rooms and those fashionable jocks with all their money in stocks and bonds. I'm just a poor, hungry old man and you're just a poor hungry little man, and you'll be that all your life if you don't use your brain and if you don't show some guts."

Hell, that Whitey's got some nerve, asking me to do him a favor. I did him a favor, and I don't mean tonight. Many a favor. Like the time the guy who owned the building raised the rent and Whitey says he couldn't afford it, it would put him out of business, and I told him he should buy the dump. Whitey says he thought of that but the bank won't loan him enough so I loaned him $10,000 for three years before he paid it back, no interest.

Many a favor. Like the night after I won that goddam Special on that Windborne I picked up the tab for one hell of a blast there. I coulda had it anywhere. I coulda had it in any fashionable joint I wanted, any one of them, but I brought it there for Whitey, and them free-loaders must have come from a hundred miles around. What the hell did I care? The only one I cared about in the whole goddam joint besides Whitey was old McGeady, because after he sold my contract for that $5,000 he knew he'd never get another boy like me and I knew I'd never know another citizen like him.

Why, I won that goddam Special because of him and all he taught me about rating an animal and saving ground and time, and he was lucky he had a clubhouse pass. Them other jocks they knew I had a hell of a come-from-behind animal under me, but they knew as well as I did that he had only one run in him so they sent that P. J. Petrie out to pull my cork. That was a joke because I knew P.J.'s animal couldn't go the distance and he'd come back to me, and then them other three they thought they'd slow that damn pace down to where they'd all have plenty left comin' home. That was a joke, too, because like I told Whitey I learned to tell time, and after we like walked that first half mile in :50 I turned that sob loose. They thought they had me locked in there pretty good, but when I set that animal to running Bobby North was lookin' over his shoulder and he hollered: "Here he comes!" and that beast just made his own hole inside Bobby's animal and that rail and win by six.

"You did all right," McGeady said to me that night at Whitey's, "but tell that owner of yours to stop talkin' about that horse bein' another Citation."

"What's that mean?" I said.

"You know damn well what it means," he said, and he was right. "You finished tryin' to make it look like you still had some horse, but he was empty. In another eighth of a mile you'da had to get off him and walked, so don't try to sell me that."

So right up there over the cash register Whitey's still got that picture of me on that animal in the winner's circle with the owner's wife at the head holding the bridle, and ain't that ridiculous? I mean my picture is on the goddam wall and he don't want me in the goddam joint, but Mister Whitey is gonna be surprised. He's gonna be oh-plenty surprised when I do it and he hears about it or reads about it or however he finds out, and then he'll be a sorry sob. There'll be a lot of sorry sobs, and that Doc Stillman is gonna be one of them but he ain't a bad guy. He's a kind of a stranger, but a gentleman, and I told him a lot, most all of it, but how could I ever tell him I hit that little colored girl?

"Her condition remains critical," they say, every day I call the goddam hospital since that first night I bought the paper to see if she died or where she was.

"But is she gonna live or die?" I say.

"I'm sorry, sir," they say, "but that's all we're permitted to release on the condition of the patient. Are you a member of the family?"

"No," I say, "but I'm a friend of the family."

"Would you care to leave your name?" they said the last time. "So that the family will know of your concern?"

"No, thank you," I said, and I hung up because I know damn well they told the cops this same guy calls every day, and the cops put them up to it to see what I'd say. Maybe they thought I'd say that this is Nick Braff, and I told that Stillman I'm off the sauce but I got loaded again that night, and when I woke up I figured I could still get to the track in time to go out with the last set and I hit that little girl when the light changed because the great Braff with the great seat and great hands and the clock in his head was afraid he'd lose his goddam job workin' horses mornings.

No, sir, that ain't the way it's gonna go. It ain't gonna go that way at all, because I ain't gonna go see that Stillman tomorrow night or any other night because if I saw him again I might tell him, the way he just sits there, a real nice quiet-type fella, asking a question now and then and nodding and just smokin' that pipe and listening. The first thing you know you're tellin' him things you ain't thought of for years, that you didn't even think you remembered any more, and it's for sure that if I told him this thing he'd get me to tell the cops or he'd tell the cops himself and what good would that do? It wouldn't make that little girl any better, and all it would do is get me ruled off and maybe sent to the can. What good would that do?

Hell, if I had the money I've thrown away I'd a told the cops. I coulda paid for everything, the hospital and all of it, and then they mighta only yanked my license and set me down for a year, if I just still had the money I tossed off, most of it, like McGeady said would happen, on that broad.

"Well," he said, after he sold my contract for that five gees and we were sayin' goodbye where he was stabled there, with him sittin' in that same old canvas chair, "I wish you luck, because you're gonna need it."

"Oh, I'll do all right," I said. "I'll win my share."

"I know you will," he said, "because you can ride, but I'm not talking about that. I'm talking about what's gonna happen to you when you begin making that dough, because you've been wantin' to spit the bit now for a year. You gotta remember that when you start wearing them silk pajamas it makes it tough gettin' up mornings. After a year you'll stop working horses mornings and start living it up late and that won't hurt your weight, because you're small boned, and the nervous type that don't put it on too much, but it will affect your whole thinking.

"Then you'll marry some broad," he said, "and she'll do the rest for you. She'll stand a hand or two higher than you, and she'll find ways to spend that money that you never even knew existed. 'Now don't take any chances,' she'll tell you every day when you leave the house. 'Don't get hurt.' So while she's out spreading that dough around you'll be going wide on the turns taking that married man's route to protect that money factory. Hell, I've seen it happen dozens of times."

It happened, too, and that was the start of it, and I'm glad McGeady wasn't around to see it. That's a hell of a way to think, though, because I ain't glad at all, because after I come out of that hospital he woulda got me outa that fall the way he got me out of the first one and just by whippin' my tail until I did it.

The first thing I remember when I come to after that first one was seeing them white-painted walls in that little first-aid room that they had there. I'm lying on that cot, and there's that nurse there and the goddam veterinarian and some doctor they called out of the clubhouse and there's McGeady.

"What the hell am I doin' here?" I said. "I'm ridin' in the seventh."

"Lie down," McGeady says. "You already rode in the seventh, if that's what you call riding."

I was some rodeo cowboy up to then, and as McGeady said later if I'd a had another mount that day I'd probably got right up on the sob and rode him like nothing happened. The next day I didn't give it a thought, going to the gate on that first one and comin' out, and I was fine until we come to that first turn and then I could see that animal stumblin' like the other one and me trying to hang on and going down and the whole goddam cavalry troop runnin' over me.

That was a hell of a four or five days. I tried, but I'd break a sweat just going to the gate, and I just couldn't put them up there runnin' and bust them in there.

"You're a coward!" McGeady would scream at me when I'd come back out of the money on something he knew should have won it or got a piece of it. "Ain't that awful? Why, those other jocks tell me you're out there hollering for room when you could put a whole set in that hole sideways. I've got stable fees and entry fees and feed bills piling up here, and I'm being ruined by a yellow little coward I gave almost three years of my life to. Ain't that awful?"

Then he gave me the silent treatment. He wouldn't say a goddam thing to me, sitting around that motel room, me watching the TV but not even knowing what I was looking at, and him going over the *Form*. In the mornings he'd just tell me how he wanted the animals worked but nothing else, until the day he finally made me do it.

"All right," he said that morning, "this is it. I'm running that Trapper in the sixth, and he's gotta win it for me to get out of town. If he don't, you and I are done. I've still got almost two years on your contract, and I'll set you down. You won't ride again, and if you don't ride how in the hell are you ever going to make a decent living? You won't, and you'll have to go home and live off your Old Lady just like your Old Man."

That did it. I wasn't going back to that sick mess, and the truth was I was more scared of McGeady if I didn't bring that Trapper Jay home on top than I was of getting killed. That Trapper Jay was a big five-year-old brute that they'd gelded and the best McGeady had, and on that turn for home I saw that opening and I just set my teeth and hit that sob, and I just put him in there and he just spread horses and made his own hole and we win by almost two.

"You see?" McGeady said, when I come back feeling like the whole world was finally off my shoulders. "That whole thing was just a bad dream, but you're over it now."

So they buried McGeady like three years ago and I paid for the plot and the stone, which wasn't a hell of a lot to do, and it wasn't a hell of a lot of funeral either. There were three of those gyp horsemen who'd known him for like forty years and a couple of grooms and that boy he was breakin' in at the end. We all went out from the funeral parlor in two cars. That's all it took, two cars followin' the hearse, and it was so goddam pathetic that when it was all over I just stood there by that grave in the sunshine in that cemetery and I was crying like a kid.

"Bums!" the Old Man screamed when I first told him I was bustin' out to try to be a jock, and when I think of him calling people like McGeady a bum I could laugh. "You wanna be a bum? They're all bums hang around the track."

That was a laugh, all right. That was ridiculous, like everything's ridiculous, because if they ever ran a World Handicap for bums, the Old Man would have to be top weighted, he's so goddam many lengths ahead of the field. Bums he called them, him sittin' around in his undershirt and, when he couldn't get the money from the Old Lady for the hard stuff, soppin' up the beer, always talkin' about how he could get this job or that job but the one guy was althief or the other was a miserable sob or the pay wasn't right, and the Old Lady taking in laundry and cleaning offices at night until, after I took off, she eventually just give out and died from being tired, I think, from just working herself to death.

"Be a jockey?" he screamed that day. "Who give you that idea? I'll split his head."

He might have, too, if he was oiled enough. Like I told that Stillman, when he was really drunk he wanted to fight everybody and when there wasn't anybody around he'd fight me. Fight, hell, it wasn't any kind of a fight, just him chasin' me around that kitchen and finally pinning me in the corner behind that goddam table, and then turnin' the table over on me and beatin' the hell out of me because I come in late or give him some lip or flunked some goddam subject in school, but probably because he was ashamed of me I was so goddam small.

"Be a jockey?" he screamed at me that day. "You can't no more be a jockey than I can be President Eisenhower! Who give you that idea? Tell me!"

"Nobody," I said. "I figured it out for myself."

That was a goddam lie, but I never told him the truth half the time anyway. Like as not, if I'd a told him it was that Al Barone, hanging around Goldman's down at the corner and making book, he'd agone down there oiled up and split his head like he said.

"Hey, jock!" Barone used to say to me. "Hey, Arcaro! How come you're here when it says in the *Form* that you're ridin' in that stake at Belmont today?"

Or sometimes it would be Santa Anita, or Hialeah or Saratoga, and then I got to reading about Arcaro and all them Derbies and all them stakes he won and all the money he made. Then I got to thinking and romancing the whole idea, and finally I got up the courage and I asked that Barone one day how the hell you get to be a jock.

"You know somethin'?" he said. "You just might make one. You meet me here tomorrow morning at eight o'clock, and I'll take you out to the track."

That might have been the greatest morning in my whole goddam life because it was in the spring and it was a clear morning and the leaves were all just out and we went down to the rail to wait for that Donovan, that Barone knew, to come back with his last set. I just stood there bug-eyed, watching those horses come by with the boys hunched over them and everything otherwise so quiet that you could hear the sound of their hoofs as they came down the stretch and then getting louder and then the boys clucking to them and then talking to them as they went by.

Then that Donovan saw Barone, and he come over to the rail on his stable pony and reached down and shook hands with Barone and then with me. Then we followed him, walking behind the pony following the set back to the stable where the grooms were just starting to sponge them off by the time we got there, and them horses just gleaming there in the sun.

"He says he ain't got nothing right now," Barone said when he come walking back from talking with Donovan, and I thought I was gonna be sick to my stomach I wanted it so much. "He says he's got three exercise boys, and he ain't got time this meeting to start teaching you."

"Tell him I'll do anything," I said. "Tell him I'll do anything around here he wants me to do, and I'll work the cheapest of anybody just to stay."

"You tell him yourself," Barone said, and he took me over to Donovan, and I don't remember all I said but he musta finally felt sorry for me because he finally said if I really meant that I'd do anything around there he'd take me on for the rest of the meeting. Then Barone drove me home and I was away up there, except that I had to tell the Old Man, and I waited until we finished eating there in the kitchen that night.

"You're gonna what?" he said, jumping up. "You're gonna quit school to be a race-track bum? You are like hell! Why, I'll split your goddam head!"

"Let the boy go," the Old Lady said.

She was standing there at the sink, starting to do the dishes, and the Old Man couldn't believe his ears. I don't think the Old Lady had ever stood up to him before in her whole life, and he just stood there with the funniest surprised look on his face like somebody had just yanked him up and choked him right down two steps out of the gate.

"I said let the boy go," she said. "There's nothing for him around here."

"I'm goin' out," the Old Man said, and he went into the bedroom and grabbed up his shirt and he was still tuckin' the tails in when he went out the door. When he came in I heard him because I couldn't get to sleep that night. I heard him bangin' around the kitchen, probably looking in the refrigerator to see if there was any beer left, but I didn't give a damn any more because I was goin' with the horses and already I was seeing myself a great jock.

Then that morning I was up at 5 o'clock, and you couldn't even get a bus until 6:15. The Old Lady made me breakfast, which I could hardly eat I was so goddam excited, and every morning for the three weeks left in the meeting I took that bus and I didn't come home again until night.

That Donovan worked my tail off, too, which was all right with me. He had me muckin' out stalls and wrestlin' those hay bales that weighed damn near as much as me and walkin' hots, which made me feel real important, and with the first money he paid me I got me some boots and new Levis and a cap, and those exercise boys were real nice and finally put me up on the stable pony one day and let me ride it around under the shed.

I rode that pony every chance I got, sittin' there on it and just making believe I was up on a real one. Then the afternoons were great, hanging around the jocks' quarters with them exercise boys between races, and then out on that balcony they have for them there on the clubhouse turn with the jocks who didn't have anything in that race out there in that sunlight in their clean, bright silks for the next race watching the pack come into the turn and go out of it and talkin' about this rider or that horse and my ears perked for everything.

"I'm sorry," that Donovan said to me when the last week of the meeting opened, "but at the end of the week I'm shipping out like everybody else and I haven't got room for you."

"But I'll work for nothin'," I said, "just for my keep."

"I know, and you're a hard-working kid," he said, and then he said: "Do you know old McGeady?"

"I know who he is," I said, "but I never met him."

"Well, he's losing his boy," he said. "Of course, you won't be able to work horses for him yet, but he's hard up and he can teach you. I'll talk to him."

So the next day he told me he'd seen McGeady, and I went over there. I was scared as hell, because if McGeady didn't take me I didn't know how I was ever gonna make it, and there he was, sittin' by his barn in that canvas chair and chewin' that tobacco.

"Well," he said, "I don't know. Donovan tells me you've never been up on anything but the pony, and I don't know."

"But I'll do anything," I said.

"I know," he said. "Donovan tells me you're a good doer. How old are you and what's your weight?"

"I'm seventeen," I said, lyin' by about six months, "and I weigh 102."

"You mean going on seventeen, or seventeen?" he said.

"Goin' on seventeen," I said.

"You see?" he said. "You were lying. I've got no use for liars around me. My life is hard enough without having my help lying to me."

"I'll never lie to you again Mister McGeady," I said, and I meant it. "I'm sorry, but I'll be seventeen in less than six months."

"You got small hands and feet," he said. "You know what that means?"

"No, sir," I said.

"It means you're lucky," he said. "You're luckier than most of them."

"How's that?" I said, because I didn't know what the hell he was talkin' about, and it was about time I found out I was lucky about something.

"You'll never grow too big for it," he said. "A lot of kids like you come around wanting to be jocks, and I can tell from the size of their hands and feet that by the time I spent a couple of years of my life making them finished riders they'd grow too big for it. You're just born lucky."

Born lucky? All my life I'd been too goddam small compared to them other kids to play in their goddam ball games, and all my life they were beatin' up on me on the street or in the alleys if they could catch me, and now I had it on all them sobs because I was born lucky.

"Then you're gonna take me?" I said, because I figured that's what he meant.

"There you go," he said. "I don't like people around me who jump to conclusions, and you're one of those people. Right?"

"Right," I said. "I mean, no sir."

"I wouldn't be able to pay you anything," he said, "just your keep. Then if I made a rider out of you you'd get your fee and the piece of the purse, but I don't know that I can make a rider out of you anyway."

"I don't care," I said. "I'll work for nothin'."

"I'm shipping out like everybody else Sunday morning," he said. "I don't know what time they'll move us, so be here by seven and don't bring any wardrobe trunk because we travel light."

Some wardrobe trunk. All I had was that old zipper bag with an extra pair of jeans and another T-shirt and underwear and socks that the Old Lady washed for me and a pair of old sneakers for when I wasn't wearing the boots. That night I didn't tell the Old Man, and he was still sleeping the next morning when the Old Lady got up to make my breakfast and cry a little when I left to make that 6:15 bus to the track.

At the track McGeady was all set to go, waiting for the railroad people to tell him when to load his two and the pony. He was sitting there in his canvas chair again in front of the barn where he was stabled, and when I walked up to him I had this cigarette in my mouth and he just reached up and snatched that cigarette out and threw it on the ground and hit it with a spray of that tobacco juice.

"That's awful," he said. "There have been more stable fires blamed on defective wiring that were started by help that smoked, and I just can't follow you around all day with a wad of tobacco in my cheek, because I've got other things to do. Why didn't you tell me you smoke?"

"I don't," I said. "I mean I won't any more."

"Not around me you won't," he said.

We were three days in that horse car goin' south, with the horsemen bitching every time we got sidetracked or hung up in some freight yard, but with me living every minute of it. The railroad allowed you one man to take care of three horses and that was McGeady, so I was stowing away along with a half dozen others in that car who shouldn't have been there, either. Whenever we'd feel that train slowin' down night or day we'd be in them holes-between the bales of hay, and it was amazing how everybody lived like that, keeping the car clean and keeping themselves clean, washing and shaving in a pail of water, and feeding the animals three times a day and the rest of the time just sleeping or lookin' out the open door or just talkin'.

McGeady wasn't a big talker, but when he talked everybody else listened. Mostly he just talked to me, though, and he sure had me captured, telling me about some of the great races he'd seen, and especially about the best jocks he'd seen and what each one could do, like how McCreary was the best at rating a horse without taking a big hold and about Guerin's rhythm, and how Woodhouse could kick and push at the same time as a horse takes off and how Georgie Woolfe had been a picture hand-ridin' a horse and how Atkinson handled the whip and how Shoe was the best of the new ones and how Arcaro was the best all around. Then, when we got down there and the meeting started and when he didn't have one of his entered, he'd have me over at the gate with him, watchin' how they broke 'em out, or at the wire, watchin how they finished on 'em.

In the mornings, after that Billy Noel had worked his two or three for him and we'd sponged them down and rubbed them with the body brace and walked them, he'd have me in that barn, sittin' on a bale of hay with the reins tied to a bucket for pressure like a horse's head and practicin' with that whip. He'd have me whackin' that bale and practicin' at switchin' hands with my hands full of the reins already but without puttin' the whip in your mouth, and practicin' how to twirl the whip because them starters won't let you go in the gate with the whip up.

"It's a matter of pride," he said. "Most of those fashionable riders can't switch without passing it through their mouths and most of them can't twirl a whip up and so they have to use rubber bands, but you'll do it. You'll do it because with the stock I can afford there's nothing I can do to make them into quality horses but maybe I can make you into a quality rider."

The first time he put me on one of his, just to ride it around under the shed, and he pulled up them stirrups from the way I'd been ridin' long on that pony, I thought I had no perch and I'd fall off. Then the first time he let me work one and it run off, with me yankin' at it and sawin' on its mouth until I was exhausted, I damn near did fall off.

"That's awful!" he screamed at me after it had run itself out and he come gallopin' up on that pony. "That first day you came around why didn't you tell me that you don't have any brains in your head? You weigh 102 pounds and that animal weighs 1,200, and you think you're going to tire it out? When one of them runs off with you let it run. Now I've spent all that time on you, and you don't even have brains enough to know that!"

It was a long time before he put me in that first race and I was proud as hell gettin' into them silks and scared as hell, too. I can't even think of the name of that animal any more, like Fly Leaf or Flying Leaf, and I ain't gonna think of it tonight. He knew it didn't have much chance and I didn't improve its chances any either, because I was all over that animal, and when I come back my silks were hangin' out at the waist and I'd lost the whip and I thought he'd give me holy hell for sure.

"Well," he said, "you had to get wet sometime, and you did. That wasn't too bad. It could have been worse. You'll learn."

That really surprised me. That's all he said, and I thought I never would learn. I rode eighteen goddam races, most of them on his and some of them on friends of his, and I got a few of them up into the money and I must have got beat a half dozen noses before I brought that thing called Spearchucker in. Hell, he had that race won on the turn for home, but I was so goddam hungry to win one that I rode him down that stretch like it was the goddam Derby and won by six when I coulda just hand rode him easy and won by two.

"Congratulations," he said when I come back to the winner's circle, listening to that applause and livin' it, "but you just gave my horse away. Now if I run him back for this price they'll bet him off the board and there'll be fourteen claims in the box for him. I just wish you hadn't done that."

Hell, there's a lot I wish I hadn't done, and there's many a time I've wished he was still around. I probably wouldn'ta seen him much any more and maybe I wouldn'ta seen him at all, but maybe it woulda been different if I'd a just known he was around.

Like with that broad, and she's gonna be goddam surprised, too. Hell, I'd never even met her yet and he didn't even know she was alive but he sure as hell called that marriage like he'd studied all her past performances in the *Form*. I don't know what the hell she did all day, but there was no way I was gonna let her run loose alone at night, and I'd get to that track so goddam hung over just in time to climb aboard that first animal that I wouldn't sober up until the sixth race, and like he said I'd be out there protectin' that money factory and that's the way the whole goddam thing happened.

"You just can't play it cozy!" he'd holler at me over and over after that first spill and before he got me out of it. "When they've got you in a blind switch you just can't be back there three feet. You've got to be six inches from the heels of that horse ahead so that when you see that hole open either side you're in there. If you're back there three feet that hole will close before you can get into it, and your animal will hit those heels and I'll have to bury you. I haven't got the money for that."

And it happened just the way he said it would, with me tryin' to play it cozy like he said and layin' back there too far, and I wouldn't even know what the hell happened if I didn't go look at the film patrol movie when I couldn't put it together afterwards. I could remember goin' to the track that day and riding the first two races, and then there's that whole goddam piece right out of my whole goddam life that I still can't remember at all. I still can't remember gettin' up on that horse, and I still can't remember ridin' that thing except what I saw in that movie where it's like I'm watchin' someone else even though I know it's me when that animal stumbles and I'm tryin' to hang on and I go down and all them other animals come over me and play soccer with me down that backstretch.

Maybe I shouldn't have watched that movie, but that Stillman says he doesn't think it made any difference, and all I was trying to do was piece together that part of my life that I can't remember at all, from coming back to the jocks' room after ridin' that second race and then wakin' up in the hospital after them five days. That's what they told me later, that I was out five goddam days, and that scared the hell out of me, because that's like bein' dead five days if you can't remember anything or that you were even alive, until I come to all wired and pulleyed up and could hardly make out anything at first, and then I saw them two nurses that was that one nurse and sometime later that I don't know when the hell it was I saw two of my Old Man and that was enough so that I didn't give a damn if I died right there.

Race-track bums. That's what he called them, and then when I started to make it good he'd be around the stable mornings at least once every goddam week and sometimes twice a week. There he'd be when I'd come back with the last set, waitin' for me, all cleaned up and shaved and even wearin' a goddam tie and smilin' to everybody and bein' so goddam nice that everybody thought he was a helluva guy, and I'd peel him a fifty or a C-note from what-ever I was carrying for walk around money.

That was ridiculous. The whole goddam thing's ridiculous, because if I just had the money he bummed off me all them goddam years I coulda just sent it to them people of that little girl. No name. Just to that Mr. and Mrs. Wade that I never even saw or wouldn't ever want to see, instead of him drinkin' it up and hauntin' me all my goddam life.

Like I told that Stillman. Like I told him about those goddam nightmares I had when I come out of the hospital and started gettin' up on those god-dam things again so chicken-scared that I was shakin' all over and there was no way I was gonna bust those sobs in there the way McGeady finally made me do it that first time. Like I told him about that one where I'm walking down the sidewalk like at noontime in this whole crowd or sometimes I'm trying to get to the jocks' quarters at like Aqueduct and I'm like six inches tall and all I see is all these big shoes and I'm gonna get walked on when I wake up shakin' all over and breakin' a sweat. That one's bad enough, I told him, but the other one is worse when I'm like six inches tall again and it's the Old Man chasin' me around the kitchen and through the rest of the flat with the goddam whip, and while he's runnin' after me he's got the goddam whip in his mouth. The first time I had that one, and right in the middle of being scared as hell, I had to laugh. I had to laugh that he wasn't even up on an an-imal and the miserable sob still couldn't pass a whip hand-to-hand without passin' it through his mouth, and I was even sayin' to myself that I bet he couldn't even twirl it comin' out of a gate without a rubber band around his finger when he gets me in that corner of the kitchen in that goddam night-mare and he takes that whip out of his mouth and I wake up screamin' and sweatin' and sometimes I even have to get up and puke.

Dreamin' is natural, that Stillman said, but I told him not like the dreams I got, and he said that's the way I'm just naturally tryin' to relieve my tension or some goddam thing. Like that time I told him about this other dream I get sometimes where I'm like ten or eleven years old and I'm in this goddam bathtub and my mother is washing me and calling me Nicky and, hell, I don't ever remember her washing me, except maybe she did when I was very small, and she never called me Nicky but always Nicholas, and this goddam dream always makes me cry. So he says that's because now I'm having this feeling of helplessness, or something, and that I'm like embarrassed and like ashamed of needing somebody or something.

So the last couple of times I seen him I told him I was gettin' better and that I was cuttin' down on the booze, and I wasn't lyin' to him, either. I fig-ured I was maybe gettin' better but, hell, I knew I was never gonna get better with me just gallopin' horses mornings, me just a goddam exercise boy after what I was and what I coulda been, and them trainers that used to run after me duckin' me now whenever they see me comin' because they're scared as I am to put me up on one, bein' scared that I'll get killed and maybe rack up their animal and maybe kill somebody else, too.

So, instead, I killed that poor little girl or maybe I didn't kill her and I don't know and I'll never know. I know one thing, though, and that's that the Old Man and that broad and Whitey and that Stillman and a lot of other people are gonna be goddam surprised, and that Schwartzman, too.

"What do you want a hand gun for?" he says to me.

"I'm gonna hold up the Valley National Bank," I said.

"I'm serious," he said. "What do you want it for?"

"For my own protection," I said. "What the hell do you care?"

"I don't know about you," he said. "Are you feelin' all right?"

All of a sudden he's Mister Nice, but he sold me the goddam thing. Thirty bucks he took for a piece of junk with a goddam plastic handle and cheap shiny barrel and after all the money he made on me from the stuff I took to him like them cuff links. Four hundred bucks he give me for them things that that stupid broad paid sixteen hundred for, except I had to pay the bill when it come with the others, and there I am with a pair of sixteen-hundred-buck cuff links with my initials on them in diamonds and I don't even own a shirt with them kind of cuffs. It's ridiculous. Everything's ridiculous.

"Those things cost sixteen hundred," I told that Schwartzman.

"You got took," he said.

"I didn't get took," I said. "They come from a high-class place."

"High-class places got a license to steal," he said. "I ain't. Besides, where am I gonna find somebody else with the initials *N.B.?* Four hundred bucks."

Some citizen he is, so I had to give him thirty bucks for this piece of junk, but I made him throw the cartridges in, too. Then I put them in right there, and scared the hell out of him.

"How do I know this thing will fire?" I said, cockin' it.

"Don't shoot it in here!" he says. "Put that thing away, please!"

So he's gonna be a surprised sob, too, or maybe he won't be but I don't give a damn. When I took the goddam piece of junk out in the park that night it fired all right and it will fire again and it ain't gonna be like the first time with that goddam razor blade when I tried to cozy it like hangin' back there three feet instead of six inches from their heels, and this time I'm gonna bust that sob right in there just like spreadin' horses.

The Head and the Heart

from *Cosmopolitan*

From the very start I have to believe that this can't be any good. I am in the kitchen, having the Mirror with my coffee and reading Dan Parker, when the phone rings and my wife takes it.

"It's for you," she says. "Lou John."

"Hello," Lou says, when I answer the phone. "Is that you, Eddie?"

"Why not?" I say.

"Eddie," Lou says. "You be at the gym this afternoon?"

"Every afternoon," I say.

"Eddie," Lou says, "I'll see you there. I got a kid I want you to look at. Maybe you'll take him."

"I doubt it," I say.

I've got nothing against Lou John. I handled two or three of his guys, but I never liked it. He's a manager, and I'm a trainer; maybe that's it.

That afternoon at Stillman's Gym I'm working with a kid who's just loosening up on the bags on the balcony. I'm through with him, and I send him down and tell him to cool off awhile before he takes his shower, and then I go down on the floor and I see Lou, in a blue overcoat and a gray fedora, over behind the two rings, just standing there and watching.

"Eddie," he says, "I got it this time. This is the thing."

"How big?" I say.

"A heavy and white," Lou says. "About a hundred and eighty and getting bigger."

"From where?"

"Syracuse," he says. "Only about two dozen fights, but he moves perfect."

"Where did he learn it?"

"College," Lou says. "Syracuse University."

"Thank you," I say, turning. "Good luck."

Lou grabs me by the arm. "No, wait a minute," he says. "What's the matter?"

"College," I say. "I'm not running a finishing school for bright young physical instructors."

"No, wait a minute," Lou says. "This kid is serious. This is really a good thing. Look at him first, will you, Eddie?"

"What for?" I say. "It's a waste of time. There are places where an education won't help you, and one of them is in a fight. A fighter is an animal and to hell with an education." I tap myself on the forehead. "They all got it here," I say, "college guys." I tap myself over the heart. "Here," I say, "when it comes to fighting, they got nothing."

"Nevertheless—" Lou says.

"Nevertheless hell," I say. "Name me one. Name me one college guy could fight."

"Danny Daniels," Lou says.

"Who?"

"Up there," Lou says. He motions his head toward the ring.

There have been a couple of guys working, but I have not been paying any attention. Now I know one of them is Lou's kid, the one he is talking about.

"In the black tights," Lou says. "The blond."

It is a nice-looking kid, tall and no fat and long muscles. The other guy is slow, and the kid is moving around in the middle of the ring. In three moves I have to know he's got it. I have to admit to myself that I like him.

You see how it is with me when I like a fighter? Take the way this kid punches. You know how it feels when you move a fine piece of silk back and forth in your hands? That's the way I feel when I see a guy who punches smooth like this kid. He puts out a jab, and then he hooks right behind it. You don't find anybody can double up a left hand like that these days, especially among the heavies. He's in and out, like Leonard in a way, and he's got a nice straight right that cracks right off his shoulder and that he can place like an arrow. The other guy starts a hook, and the right goes right in ahead of it.

"Well?" Lou says, watching me watching.

"It's too bad about the college," I say.

"Nevertheless," Lou says.

With that Stillman rings the bell for the end of the round. Lou nods to me, and I follow him up the stairs onto the apron. The kid is coming over to the corner, breathing good. He is a blond all right. He has short hair—one of those college haircuts—and it sticks up around the straps of his headgear. He has very blue eyes and a nice nose, and he is really a handsome kid.

"Danny," Lou says. "This is Eddie Brown. Trained four world champions."

"I'm glad to know you, sir," the kid says, looking at me and smiling.

When I wince inside I have to show it. What is there to hide? This is a kid who will say that some night to a guy he's supposed to be fighting.

"Look," I say to him. "You pick off punches nice, but let me tell you something. Does it ever occur to you that while you're catching a punch you can't be throwing one and that that's when the other guy is open?"

"Yes, sir," the kid says, "but Jack Johnson used to. He would catch a punch, and with the same motion he'd—"

The kid has seen me looking at him, and he stops.

"Listen," I say. "Forget Jack Johnson."

"That's right," Lou says. "Listen to Eddie."

"Oh," the kid says. "I'm sorry. I didn't mean—"

"That's all right," I say. I have to like the kid. This is a real nice kid. I can see he is embarrassed and that it hurts him a little.

"Now what I want you to do this round," I say, "is this. I notice you feint very good with your head. If you can use your head for feinting like that, yau can use it for slipping punches. This time go out there and take a couple of those left leads for distance and then slip the next one. Slip it either side; it doesn't matter; and then counter the guy quick, either under or over. Understand?"

"Yes," the kid says, nodding his head, and I can see he is thinking about it.

I turn and go down the steps and with that Stillman rings the bell for the round, and Lou comes down after me. The two are out in the center of the ring, and we stand there watching. The kid has his hands up high, but he does like I tell him. He takes the guy's jab. Once, twice and he kind of makes a move to slip the next one, and then I see his left glove come up and he catches it.

"He's new," Lou says. "He'll get it."

"Maybe he'll get it," I say, "but other-wise this is a guy who'll never get it."

"What do you mean?" Lou says.

"Like all college guys," I say. "This is a guy who's big in the brains and small in the heart. This is a guy knows too much and doesn't have to give out from inside. This is a guy doesn't have to let himself get hit to learn anything. This is a guy who knows how Johnson did it."

I do not want to make it appear that I was mad. I was just making the point that in the fight game what the head can't give the heart has got to give, and in this racket it is mostly heart.

"But still," Lou says, "you'll work with him."

"I won't like it," I say. "I'm warning you now."

"Nevertheless," Lou says because he is pleased and the type that understands neither me nor his own guy.

When I think now of what I know about this game and the way I went along with this thing! All the chances I had to blow and I stick. Why?

That Friday night, after I see the kid in the gym, Lou has him in at the Garden. It is just six rounds underneath, and he's in because this is an allheavy card, and the heavies are always scarce. As is usual when I haven't anything big going I am out front watching most of the time, but about ten minutes before the kid goes, I go back, and he and Lou are sitting in a corner of the room they are using for this half of the preliminary guys.

"How do you feel?" I said to the kid.

"All right, I guess," the kid says. "I'm a little nervous."

"So's the other guy," I say. "They all are."

"I guess so," the kid says.

While I am talking with Lou, I watch the kid. He keeps knocking his gloves together in front of him. I watch his feet shuffling back and forth. In the fight game there are two kinds of nervous guys. Dempsey was the other kind.

Pretty soon they call the kid, and we go out and down the aisle. The kid is wearing a light blue robe, which is a bad move, but that's like Lou. It's like calling the kid Danny when his name is Dan. It doesn't help the kid any. I mean not down inside.

When he climbs up the steps and into the ring I know what is happening because I have seen it happen before. The crowd gets one look at him, and then it goes "Oooh!"—loud and all over the house. They have got to be impressed with this kid's looks, because he's hand-some, but they don't have to like him for it. You know what I mean?

The guy he's fighting is a bum. This I know because I've used him against other guys. Everybody uses him. This is what the newspapermen call a "trial borse," short, rough, stumbling, but you can't knock him down and, best of all, he can't knock you down either. I let Lou do the talking in the corner because, after all, this is the first time for me with the kid. I slip off his robe, and I hear the crowd give it that "Oooooh!" again, but this time with whistles, and then there's the buzzer, and I get the stool. I'm down the steps getting settled, and there's the bell, and Lou comes down winking at me.

I must say the kid puts on a beautiful show. For three rounds he moves around this other guy, and he has his left in the other guy's face so much I'm afraid it's going to grow there. This is, I must say, as good a left hand as there is in the ring today, but after three rounds of this—jab, hook, move away, only now and then a cross—I can feel the crowd is getting a little weary of it, and I am, too.

Near the end of the fourth round I pull Lou by the sleeve, and I lean over to him. "Lou," I say, "what kind of a one-two has this kid got?"

"A good one, Eddie," Lou says. "It's, a beaut."

"Why doesn't he use it?"

"I don't know," Lou says, watching the ring and shrugging his shoulders. "Ask him this round."

When the kid comes back this time Lou takes out the mouthpiece and gives him the bottle. I watch him rinse out his mouth and then, while I'm squatting in front of him, holding his trunks away, I look up at him. "Look," I say, "stop fooling around. Get rid of this guy this round."

"What?" he says, looking at me surprised.

"I said get rid of him. Go out and move around for about ten seconds, and then throw your one-two. Lou tells me you got a good one. Take it out."

"Why?" he says. "I'm winning this fight."

"Listen," I say. "This isn't a fight. This is a dance. This guy hasn't laid two gloves on you. The crowd is starting to get on. They know you can call it on this guy. They want to see it. Now go out and mix a little."

The buzzer sounds, and Lou shoves the mouthpiece in before the kid can say anything. The kid goes out, and we wait. We wait for three minutes. I'm nudging Lou, and nothing happens, and at the end of the round I'm a little mad.

"Listen," I say to the kid when I get up there. "Didn't I tell you to mix it?"

"I know," the kid says, "but I don't see the percentage in that."

"You don't see the percentage in what?"

"In mixing with this guy," the kid says. "He's got me eighteen pounds, so it stands to reason he's at an advantage inside. I've got the speed on him so the percentage with me is outside. That's what I mean."

I don't say anything. Lou says something to the kid, but I'm not even listening. I'm talking to a couple of guys I know in the press row, but when we get down for the next round I lean over to Lou again. "You got a fighter?" I say. "You got a debater. Everything is upstairs. A college guy."

"Nevertheless," Lou says. "Just watch him."

I have to say again the kid can box. He hits this guy with everything that comes in ones. He's got his nose bleeding. He closes one eye, and by now the crowd knows he is not going to do anything else, so they just sit back and watch him move around. When it's over they are very satisfied, and they give him a real good hand.

"Well," Lou says, "they like him."

"They like Fred Astaire, too," I say. What else can you say? The star bout is a stinker, and the next day the news-paper guys all have space to say that this Danny Daniels looks like he may be the new class of the division and all he needs is experience. He needs experience like I need an opera cape. Believe me, there are other things I need more.

Anyway, that is the way the fight game moves. It happens that Harry Wallace from Cleveland is in the Garden that night, and he wants Danny on top in a Christmas show. The Garden wants him back in the semi-windup in two weeks, but now Lou is figuring he'll go for the full, fast ride.

"Listen," he tells the Garden. "We're taking the kid out of town. When we come back we come in on top, or we don't come back at all."

I figure what he doesn't know has got to hurt him someday, but right now what the hell! He's like all the rest of them. All he knows is what he sees. He sees he's got a white kid who is young and clean and fast and strong and moves more ways than Louis, so what does he care?

"Nevertheless," he says if I start to talk, and that ends it there.

So we go out to Cleveland, and do better than I expect. I've been working with the kid, and he listens and there are a lot of things he learns fast. I change his feet a little. I widen them maybe an inch or two to slow down that bicycle and so he gets a little more leverage, and I find in the gym that he hits real good and stiff with the right hand.

As it works out in Cleveland, the kid gets away easy. He is very nervous about the whole thing, but in the third round he hurts the guy with that straight right over a hook, and I find out now that when he knows he's got a guy going and has pulled the guy's stinger this is a pretty good axman at that. He drops a left into the first floor, and when the guy goes to grab he bends him over the rope, and that is all.

Of course the roof goes because he has shown them he can box in the first two rounds and that he can hit, too. Beyond that he is such a nice, handsome kid, so they want him back a month later, and Lou takes it with the choice of the opponent.

Now I am not going to tell you the guys he licks because it is all in Nat's record book. You know who they are. They are not bad. He outclasses the guy we go back with in Cleveland, and in Chicago he does a job like Tunney did on Carpentier, if you remember, only better.

We go back in Cleveland again for that big gate, and then Lou rests him six weeks. Meanwhile Lou is in and out of the Garden, and the first thing I know we've got this match with this Joe Warren which, I read in the papers, may decide the opponent for the outdoor title shot in June.

Well, I don't know. Maybe I'm the one who's crazy. Maybe I'm a little twisted on this business of what makes a guy go inside. Maybe the inside has nothing to do with it when a guy moves so good on the outside, but I know fighters pretty good—I give my life to them—and I somehow can't figure this guy fighting for the title, not even fighting up near there.

Mind you, I kind of like this kid. I even think it's a little stronger than that. I get so that in the dressing room the last time in Cleveland I am almost as nervous as he is. I take that to mean that that's how much I like him because that never happened to me before. Still I can't figure it, and it makes me uneasy when we go into camp for this Warren.

We are out at the camp in New York. It is a nice camp but deader than I like things to be, and one evening we're sitting in that little lobby. I've been listening to the radio, and the kid has been looking through a couple of magazines. Then he puts them down, and we get to talking, him asking me how I got into training fighters. "What about you?" I say finally. "You like it out here?"

"Yes," he says. "I like the country. I like it here."

"Some don't," I say. "Once in the summer, one guy said the cricket noises drove him crazy."

"Guys," he says, "is Guys."

"Danny," I say quickly, "do you like fighting?"

There is nobody else there. I'm sitting in an easy chair, and he's stretched out on the sofa, a real handsome kid in a sports jacket and a pair of slacks. He kind of fingers the lapel of the jacket, looking at it. "No," he says slowly. "I don't think I do."

"I know you don't."

"How do you know?" he says, looking at me.

"How the hell don't I?"

He doesn't say anything. As a matter of fact he kind of half smiles.

"Danny," I say, "how did you get interested in fighting?"

"Oh," he says, "reading about it."

"Reading about what?"

"Tunney," he says.

"That's enough," I say.

"That's enough what?" he says, looking at me.

"Nothing," I say. "I don't mean to pry into your business, but Lou hires me to, help you, and maybe I can help you better if I know a little more."

"Maybe you can," he says.

I don't say anything, and he's quiet for a minute.

"I used to read about Tunney," he says finally. "I figured he was pretty smart."

"He was," I say.

"So I figured I'd try it like he did," he says.

"Did you ever fight much on the streets?"

"No," he says, "No. I never was a kid for fighting."

"I don't understand that."

"Well," he says, "fighting is a science."

"You're talking about boxing," I say.

"What's the difference?"

"I won't argue," I say. "You tell me."

"Well," he says, "as a kid I read about Tunney, and I used to go to the Y.M.C.A., and I started boxing there. In high school I played football, but I was boxing at the Y. Then I went to college."

"I know," I say.

"I had a scholarship for playing football," he says, "but I was also on the boxing team. When it came time for me to get out of college I just looked the thing over, and I figured boxing was my big bet."

"How's that?"

"I mean," he says, "that it's like anything else. You look at the things you are good at, and you look over the things you can go into, and you decide. Then you live clean, and you work hard."

How do you like that? That's exactly what he said.

"Do you think that's all?" I say.

"Well," he says, "I think so. I think it's that way with everything."

"Well," I say, "what the hell!"

We do not talk about it any more right there. We get along very well. Every morning the kid runs, and he works every afternoon. Lou stays in the city because he is smart. He knows that if he comes around and gets in the way I will walk out, so he just calls me every night, and I let him know what the kid has done that afternoon. This is so he can call the newspapermen, who will not be out themselves until the week of the fight.

It is now about a week after the night we got there. We are just getting up from the table, and the sun has gone down, and it is starting to get dark.

"Well," I say, "I feel nice and relaxed. If there is one thing I do good out here it is sleep."

"For you that's good," the kid says, "but it doesn't go for me."

"What's the matter?" I say. "You don't sleep?"

"Not well," he says. "It takes me a long time to get to sleep at night, and lately it seems like I'm always tired."

"Let's get some air," I say. "Maybe each night we should take a little walk."

There has been a little snow, but the road is clear, and the snow is only in patches under the trees. It is a very clear night, with no moon but very bright stars, and we walk out the road where the kid runs each morning.

This is the road that makes the turn by the gas station and the stores. We walk out past the dirt road that goes into Gleason's cabin where Conn stayed, and about a quarter of a mile further this black and white dog comes barking out of the yard. This is the dog Conn used to throw stones at when he was running, but the kid has made a friend of the dog, and when the dog comes up he bends down and pets it and talks to it, and the dog follows along.

"Eddie," the kid says finally. "What kind of a fighter is this Warren I'm going to fight?"

"Well," I say, "we weren't going to start to work on his stuff until next week."

"I understand," the kid says, "that he's a good hooker."

"Well," I say, "the truth is that he's a turned-around southpaw. They don't say so, but a lot of these so-called great hookers are."

"I guess he can hit," the kid says. "I was looking at his record."

"Sure he can hit," I say, "if you put it out there."

"I don't know," the kid says.

"Listen," I say, "with a guy like this we go to his right hand instead of the other way around. It'll be a little different, but we'll work on it."

The kid doesn't say anything. When we reach the mile point we turn around and start back. The dog is following at the kid's heels.

"Eddie," the kid says finally, "You don't really like me, do you?"

"You're wrong there," I say. "If I didn't like you I wouldn't be out here."

"I don't know," he says. "It's your business."

"No it's not," I say. "It's not my business if I don't like it."

For a moment he doesn't say anything. "It's not like that with me," he says then.

"I know," I say.

"You don't know."

I can see it coming, and I think it may do some good.

"Eddie," he says, waiting, "you won't say anything about this."

"No."

"Eddie," he says—and I feel sorry for him—"I hate fighting."

"I know," I say. "I knew that the first time I saw you in Stillman's."

"You don't know," he says. "Eddie, you think that fighting is fine."

"It's my business," I say.

"You don't know how I hate it," the kid says. "I hate everything about it." He turns his head so he is looking at me as we walk along. "I don't mean you," he says. "You're all right. It's your business. You're all right to me."

He's talking faster now.

"But I hate everything else," he says. "I hate Lou John. I don't know why, but I hate him. I hate hitting other guys. I hate the people who come to see me hit other guys. I hate the places where I fight. I hate the people shouting, and when I win and I come out of the ring and they shout at me I could spit in their faces, and I'm a nice guy."

"That's right," is all I say.

"Eddie," he says, "what can I do?"

"You can get out," I say. "I'm working for Lou John, and I shouldn't tell you that, but you can get out."

"No," he says, "I can't."

"Why?"

"It's like anything else," he says. "I'm too good a fighter to get out. Isn't that right, Eddie?"

"No," I say. "You're too good a boxer, maybe."

"But I'm a real good boxer," he says. "Isn't that right, Eddie?"

"Yes," I say, "for a boxer you can be as good as I've seen."

"It's like anything else," he said. "It's as if I found I could play a violin as well as I can box. Then I'd be a great violinist, maybe the best in the world, and everyone would know I was a great violinist. Then I'd be crazy to quit playing the violin."

"No, Danny," I say. "You're wrong."

"I don't know," he says. "I don't see why."

"Danny," I say, "fighting is just like playing the violin. When you are a great violinist the music you make is what comes out of you from the inside. It isn't just what you read off the paper in front of you, and the people know this because they know music."

"I don't know," he says.

"Danny," I say, "do you know what you would be doing if you played a violin the way you fight now?"

"No," he says, "I don't know."

"Danny," I say, "you would be playing a fiddle on a Staten Island ferry. No violin in Carnegie Hall. With fighting the people don't know. All they know is what they see. If the people knew fighting the way the people know music, you and me wouldn't be here together now."

The kid says nothing. I have not noticed how far we have walked, but when I turn and look I notice the dog is gone.

"Believe me, Danny," I say finally, "I don't like to say that. I only say it because I love fighting like people love music."

"I don't know, Eddie," the kid says then. "I don't know what to do."

"I told you," I say.

"Eddie," the kid says, "I can't."

"Why?"

"Eddie," he says, "this is the thing I'm good at. This is what I can do the best. If I beat Warren they say I get a crack at the title. If I don't get it right away, and I keep winning, I get it someday. If I just fight a few years I'm fixed all my life. If I quit, if I kick this away, Eddie, I'll kick myself all my life. This is what I have to do."

"I see," I say. "And if you get beat?"

"If he licks me good," he says, "then I guess I can get out. Then I guess I know."

"I see," I say.

We walk a little further.

"Eddie," he says finally. "Would you like to see me get licked?"

I might as well tell him the truth. "For yourself," I say, "and for the fight game, which is my game, I have to say yes."

"Eddie," he says, after a couple of seconds, "what will you do?"

"What will I do?" I say. "Like I always do."

The kid says nothing.

"Danny," I say, "I work for Lou. Lou hires me to get you in shape to win this fight. I get you in shape to win this fight."

"Do you think, Eddie," he says, "that I can win it?"

"I think so. Do you?"

"I don't know," he says slowly. "I'm nervous. Maybe I'm kind of scared."

"You're always scared."

"You know that?" he says, looking at me.

"I know it. Nobody else knows it. You don't show it, and nobody knows, but I know."

"I try not to show it," he says. "Sometimes, Eddie, I'm so scared when I climb in the ring I'm afraid I won't be able to move."

"You move good."

"Nobody knows," he says. "When I walk down the aisle, and they shout at me, I hate them. They have nothing to be afraid of, just grinning and shaking, and I have to be afraid so they have something to shout at."

Now I have to find out for myself. "Danny," I say, "what will you do if you have to go for the title?"

"I'll go," he says slowly. "I'll die, but I'll go. Even now I'm dying thinking about it, but I'll go."

We walk along, then, until we can see the camp. We walk up almost to the front door.

"Eddie," he says, "you'll forget what I told you."

"No," I say. "I won't forget it."

"That's not what I mean," he says.

"I know what you mean."

"Eddie," he says, "you're a good guy."

We have two weeks to go. With the fight, on a Friday, and laying off on that Wednesday, that gives us two weeks. The kid works good. I have to tell him a thing only once, maybe twice, but that is all. Lou sends a couple of new guys out to work with him, and I keep them hooking and crowding, and after the first couple of minutes the kid has them figured and knows how to move.

"Eddie," he says after one workout, "maybe they'll cross us."

"I don't get you."

"Maybe," he says, "Warren is working on his right."

"No," I say, "they won't try that."

"How do you know?" he says.

"I know," I say. "Fighters—the rest of them—fight the way they feel. This other guy is a guy who's a hooker. Maybe they'll try to change him, but it won't do any good. He hooks too good, and he likes it that way. That's the way he'll fight."

"Yes," he says, "I guess you know."

The last week the sports writers and the photographers are out every day. The kid can talk good, and he is good for pictures, and I watch them and say to myself that that is how much they know.

Actually the kid and me we never talk about it again. He reads a lot, in the magazines, and I let him have the papers. Most of them say that Warren hits too hard, but what the hell? The papers don't know what the kid knows himself. What am I trying to hide from him? Nothing, if you want to know.

The morning of the fight Lou comes out with his car to drive us in to the weigh-in. When he gets there he comes up to my room. "Eddie," he says, "what do you think about it?"

"I don't know," I say.

"Isn't he right?"

"He's as right as anybody can make him."

"So what do you mean," he says, "you don't know?"

"Listen," I say. "You hired me to get him in shape. I got him in shape. Tonight he goes."

"I want to get a bundle down," Lou says. "That's why I ask you."

"It's your money."

"Listen," Lou says, looking at me. "Is there anything wrong? What's wrong with him?"

"Nothing," I say, "except what I told you the first day."

"Oh, that," Lou says, tossing his head. "Listen. Forget it. Why this kid should tie this other guy up in ribbons. You see the other guy. He can hit, but this kid has too much. Why this kid may be the best of all time. Forget it, will you Eddie?"

"Let's forget the whole thing," I say.

I do not leave the kid for a minute all day. This thing we have between us, believe me, works only one way, and this is for me, too, a tough day. What holds this kid up I do not know, but I watch him and while the fight game is my game and this kid has no right to it, still this is a guy, and I have to see it that way.

All day it seems to me I must be seeing it his way. At the weigh-in I listen to the commissioner call off the weights, and I wonder what difference it makes to him. Next week he'll be weighing two other guys. It is that way when the photographers pose the kid and Warren. Next week they pose two other guys. With me it should be the same. Next week I'm working with somebody else or, if not then, the week after that. All of a sudden now I find myself loused up with one guy.

I do not say anything about this during the day. After the weigh-in we go to the hotel where Lou has got us a room, and Lou leaves us alone. We eat in the room and then we walk up Sixth Avenue to the park and back again. We look in the store windows and, when we get back to the room, the kid flattens out on the bed and shuts his eyes. He doesn't sleep. I know this, but I look through the papers and leave him there until it is almost time to walk over to the Garden.

The commission says you have to be in the Garden by eight o'clock, which is good, because that way you miss the crowds. I find Sol Bimstein, and he tells us what dressing room, and we go in. My brother and Frankie White, who are going to work the corner with me, are there, and after they lay out the kid's stuff I tell them to go out front and come back about nine thirty or so.

The kid is sitting down and then getting up and walking around, so I tell him he might as well get into his things. He takes off his clothes, and I hang them up. He climbs into his trunks and his socks, and I put his robe over him, and he sits on the table, and I lace up his shoes.

After that I start on his hands. We don't say anything, and I do his left, and I am starting to wrap his right when Dummy comes in with the pail of ice. I tell him to put it over by the wall, and I tell him to bust up a little in a towel and to put it in the ice bag. When he finishes and goes out, I am through wrapping, and I am putting the tape on the right hand.

"Eddie," the kid says, when the Dummy closes the door, "don't you see what I mean about this part being so lousy?"

"What part?" I say.

"This part," he says. "The ice and taping my hands. This is a dirty, lousy part."

"No it isn't," I say. "Maybe this part is right, and maybe you're the lousy part, going along with it when you don't belong." As much as I like the kid maybe I am a little sore.

"Eddie," he says, "I'm sorry. I didn't mean to get you mad."

"You didn't get me mad," I say. "I just say what I believe."

"Eddie," he says slowly, "I guess I should get a good going over tonight, shouldn't I?"

"Well," I say, "it's like I told you at camp. For the best of everything I gotta believe you should."

"Well," he says, "maybe, Eddie, I should—you know what I mean?" He is looking at me, and he waves his hand out in front of him flat.

"No," I say, "I don't know what you mean."

"Well," he says, "I mean, Eddie, that maybe I should—you know—maybe get it over with and do a job."

I have finished the hand now, and I am standing in front of him, looking at him. "Look," I say, "let's get one thing down, Danny. If you quit you quit here. Every guy I ever handled gave it the full try. Once you start for the ring that goes for you, too. Are we straight on that, now?"

"Eddie." he says. "I'm just talking. I'm sorry and don't worry, Eddie."

"Forget it," I say.

"Eddie," he says, "you don't know how I feel."

"I know how you feel."

"Eddie," he says, looking at me. "You're a good guy."

That's all we say. I get him warming up, moving around a little, and at nine thirty my brother and Frankie come in. I sit the kid down and vaseline him a little, and then we check the kid and the pails.

At ten o'clock Sol sticks his head in the door. "You're on," he says.

We don't say anything, and we go out, and we start down the aisle. They got a good house—full—and as we walk down the aisle, the kid in front and me rubbing my hand over the back of that light blue robe, I know what he means. They are all turned around to see him, and they are shouting, and these are the guys supporting me and my racket, and I want to swing at every face that is turned to the aisle.

The way the kid stands up is a great thing. He is doing a little jig step down the aisle, and the way he goes through the ropes you would think he lives there. He gloves the crowd as nice as you'd want, and when he goes to our corner, as he is the first in, I put him down on the stool. I keep my hand on him, and when I hear the crowd and see the other guy climb in, I don't feel a thing move under my hand.

The other guy, this Warren, is a fighter. Just believe that. His weight is about the same, but he is half a head shorter, and this is just a rough, tough guy who likes it. This is a guy who would cut your heart out, I think, and when we are up close for the instructions, and I can see him good, I know. Do you want to know what the fight game is? The fight game is Warren. It is this guy.

When we go back to the corner, we don't say anything. What are we supposed to say? I can hear Lou John hollering somewhere a couple of rows back on the aisle, but I don't pay any attention. With the buzzer I give the kid a slap on the back, take his robe, and go. I am turned around when the bell rings, and I see the kid walk out.

It has been about twelve weeks, and I have forgotten—what with everything—just how this kid looks in a fight. The way he moves, like we figured it, and with that left hand, the other guy won't hit him all winter. On the arms, yes. On the gloves. High on the head. He'll give him those, but that's all.

For three rounds, if you like guys who are good with cards, this is a thing to watch. Even I have to watch it, although I know this is just a guy playing a lot of notes Corbett and Johnson and Gans and Leonard and a few others wrote. This is a guy who can't write two notes of his own, but he hasn't missed two counters, and the other guy is beginning to redden on the cheekbones and puff over the eyes. This thing is no match, but the crowd, which can't even read music, loves it. Then in the fourth it happens like I felt it had to all the time.

They are out in the middle, with less than a minute gone, the kid circling and the other stalking. The other guy, like I say, is a hooker all the way, and he starts one, and the kid sees it and throws that good, straight right. As he does, though, the guy is turning, and the kid's right goes over his shoulder, and his hook catches the kid, maybe just a half inch too high but right here.

It is a punch, no matter where it lands, and at first I think the kid will go. I see the knee start and the hands drop, and then I see his face. Afterwards I remember a movie I saw. It was about the old times in England, and they were going to burn a guy at the stake. The movie showed them walking up with the torches, and then it just showed the guy's face. That is where I saw this face before. Now what I see is the kid going, then holding himself up, and I see the other guy, surprised and off balance, recover. I see him move in and that left go back.

Then I see the kid's hands come up. You know what it is like? It is like a woman trying to shove off a guy in a parlor game, but behind it there is that face. For the first time in a ring, now, the kid shows it, and I know now that this is it, that my game will stand still just so long for a guy like this. This is a woman pawing, a kid all upstairs and forgetting everything he knows, and now I see the other guy's left come over, and I know that here is the one punch that will solve it, solve everything for me and my game and the kid.

Ruby Goldstein is the referee, and he is one of the best. As the other guy has thrown the left the kid, grabbing, has fallen in, and it has gone around his neck. Now the other guy is trying to push him off, and Ruby steps in and breaks them quick, and as the kid backs off I see the face is still there. There are the gloves, both out, pawing, and here is the other guy, arm cocked. Almost running in. This is it, now, I know, and I must be glad. This is it. And then the other guy starts the left, but the kid, with that face I remember, brings up his right like you would throw a horseshoe, off the knee.

This is a straight right-hand puncher. Remember that. This is a guy who wouldn't throw one like this except that fear makes him. But he throws it, a pure sucker pitch, but it is inside, and when it hits and I see the other guy's eyes pop open I know it is over. He goes straight back and his left hand is still halfway home when his head hits.

In the noise and the uproar I look for the kid. He is standing in the neutral corner looking at Ruby counting over the other guy, and that face is still there. It is there when Ruby finishes, and they are piling into the ring, and my brother, Frankie and I get to the kid.

What does my brother know? He's a kid himself. What do any of them know? In our corner the cops are pulling a guy down from the stairs. The guy is Lou John. "Danny!" he is hollering. "Danny!" And then he sees me. "Eddie," he is hollering. "Eddie. You see? I told you."

Down the aisle they are pounding on the kid's back, and I think how much the kid must hate them, and how much I must hate them, too. This is what this kid has done to me, and when we get to the dressing room I have them lock the door. We sit the kid down and he is shaking. I do not think he can talk, and I think he may cry. "Eddie," he says.

"Yes," I say, and I have his right hand and I am cutting the tape.

"Eddie," he says. "I'm sorry, Eddie."

"What the hell!" I say. "This must be best."

Here I am telling a lie, me, and I got a frightened fiddler off a ferry boat, and we are on our way now to con them in Carnegie Hall.

One Throw

from *Colliers*

I checked into a hotel called the Olympia, which is right on the main street and the only hotel in the town. After lunch I was hanging around the lobby, and I got to talking to the guy at the desk. I asked him if this wasn't the town where that kid named Maneri played ball.

"That's right," the guy said. "He's a pretty good ballplayer."

"He should be," I said. "I read that he was the new Phil Rizzuto."

"That's what they said," the guy said.

"What's the matter with him?" I said. "I mean—if he's such a good ballplayer, what's he doing in this league?"

"I don't know," the guy said. "I guess the Yankees know what they're doing."

"He lives here in this hotel?"

"That's right," the guy said. "Most of the older ballplayers stay in rooming houses, but Pete and a couple other kids live here."

He was leaning on the desk, talking to me and looking across the little lobby. He nodded his head. "Here he comes now."

The kid had come through the door from the street. I could see why, when he showed up with the Yankees in spring training, he made them all think of Rizzuto. He isn't any bigger than Rizzuto, and he looks just like him.

"Hello, Nick," he said to the guy at the desk.

"Hello, Pete," the guy at the desk said. "How goes it today?"

"All right," the kid said, but you could see that he was exaggerating.

"I'm sorry, Pete," the guy at the desk said, "but no mail today."

"That's all right, Nick," the kid said. "I'm used to it."

"Excuse me," I said, "but you're Pete Maneri?"

"That's right," the kid said, turning and looking at me.

"Excuse me," the guy at the desk said, introducing us. "Pete, this is Mr. Franklin."

233

"Harry Franklin," I said.

"I'm glad to know you," the kid said, shaking my hand.

"I recognize you from your pictures," I said.

"Pete's a good ballplayer," the guy at the desk said.

"Not very," the kid said.

"Don't take his word for it, Mr. Franklin," the guy said.

"I'm a great ball fan," I said to the kid. "Do you people play tonight?"

"We play two games," the kid said.

"That first game's at six o'clock," the guy at the desk said. "They play pretty good ball."

"I'll be there," I said. "I used to play a little ball myself."

"You did?" the kid said.

"With Columbus," I said. "That was twenty years ago."

"Is that right?" the kid said. . . .

That's the way I got to talking with the kid. They had one of those pine-paneled grillrooms in the basement of the hotel, and we went down there. I had a cup of coffee and the kid had a Coke, and I told him a few stories and he turned out to be a real good listener.

"But what do you do now, Mr. Franklin?" he said after a while.

"I sell hardware," I said. "I can think of some things I'd like better, but I was going to ask you how you like playing in this league."

"Well," the kid said, "I guess I've got no kick coming."

"Oh, I don't know," I said. "I understand you're too good for this league. What are they trying to do to you?"

"I don't know," the kid said. "I can't understand it."

"What's the trouble?"

"Well," the kid said, "there's nothing wrong with my playing. I'm hitting .365 right now. I lead the league in stolen bases. There's nobody can field with me, but who cares?"

"Who manages this ball club?"

"Al Dall," the kid said. "You remember, he played in the outfield for the Yankees for about four years."

"I remember."

"Maybe he's all right," the kid said, "but I don't get along with him. He's on my neck all the time."

"Well," I said, "that's the way they are in the minors sometimes. You have to remember the guy is looking out for himself and his ball club first."

"I know that," the kid said. "If I get the big hit or make the play, he never says anything. The other night I tried to take second on a loose ball and I got caught in the rundown. He bawled me out in front of everybody. There's nothing I can do."

"Oh, I don't know," I said. "This is probably a guy who knows he's got a good thing in you, and he's trying to keep you around. You people lead the league, and that makes him look good. He doesn't want to lose you to Kansas City or the Yankees."

"That's what I mean," the kid said. "When the Yankees sent me down here they said, 'Don't worry. We'll keep an eye on you.' So Dall never sends back a good report on me. Nobody ever comes down to look me over. What chance is there for a guy like Eddie Brown to see me in this town?"

"You have to remember that Eddie Brown's the big shot," I said, "the great Yankee scout."

"Sure," the kid said, "and I'll never see him in this place. I have an idea that if they ever ask Dall about me, he keeps knocking me down."

"Why don't you go after Dall?" I said. "I had trouble like that once myself, but I figured out a way to get attention."

"You did?" the kid said.

"I threw a couple of balls over the first baseman's head," I said. "I threw a couple of games away, and that really made the manager sore. So what does he do? He blows the whistle on me, and what happens? That gets the top brass curious, and they send down to see what's wrong."

"Is that so?" the kid said. "What happened?"

"Two weeks later," I said, "I was up with Columbus."

"Is that right?" the kid said.

"Sure," I said, egging him on. "What have you got to lose?"

"Nothing," the kid said. "I haven't got anything to lose."

"I'd try it," I said.

"I might," the kid said. "I might try it tonight if the spot comes up."

I could see from the way he said it that he was madder than he'd said. Maybe you think this is mean to steam a kid up like this, but I do some strange things.

"Take over," I said. "Don't let this guy ruin your career."

"I'll try it," the kid said. "Are you coming out to the park tonight?"

"I wouldn't miss it," I said. "This will be better than making out route sheets and taking orders."

It's not much of a ball park in this town—old wooden bleachers and an old wooden fence and about four hundred people in the stands. The first game wasn't much of a game either, with the home club winning something like 8 to 1.

The kid didn't have any hard chances, but I could see he was a ballplayer, with a double and a couple of walks and a lot of speed.

The second game was different, though. The other club got a couple of runs and then the home club picked up three runs in one. In the top of the ninth the home club had a 3–2 lead and two outs when the pitching began to fall apart and the other club loaded the bases.

I was trying to wish the ball down to the kid, just to see what he'd do with it, when the batter drove one on one bounce to the kid's right.

The kid was off for it when the ball started. He made a backhand stab and grabbed it. He was deep now, and he turned in the air and fired. If it goes over the first baseman's head it's two runs in and a panic—but it's the prettiest throw you'd want to see. It's right on a line, and the runner is out by a step, and it's the ball game.

I walked back to the hotel, thinking about the kid. I sat around the lobby until I saw him come in, and then I walked toward the elevator as if I were going to my room but so I'd meet him. I could see he didn't want to talk.

"How about a Coke?" I said.

"No," he said. "Thanks, but I'm going to bed."

"Look," I said. "Forget it. You did the right thing. Have a Coke."

We were sitting in the grillroom again. The kid wasn't saying anything.

"Why didn't you throw that ball away?" I said.

"I don't know," the kid said. "I had the idea in my mind before he hit it, but I couldn't."

"Why?"

"I don't know why."

"I know why," I said.

The kid didn't say anything. He just sat there, looking down.

"Do you know why you couldn't throw that ball away?" I said.

"No," the kid said.

"You couldn't throw that ball away," I said, "because you're going to be a major-league ballplayer someday."

The kid just looked at me. He had that same sore expression.

"Do you know why you're going to be a major-league ballplayer?" I said.

The kid was just looking down again, shaking his head. I never got more of a kick out of anything in my life.

"You're going to be a major-league ball-player," I said, "because you couldn't throw that ball away, and because I'm not Harry Franklin."

"What do you mean?" the kid said.

"I mean," I explained to him, "that I tried to needle you into throwing that ball away because I'm Eddie Brown."

Man's Game

from *A Treasure Chest of Sports Stories*

Eddie looked at the drink in his hands and tasted of it. It was bitter in his mouth, but it was as he had expected. It never does taste good, he thought, unless I am all right myself.

"So you can quit, Eddie," his wife was saying. "You can call Bud Walker and in a minute you can go with the pros." She was sitting across from him, her legs curled under her, at the far end of the sofa.

"I know," he said.

"Paul Brown did it. He left Ohio State and he's happy with the pros."

"Paul was ahead."

"What difference does it make?" she said. "You'll win games. You'll be ahead. Even when you're ahead it will always be the same thing over and over. I don't think you realize what you are."

"Oh, I don't know. I pass myself off as a football coach."

"Eddie," she said, "we've talked about it so much. You're so close to yourself that sometimes I don't think you see it."

"See what?"

"That you're just like the artist or the writer or anyone else."

"Oh, I see that," he said. "Once when I was about ten years old I wrote a composition called What I did on My Vacation. And as for my being an artist, why I can walk up to a blackboard and diagram a play so—"

"Eddie." She smiled. "Honestly. The only place you have to express yourself is on the field, and when you can't express yourself there, then there's nothing in it for you to be coaching in college."

He leaned forward in the chair and, holding up the cocktail glass, looked over the top of it at her.

"You know something?" he said. "I'm not knocking these, but the way to mix Martinis is by color. You add just enough of the vermouth to give it the color which, you know by experience, assures the dryness you have come to appreciate."

She looked at him and said nothing, and he laughed. "And then," he said, "you add the ice."

When he walked into Stratfield's office the next morning he knew he was not going to quit and he knew they were not going to buy his contract either. He knew that nothing would be accomplished on this day, but he would go in there and fight a little, not for himself, but for the next guy—maybe it would be Angelo—the way Bud Walker had fought a little for him.

Maybe that way, after a long while, after a lot of them had come and gone, all of them fighting a little, these others would see it. He could kid about it with his wife, but it was nothing to kid about. It was a serious thing to all of them who had chosen football as their medium, who wanted the right to be judged as professionals by professionals and not by amateurs who understood only games won and games lost, who went only by scores.

"Good morning," he said.

"Good morning, Eddie," Stratfield said.

Stratfield was sitting behind the big desk; he was white-haired, but his face was still young and handsome. Always the picture president, Eddie thought, glancing around the big room at the big oil portraits on the paneled walls, the wall-to-wall carpeting, the heavy leather furniture. He looked over toward big Enright, and then he walked over to him and stuck out his hand.

"How are you, Cap?" he said.

"I'm all right," Enright said.

Eddie sat down in the chair near the desk. He waited for Stratfield to start it. He was thinking about Enright. Enright had probably been a pretty good football player, he was thinking. Big enough anyway, and not dumb. Smart enough to sell insurance and then to get other people to sell it for him, to stick close to the university for a stage on which to strut.

"Eddie," Stratfield said. "I dislike this business of calling you in here rather regularly, but I'm afraid that I'm finding this situation embarrassing."

"That makes two of us," Eddie said.

"Now wait a minute, Eddie," Stratfield said. He picked up a pencil. "I'm afraid you don't understand. This whole thing puts me in a very awkward position. I'm the one who's responsible for your presence as football coach here. I'm the one who accepted the recommendation of Walker, when he left, and of a rather large section, at the time, of the alumni—including Cap here."

"That's right," Enright said, nodding.

"This—these losses—reflect on me," Stratfield said. He put the pencil down on the desk.

Eddie knew they were waiting for him to say something. "It's not increasing my popularity, either," he said.

"Look," Stratfield said. "Let's stop sparring and be frank about this. Your first year, even last year, there was some basis for understanding. I suppose it takes time for you to put in your system, or whatever you call it, but it seems to me that you've had time. It seems to me that you've had assistance. It was my belief that the alumni—and Cap will bear me out—had succeeded in convincing, shall we say, some rather promising football players to matriculate here."

"That's right," Enright said.

"That was my understanding, too," Eddie said.

"Now," Stratfield was saying, "let's get down to cases. What about this"—he turned to Enright—"this fellow you were mentioning?"

"Benson?" Enright said, sitting back. "The guard?"

"Yes," Stratfield said. "Benson. What about him?"

"Benson?" Eddie said. "Well, he's big enough, and I suppose he's kind to his mother."

"It's now my understanding," Stratfield was going on, "that he is being sponsored here by one of our groups—the Milwaukee group, I believe Cap has told me. They're seeing to it that he has the necessary funds to meet his bills. Employment has been found for him here. What's the matter with him?"

Eddie stood up. Here we go, he thought.

"Ask Ferris," he said.

"Ferris?" Stratfield said. "Ferris is a professor of mathematics."

"Sure. Ask him."

"Why?" Stratfield said. "I don't see what that has to do with it."

"It has everything to do with it," Eddie said. "Ferris has been trying to teach Benson mathematics. No calculus, mind you. Just that minimum of simple mathematics incorporated in that baby math course that someone—you tell me why—has told Benson he should take."

"So?" he heard Enright say.

"So Ferris and I," Eddie said, looking from one to the other, "are enjoying a common lack of success—Ferris trying to teach Benson just a little about math, I trying to teach Benson just a little about football, and the T formation in particular. I doubt very much, however, that you, Dr. Stratfield, have had Ferris in here, asking him why Benson can't learn mathematics. I doubt very much that anyone is blaming Ferris."

"Oh," he heard Enright say, "it isn't quite the same."

"No," Eddie said. "It isn't. Ferris plays his little game of X's and O's in the privacy of a classroom. I play mine out in the middle of that white elephant—with sixty thousand undergraduates, clothing salesmen, bank tellers and their girl friends or wives, sitting in judgment. They don't really know any more about what I consider my science that they do about what Ferris is trying to teach. You wouldn't accept their opinion of Ferris' abilities, but you'll accept their opinion of mine."

"And I suppose," he heard Enright say, "that you might have mentioned insurance salesmen."

"Yes, I might," Eddie said.

"All right, Cap," Stratfield said, looking at Enright. "We're going to forget Benson. I merely mentioned his name."

Eddie said, "Oh, no. Let's not forget Benson. You hired Ferris and me as professionals, proficient at our sciences, and then you threw Benson at us. Unfortunately, again, Benson is very important to me, because he's my right guard. His age is twenty, and I think his I.Q. is about the same. Most of them, I'll admit, are more intelligent, but in one respect they're all Bensons. They're all adolescents. Maybe they don't look that way to you people, because when you see them on the field they look like gladiators, but when you see them in the locker room, before they get dressed, when you talk with them, you know they're just a bunch of kids. Football is a man's game.

"We put them in a big stadium with sixty thousand people shouting, and speculators walking around outside getting forty dollars for a pair of tickets, and then we're selling them as men and we're selling their game as a man's game."

"Oh, I don't know," Enright said. "We've got to go by results. I make a good living in the insurance business, I might say, but I played football, and what you've got to go by are the sales or the scores. Furthermore, I don't know if football is any more of a man's game today than it was when I played it."

"You don't?" Eddie said. He knew now that the rest would be useless. He hadn't moved them a yard, and now he would just stay in there, disliking Enright, waiting to snipe at him.

"No, I don't," Enright said. "We weren't any older than these kids and we played good football in my day."

"You did?"

"Certainly we did. Old Doc Harris knew how to coach, and he taught good football."

"He did?"

"Of course he did. My senior year we were undefeated."

"I know," Eddie said. "And would you like to go in with me right now and look at some of the movies of your games?"

"The movies of our games?" Enright said. "They didn't take movies of games in those days."

"I know they didn't," Eddie said.

"Look, Eddie," Stratfield said. "That doesn't solve anything. You've already lost five games out of seven."

"I have?"

"Let's say the team has, then. There's a lot of agitation. I get letters. The things in the papers. Cap has to make a special trip down here. It embarrasses me. It puts me on the spot."

"I'm sorry it does."

"Don't you think you can win Saturday?"

"Of course I think I can win Saturday," Eddie said. "I never saw a game that I didn't think I could win. If I didn't think I could win Saturday what would be the point of us playing the game?"

"Well," Enright said, "I'm sorry I don't share your optimism."

"It isn't optimism," Eddie said, turning on Enright, mad again. "I didn't say I'd beat them. I said I thought I *could* beat them."

"If you could beat State, Eddie," he heard Stratfield saying through it, "it would solve everything, at least for now."

"It sure would," Eddie said.

He walked home across the campus. It had started to rain, the water beginning to drip from the trees, to wet the leaves on the paths. He could think of the rain as out of the way now by Saturday, the field the way it should be.

He met his wife getting out of the car and they carried the packages of groceries into the house together.

"You know," he said, "I'm surprised they'll even sell you anything any more."

"They'll sell to anybody who can pay," she said. "They'd sell even if they thought we'd stolen the money."

"They probably think we have," Eddie told her.

"What happened?"

"The same. He and our fat friend want us to win Saturday and I want us to stop kidding ourselves."

"They'll never understand, Eddie. What you see in football or what Bud sees or Angelo sees will never mean anything to them. It will never mean anything to anybody until you have the tools. Bud told you that."

"Oh," Eddie said, "we might make a game of it Saturday." . . .

After lunch he walked through the rain to his office in the athletic build-ing and he picked up where he had left off on Sunday night. He sat there with his assistants, Harry and the Moose, looking at the movies of last Satur-day's game, looking at the movies of last year's game with State, stopping them, running them over, talking about them. Then he called in Angelo.

Angelo is the best, he thought, when he saw him walk in: short but strong, black hair and dark eyes and even white teeth, young and still smiling. He thought about him, once a good ball-player and now giving a whole season to tailing State, learning football but never seeing his own club play, scouting State for two months in the hope of helping to lick them in one game.

"Well, Angelo," he said, "this is your game."

"Thanks for the present, Chief," Angelo said, smiling, "but maybe I don't want any."

"Why?"

"You know me, Chief. I'm just kidding. I always think anybody can be licked. I always think we can win any one game."

Angelo handed Eddie his reports, twenty pages carefully typed, the dia-grams carefully drawn. He gave out the copies to the others and they sat back, scanning them.

"Hopkins is a good coach," Angelo said, after a while. "This year he's got the material, too. Big guys and fast. They run the T the way you're supposed to—tackles downfield leading plays—if you know what I mean."

Angelo went to the blackboard, then, diagraming plays, erasing them, dia-graming others, answering questions, enlarging on the things in his reports. Eddie kept rubbing his chin, thinking.

When Angelo had finished they went downstairs together and got into their sweat clothes and football shoes and hoods, and walked out onto the practice field.

The rain had stopped, but it was damp and raw on the field and he took it easy with the kids because it was Monday. On Tuesday and Wednesday he really gave it to them, the second team running the enemy plays against the first, Angelo behind the second team, he behind the first, walking back and forth, starting them, stopping them, applauding them, criticizing them.

"Look, Murray, what are you doing up? Get down and come up under them. When you see that coming you're supposed to pile it up, slow it down. Didn't we just go over that play?

"All right, Pardini, that's fine. Don't forget to go wide with that man in motion. Don't let them get outside of you. Keep them down the middle. That's fine."

On Wednesday he also put in the new stuff, the stuff he'd been saving all year. There was nothing very different about it, just a few variations and one new pass to Luomo. Eddie watched them practice the Luomo pass play; he still fingered his chin. He had not yet, in his own mind, won the game.

He fell asleep that night playing the game, stopping strength with what strength of his own he could muster, playing his strength against State's weaknesses.

On Thursday he was looking over Angelo's reports again when Angelo came in. "What about this big tackle?" Eddie said. "This number 74?"

"Number 74?" Angelo said. "His name is Kradyk."

"It says here: 'Good initial charge.'"

"That's right. He comes in high, but real strong."

"Any lateral mobility?"

"Oh, enough. They only use him on defense and he bulls you."

"Can you trap him?"

"I don't know for sure, because nobody has tried it, but I would think so, now that you mention it."

He kept working it around in his mind. He went to lunch thinking about it and, after lunch, he talked it over with the others.

"Just two plays," he said. "We'll let this 74 come through the first time, with a little pressure on him, but let him make the tackle. Angelo says he likes to bull in there, pretty straight, so the second time we'll trap him. It might be very good, say inside the twenty."

He tried it on the blackboard, against a six- and then against a five-man line, his left halfback in motion to the right, his left guard pulling out to make the trap block. He changed the downfield assignments a couple of times, and then he put the chalk down.

"Well," he said, "what do you think?"

He could see they liked it, Harry and the Moose sitting there and studying it and nodding their heads.

"Chief," Angelo said, "I don't know how you do it."

"With a piece of chalk and a blackboard," he said, smiling. "I'm an artist."

"That'll open their eyes at the coaches' meeting this winter."

"I just hope," Eddie said, "that it opens a hole on Saturday."

"It will," Angelo said.

Eddie put it in that afternoon, working them late under the lights. He had given it to them on the blackboard in the locker room, and then on the field he ran them through it again and again, talking to them individually.

"That's right," he told his left end. "You just brush that end long enough to keep him from crashing around behind. You give him that two-count block and then you tear down on that halfback, who'll be starting to float in, and you've got to take him out.

"Now you, Marino"—he turned to the big tackle—"you've got to keep some pressure on this 74, especially the first time. Let him bull you back and let him fall into that first tackle. The second time give him just a little fight at the start. If you don't he'll get wise. If you're not there at all he'll take two steps and stop. I'm sure he knows that much. So you fight him a little and then as you slide by he thinks he's free. Then you go down and take that fullback.

"Now, Price, you have it pretty easy on that trap block, because the big guy thinks he's free, and Fordy, handing off the ball, is cutting off his view of the play. He's looking to see which way it's going when you, Price, you hit him a reverse shoulder—in other words, with your right shoulder.

"Which reminds me of something," he said. "Benson!"

"Yes, sir."

He saw Benson in the line on one knee, his helmet off, his blond hair flat and gray now with sweat. In spite of what he had said in Stratfield's office, Eddie had no strong feeling against Benson. He had seen too many of them, good enough kids but kids whose ineptness he always had to disguise and accommodate with the simple enough jobs.

"You have to remember only one thing," he said, walking over. "You take that guard with a straight left shoulder, not a reverse shoulder, so that if he does slip off then you've still got your body between him and the hole. The hole has got to be permanent. Is that clear?"

When he sent them in, dirty and tired, he had won his game. They would play it on Saturday, but he had already—in his own mind—won his part of it because he saw now how it might be done. The playing of it would still excite him, but he had carried his science to the last decimal point. If the tools they had given him should fail him, that would not be his fault.

He slept well that night, and on Friday he tapered off. He ran them through a few plays just to keep them loose. He worked with his kicker for a while; he ran through the Luomo pass play a few times, and then he sent them in. He passed up the rally that night; it would be, he knew, a quiet one, dispirited. Instead he and his wife stayed home and played chess until eleven. . . .

The next morning they drove out into the country and back. It was a fine morning, cold and clear, the color still in the hills. When they got back to town the streets were crowded with the game traffic, horns blowing, the people laughing. She dropped him off at the stadium.

"Remember," she said. "Whatever happens it doesn't really make any difference."

"I know," he said.

He went into the dressing quarters and back into Gus's room. The walking wounded were already in, Gus bandaging their ankles, their wrists, putting pads on their thighs. At noon the healthy started coming in to have their wrappings put on, to get into their uniforms slowly and meticulously. He walked around, not to tell them anything but just to talk to them, one at a time, and at one fifteen he took them out onto the field.

He watched them loosen up. The big bowl was already almost filled, and he could feel the pressure growing inside of himself. All week, he was thinking, you retain your objectivity. Then you see how it can be done, and when you take them on the field on Saturday it burns in your stomach.

He walked around among them as they ran up and down, bringing their knees up high, rotating their shoulders, and he felt his closeness to them. They were his tools, not perfect, but he had shaped them to their uses the best he could. He and they had not the same purpose—his being in the manner of the playing of the game, theirs only in the winning, somehow—but they shared a common anxiety close to fear, and it brought them together as it does men in war.

He could imagine how they looked from the stands—plastic helmets, big shoulders, tall and strong and mature.

At one forty-five he took them back in and he saw them again as they were— good kids, but kids on whose decisions no one in the stands would want his life depending. They were already too excited, and he tried to quiet them.

"These people aren't any bigger or stronger than you are," he said. "They play the same game you play. Actually you've got the drop on them because they're out there undefeated and cocky. The time to get them is before they wake up."

If they can do that, he was thinking, they will see how possible everything is. Then he saw Ford wanted to speak.

"Fordy?" he said. "You have a question?"

"No question, Coach," Ford said. "I just wanted to say that we don't go along with that stuff they're saying around."

"Oh."

"We think we know you better than anybody, and we think you're a great coach. You've taught us good football, and if we don't play it then it's our fault."

Eddie scuffed his toe delicately against the concrete floor. "Well, not exactly."

"Anyway," Ford was saying, "we're gonna give 'em hell for you today."

Now they were all standing up and shouting and that was the way he sent them out. He walked down the tunnel after them with Ford, the sounds of stamping feet and of cheering overhead, his arm over the kid's shoulders, the kid listening and nodding his head as they walked.

"Receive if you can," he was saying. "Our best chance will be in the first five minutes. If you can get inside their thirty-five, use Luomo on that wide cutback. Then throw him that short pass we just put in."

"All right," the kid said. "I know."

It seemed now as if they would never get it started. Eddie stood watching them in the center of the field, Ford and the other captain and the officials shaking hands, then the coin going up in the air and coming down. He saw the official's hand come down on Ford's shoulder and when the kid came running back, strapping on his helmet, Eddie met him at the side lines with the rest of the team.

"Fine, Fordy," he said. "This is our day."

When they ran out on the field and spread out, the noise seemed constant to him. At the peak of it he saw the kick go up in the air and start coming down and now he was all right. They were keeping it away from Luomo, and Ford had it on the five. The other people—the State people—were sloppy, finding it hard to get started. Ford was at midfield before they dragged him down.

Now Eddie was conscious of nothing but the game. Ford might have gone all the way, he thought. Now is the time.

Ford, on a sneak, made five. Luomo, on a reverse to the weak side, made a first down. He could see the other people, the big guys wearing red, trying to stir themselves now, hollering at each other in the line, nodding their heads in answer. They hit Mancini at the line, but he kept digging and he dragged them for five before they really stopped him. On the thirty-five-yard line.

All right, Fordy, he thought. Now.

Ford called the cutback and they ran it just right—Luomo starting wide, cutting perfectly, the tackle swept out of it, the secondary sucked over. He saw Luomo streaking back across the field before they grabbed him by the ankles on the 20. He saw the other people call time out.

That's fine, he thought. He knew they would work over quickly all the possibilities, and he recognized that their calling time was his ally. He knew that as they talked about it they would only set themselves more firmly in their practiced patterns of stopping what they had been told he might use. They would never suspect he would pass to Luomo. There was no record of Luomo ever receiving.

He saw Ford looking toward him from the field and he nodded. He heard the whistle go and saw them lining up. He heard Ford calling off the count, saw it start with the fake to Mancini, Ford keeping it. He saw Ford run to the right—the fake sweep—and then he looked for Luomo. He saw him cutting across just beyond the line of scrimmage, the pass coming to him alone on the ten. He saw Luomo catch it on the run and go over. He heard the roar and he sat down for the first time in the ball game and watched Ford kick the point.

After that it got very tough. He knew it would be that way, that even if he succeeded early he would only succeed in waking them up, but that was the only way to do it.

He watched the other people come back, fumbling the first time in their anxiety. It was that way through all of the first quarter and almost into the half. They didn't fumble again, but their timing was a little off; his kids kept kicking out—and then, thirty seconds from the end of the half, State evened it.

I almost had them at the half, he thought. I could have had them at the half. That is the way it always happens.

"All right," he said to them in the locker room. "Now you've seen how you can do it. For all but thirty-five seconds you had them beaten. This second half they'll be thirty-five seconds too late. You know now that it's possible to hold them off for just two periods."

He walked around them, then, as they sprawled on the floor, some of them lying down, others leaning against the lockers, their heads back and their eyes closed, their bodies cluttering the room. The air was heavy with their breathing and with the smell of their liniment-logged sweat, and he talked to them individually, praising them, not criticizing them, only advising.

"Remember, Marino. If we get a chance to pull that 33-trap, it depends on how well you convince that 74 that he's actually moving you, that you're not giving ground away free.

"And, Benson, I'm talking about that trap on that tackle. You have to hold that hole open on the inside. You've got to move that guard there with a left shoulder. Is that clear?"

"I know," he said.

He talked to them all again, then making the adjustments the Moose had brought down from the top of the stands. He walked out again with Ford.

"You can use Luomo for a threat on that pass again, but you won't be able to throw to him. . . . Don't try that 33-trap unless you're inside the twenty, if you get that far. They'll go into a five-man line on second down because they'll be looking for that Luomo pass again."

The second half was the way it had to be, the other people driving for two or three first downs, his own kids hanging in there and, finally, taking the ball. His own kids would make a first down now and then, but for the most part they would run a couple and then kick, waiting for the break, until then settling for a tie.

It came with all but three minutes gone. Ford had kicked from his own twenty; it had been high and long, and when it had landed it had come down on a point, bouncing crazily, down to State's 30 and then the 25. If the other people had been ahead they would have let his ends ground it, but one of their backs tried to pick it up, angling back toward his own goal with the ball dancing on the tips of his fingers, looking for blockers. Now Eddie saw the ball hit the ground, his own right end on top of it.

He heard the great noise come out of the stands and he realized that he, too, was standing. He felt the moment in his stomach again, and he waited for Ford to look toward him. He saw Ford clapping his hands, calling them back in a hurry. He knew Ford would call it.

"Chief," he heard Angelo saying at his side, "here we go."

They set it up beautifully. He watched the big red 74 bulling in and Marino, giving ground, letting him fall in to make a tackle. He watched them line up again, State going into a five-man line. He saw 74 charge, Marino contacting him, then slipping off and going for the fullback. He saw Price pull out and come across and hit 74, the big guy going down, and he saw the hole, as big as a highway. He saw his halfback, the others, too, now starting downfield. He saw Luomo wheel into that hole and then he saw a red helmet and red jersey—State's other guard—slide over, filling the hole, pulling at Luomo, Luomo dragging him for about two yards, all of his fine speed halted, Luomo hauled to the ground.

Suddenly, standing there, Eddie felt very empty, as if something had punctured him, leaving him loose and weak.

"Benson!" he heard Angelo saying, shouting it at him.

"I know," he said. "I saw it."

"He tried to reverse shoulder that guy. You told him, and he didn't do it."

"I know," he said, turning on Angelo. "Don't tell me. Run up in the stands and tell Enright. I can see."

"I'm sorry," Angelo said.

"Forget it," he said. "It's my fault."

He was conscious, standing there then, of how quiet it was. In the stands there was so little noise between plays. He knew that in their ignorance they did not know that right there the thing to be won had been lost.

She said it is my only means of expression, he was thinking, this thing that happens on the field. It is all I have and if I cannot prove it on the field I cannot explain it otherwise. I cannot, by talking, make Stratfield and Enright and the rest of them understand.

Then he heard them shouting and, looking up, he saw what he had been looking at but not seeing. He saw Ford, the ball in his hands, running back with the other ends on him, circling, going back again, back to the thirty-five.

As he watched it he saw in his mind the uniform stripped from Ford now, leaving him not the gladiator but the kid, naked in his panic.

No, he said to himself. The short pass on third down thrown to a man. Not the long one the other people can intercept, that can give them possession in a broken field.

Then he saw the ball going—high and wobbling and poorly thrown, anybody's ball, and he knew that some one of the other people would grab it and run it back all the way and that the debacle would be complete. He saw it start to come down, and on the five he saw his right end—the blue—going up in the air with two of the other people in red. He saw the ball come down in the middle of them, his end clutching the ball, twisting and turning with the other people on him, falling over the goal line.

When it ended that way—13–7, the great place full of noise—the people started to flock onto the field, flooding it, carrying his shrieking players, trying to reach him. He remembered Hopkins on the other side of the field, but the mob was in his way, carrying Ford, and he heard Ford shouting to him.

"Coach! Coach! That was for you."

He hollered something to Ford, and then he saw Hopkins coming toward him, his hand out.

"Congratulations, Eddie," he heard Hopkins say.

"I was lucky," he said. "I shouldn't beat you."

"You should today," Hopkins said. "It was your ball game on that trap on the twenty. You should have won it then, but that big, slow guard of yours didn't hold your hole for you."

"Thanks," he said.

The locker room was noise. The kids, naked now, were shouting, jumping up and down, the place hot and steamy, the newspaper writers on him.

"Yes," he was saying. "Ford called a fine game. . . . No, I don't ever remember seeing a more dramatic pass than that. . . . Yes, they were just as tough as we thought they'd be. . . . Yes, their 74 gave us a lot of trouble. . . . They're a fine ball club."

Then the alumni were on him, flabby people getting misty-eyed in their excitement, slapping him on the back, shouting to him, grabbing his hand. He saw Stratfield and Enright come in together, Stratfield immaculate, Enright flushed and expansive, both of them smiling, greeting people, looking for him.

"Eddie," Stratfield was saying, "you did it."

"You sure did, Eddie," Enright said. "That was a hell of a pass."

"You don't know how relieved this makes me feel," Stratfield said. "Just forget everything. We knew you could do it, and everything is all right."

"Yes," Eddie said. "It is. May I see you alone for a minute?"

"Certainly," Stratfield said. "Certainly."

His wife was waiting in the living room, the mixer and two glasses on the table. He left his overcoat and hat in the hall and she handed him a drink and sat down.

"Well, do we toast the hero?"

"Let's not kid about it," he said.

"Oh?"

"I saw Stratfield."

"I suppose," she said, "that he's greatly relieved."

"I don't know," Eddie said. "I quit."

They sat there for a moment, not saying anything.

"Eddie," his wife said, finally, "are these dry enough for you? I put hardly any vermouth in them."

"BEER DRINKER" AND OTHER COLUMNS

Beer Drinker

from the *New York Sun*

Some song peddlers were sitting at the tables along the wall, and being regular patrons who would have eaten there anyway they did not pay much attention to the screen over the bar. Along the bar, though, the guys who were sitting on the stools and standing between them had bought the ball game with drinks for which they had no great desire and they watched the screen with the avidity of real fans.

"What's the matter?" a new one who had just walked in off Broadway said. "You got no draft beer?"

He motioned toward the beer taps. They had spread two bar towels over the taps as a signal that a dime will not get you a seat at a world series game.

"No," the bartender said. "Only bottle beer."

"Why should I buy bottle beer?" the one who had just come in said, turning to the others at the bar. "Somewhere else I can get draft beer."

No one answered and he started for the door. He took two steps, watching the screen, and then he turned and walked back to the bar.

"All right," he said to the bartender. "Give me a bottle of beer."

He put 35 cents on the counter and the bartender opened the bottle and poured the beer. On the screen the figures were small and Jim Hegan, the Cleveland catcher, had just grounded to Bob Elliott, the Boston third baseman, and now the camera was following Hegan, running to first.

Elliott Needs Some Help

"But Elliott can't find the ball," Red Barber, the announcer, was saying.

The camera did not shift back to third. You could not see what was happening because the camera remained on Hegan, who was crossing first without a play.

"And Elliott still can't find the ball," Barber was saying.

"I can't find it, either," the guy who had bought the beer said. "If you ask me, nobody can find the ball."

Up the bar somebody laughed. The guy with the beer did not say anything, then, until the next inning—the fourth—when Ken Keltner, the Cleveland third baseman, fouled one back and as the ball approached the screen the beer drinker reached up toward the screen and then he cupped his hands as if he had caught the ball.

"Actually," the voice of Barber said, "your commentator has that ball."

"How do you like that?" the beer drinker said, addressing the others at the bar. "The guy steals it right out of my hands. That should have been my ball."

No one laughed this time, Bob Feller and Johnny Sain were hooked up in a pitching duel and the game was moving quickly. As it moved the bar filled, with men and then with smoke, and they said very little until the last of the eighth when the Braves scored their run.

"All right, Johnny," the beer drinker said, talking to the Boston pitcher as the camera followed him to the mound. "All you have to get now is three more."

Elliott Finds Ball, But—

"Quiet," somebody else said. "You might make him nervous."

Sain got Lou Boudreau, the Cleveland shortstop and manager, and then he got Joe Gordon. When Keltner bounced to Elliott, however, Elliott threw over the first baseman's head, although you could not tell why because the camera was not following the ball.

"Who did that?" the beer drinker said.

"Elliott," some one else said.

"They ought to take him out and shoot him," the beer drinker said. "He does better when he can't find the ball."

They were watching Sain pitch to Walt Judnich now and when he threw a third strike past him, ending the game, they shouted and some of them threw up their hands. The beer drinker said nothing. He had coaxed a world series ball game out of one bottle of beer and when he walked to the door he still left a little in the glass.

"What about last Sunday night?" one song plugger was saying to another at one of the tables. "Did you listen to my song."

"What's the matter with you," the other said. "I was listening to my own. Don't you think I got songs?"

On that afternoon of October 6, 1948, while the perambulating protagonist of this piece was contributing his commentary to the TV reception from the Boston Braves Field of that opening game of that year's World Series, Phil Masi, the occasional catcher of the Braves, was becoming a cause celebre on his own. In the bottom half of the eighth inning, as a pinch runner, he was strolling off second base and was tagged out before getting back by a pickoff throw from Bob Feller to Lou Boudreau. The problem was that he was called safe by umpire Bill Steward and scored when Tommy Holmes, his on-the-road roommate, drove him home with the game's only run, spoiling Feller's two-hitter. Years later, Steward would admit he was wrong, and Masi, on his deathbed, would confess to Holmes that he was out.

w.c.h.
January 2001

A Different View
of Football

from the *New York Sun*

Red Strader and Jack White, who coach the football Yankees, were working the squad in the clean morning sunlight that flooded the field. Around them the stands of the Yankee Stadium were empty and on one of the sideline barriers, watching, sat a little guy in work clothes with a dark blue baseball cap on his head.

"Footballs," he said, and he shook his head. "Footballs."

His name is Jimmy McGrane and he is one of Walter Owen's ground crew. He was talking about the footballs lying on the grass near the goal posts, in front of which the members of the squad were running through plays.

"What do footballs cost?" he asked.

"I think they pay $12 apiece for them," the one standing with him said.

"Then why does a guy want to give me $15 for one?"

"I suppose that's the retail price."

"Then why do the kids on my block pay $23 for a football this year?"

"I don't know."

"It's funny," the little guy said, and he started to laugh. "Because I work at the Yankee Stadium everybody thinks I get a lot of footballs and baseballs and bats and gloves."

He looked at the other.

DiMaggio's Old Glove

"I never get any," he said, laughing. "Last summer a neighbor come to my wife and she said: 'Listen. Your husband works at the Yankee Stadium. Tell him to get a catcher's glove after some ball game.'"

257

The little guy still liked the idea and the other started laughing.

"I told my wife," he said. "I told her: 'Tell her the ball players don't give away no gloves. They use the same gloves all their life. Tell her the gloves gotta be broke in and they keep them.'"

He looked back at the other.

"Did you ever see DiMaggio's glove?" he said.

"No."

"It's about this thick," he said, barely opening his fingers. "It's all old and the inside is so dry and cracked that it scratches your hand. Across the back there's an old piece of canvas for a strap.

"One day I said to DiMaggio, I said: 'Why don't you get a new glove instead of using this old rag.' DiMaggio didn't say anything, but Walter said: 'Don't talk to him like that.'"

He shrugged his shoulders.

"DiMaggio don't care," he said. "Me and Joe get along good. We never have no trouble."

He watched the players on the field. Strader and White were shouting at them and the players were hollering, and he watched Bud Schwenk throw a pass and Lloyd Cheatham turn and drop the ball.

"What's the matter with that Cheatham?" he said. "Why does he hold his arms out like that?"

"Because he's a blocking back," the other said. "He's used to blocking with his arms."

The Kid Has Fun

"I thought he had boils," the little guy said.

He thought a moment, watching the next play on the field.

"Did you ever see Cheatham's kid?" he said.

"That little kid?"

"That's right," he said. "What a kid. One day he's up in the office and he has a baseball in his hand. Somebody says: 'Don't throw that baseball in here' and he lets it go and almost hits the guy on the chin. The guy just gets his chin out of the way in time."

He waited for the other to enjoy the story.

"The other day," he said, "there's a guy painting that door just before you get to the locker room. Cheatham's kid is throwing a baseball against the door while the guy is trying to paint it and the guy says: 'Hey! Don't throw that ball against this door,' and the kid throws it at the guy and hits him in the head with the ball."

He watched the field, the three teams of players running up and down, the green turf flying from under their cleats and marring the fine surface of the baseball field.

"Football," he said. "Who invented football?"

Setting the Pace

from the *New York Sun*

That Was Hoot Mon's Year

Well, they have added another line to the history of the Hambletonian. It is the twenty-second line in the story that goes back to 1926 and as long as the Hambletonian Stake is trotted it will be in there, and, in the cryptic way in which they confine the story of a race for posterity by settling for year, horse, driver, time and value, it will always read:

1947 . . . Hoot Mon . . . Sep Palin . . . 2:00 . . . $46,267.93.

To that line they will, of course, as the years roll by, add other lines. The importance of that twenty-second line, however, is that the name of the black colt, Hoot Mon, is in there to stay now with the names of such harness greats as Spencer . . . Hanover's Bertha . . . The Marchioness . . . Greyhound . . . Volo Song . . . and Titan Hanover. And remember that as long as harness men who were here for this one get together some one is bound to say: " 1947? That was Hoot Mon's year. I remember."

Well, what any one man remembers out of any one day is his alone and no one can infringe upon it. There is one guy, though, who, when he remembers that 1947 was Hoot Mon's year, will remember it something like this:

He will remember, first of all, a Hambletonian eve. That will be a memory of a warm summer evening and cars parked on all the streets leading to the Goshen green where they were holding a band concert, bazaar and block dance and where, under the elms and under the lights, a clarinet wailed until late into the night. Then there will be a remembrance of a Hambletonian morning, the sun streaming through a bedroom window and then falling flat and warm on a cement street where cars were still pouring in from Indiana . . . North Carolina . . . Kentucky . . . Michigan . . . Pennsylvania . . . Ohio

... New Jersey ... Connecticut. They were still pouring in two hours later, to the resentment of the operator of the Goshen diner who barred his door and the old woman who stopped at a curb-stone to pat a black dog and say:

"Here now. You get right back home. This is no day for a dog to be out and wandering around."

A Memory of Two Old Men

There will be the memory, then, of two old men, sitting on a park bench in the middle of this madness that had descended upon their town. In their own way, or in Goshen's way, on Hambletonian day, they seemed to be settling the problems of the world, for one of them said:

"The Russians? Why, if a Russian came in here now and lay down on the grass nobody would pay any attention. Let a horse lay down here, though, and there'll be a crowd around as big as you ever saw."

Now those things, of course, have nothing to do with the trotting of a race. It is only that a part of trotting seems to be tied inseparably to the color and character of the places where they hold the races, and so the picture of 1947, Hoot Mon's year, must always contain the memory of the crowds streaming on foot toward the track entrances. . . . The hot sun. . . . The dust on the ground. . . . On their shoes. . . . On the legless begger crying: "Please, please don't pass the cripple by." . . . As the crowd streamed on.

What will remain, then out of seven hours spent within the fences of Good Time Park contains a recollection of a moment when somebody said that a section of the stands had just given way, and a "score" had just been in-jured. Now a "score" is always an unknown number and there was no way of fighting through the crowd to find out, and so the next hour gave vent to the feeling that, perhaps, this would after all be a year, not known by the name of the winner, but by the title of: " 1947. The year the stands collapsed."

That will be remembered, though, only as a feeling that came before they trotted off the Hambletonian. Sure to supersede it in memory will be the re-membrance of Rodney, pre-race favorite, winning the first heat easy and as he pleased, and then, top-heavy favorite in the second, standing off Hoot Mon's first drive, to fall before the second drive in the stretch that brought Hoot Mon home in two minutes flat, a record for a Hambletonian.

So the third, and final heat, then, will be remembered as a toss-up. There will be Rodney in front the first time by the stand. . . . Then Volotone on top as they became small, slow figures down the back stretch. . . . Then Hoot Mon passing Rodney and Volotone going into the far turn. . . . Then Rodney passing Volotone. . . . But Hoot Mon holding it easily with the crowd shrieking at the wire.

Hoot Mon? Why that was the horse that Fred Egan pointed to in a barn in Aiken on a rainy morning last April when he said: "And there is the winner of this year's Hambletonian."

1947? Why, don't you remember? That was Hoot Mon's year.

Down Memory Lane with the Babe

from the *New York Sun*

The old Yankees, going back twenty-five years, were dressing in what used to be the visiting clubhouse in the Yankee Stadium, some of them thin, some of them stout, almost all of them showing the years. Whitey Witt was asking for a pair of size 9 shoes. Mike McNally, bending over and going through the piles of uniforms stacked on the floor, was looking for a pair of pants with a waist.

"Here he is now," somebody add but when he said it he hardly raised his voice.

The Babe was the last to come in. He had on a dark suit and a cap oyster white. He walked slowly with a friend on either side of him. He paused for a moment and them he recognized some one and smiled and stuck out his hand.

They did not crowd him. When some one pointed to a locker he walked to it and it was quiet around him. When a few who knew him well walked up to him they did it quietly, smiling, holding out their hands.

The Babe started to undress. His friends helped him. They hung up his clothes and helped him into the parts of his uniform. When he had them on he sat down again to put on his spiked shoes, and when he did this the photographers who had followed him moved in. They took pictures of him in uniform putting on his shoes, for this would be the last time.

He posed willingly, brushing a forelock off his forehead. When they were finished he stood up slowly. There was a man there with a small boy, and the man pushed the small boy through the old Yankees and the photographers around Ruth.

Youngster Meets Babe

"There he is," the man said, bending down and whispering to the boy. "That's Babe Ruth."

The small boy seemed confused. He was right next to the Babe and the Babe bent down and tool the small boy's hand almost at the same time as he looked away to drop the hand.

"There," the man said, pulling the small boy back. "Now you met Babe Ruth."

The small boy's eyes were wide, but his face seemed to show fear. The led the Babe over to pose him in the middle of the rest of the 1923 Yankee. Then they led him into the old Yankee clubhouse—now the visiting clubhouse—to pose in front of his old locker, on which is painted in white letters, "Babe Ruth, No. 3."

When they led him back the rest of the members of the two teams of old Yankees had left to go to the dugouts. They put the Babe's gabardine top coat over his shoulders, the sleeves hanging loose, and they led him—some in front of him and some in back in the manner in which they lead a fighter down to a ring—down the stairs and into the dark runway.

They sat the Babe down then on one of the concrete abutments in the semi-darkness. He sat there for about two minutes.

"I think you had better wait inside," some one said. "It's too damp here."

Returns to Clubhouse

They led him back to the clubhouse. He sat down and they brought him a box of a dozen baseballs and a pen. He autographed the balls that will join what must be thousands of others on mantels, or under glass in bureau drawers or in attics in many places in the world.

He sat then, stooped, looking ahead, saying nothing. They halted an attendant from sweeping the floor because dust was rising.

"I hope it lets up," the Babe said, his voice hoarse.

"All right," somebody said. "They're ready now."

They led him out again slowly the topcoat over his shoulders. There were two cops and one told the other to walk in front. In the third base dugout there was a crowd of Indians and 1923 Yankees and they found a place or the bench and the Babe sat down behind the crowd.

"A glove?" he said.

"A left handed glove," someone said.

They found a glove on one of the hooks. It was one of the type that has come into baseball since the Babe left—bigger than the old gloves with a mesh of rawhide between the thumb and first finger—and the Babe took it and looked at it and put it on.

"With one of these," he said, "you could catch a basketball."

They laughed and the Babe held the mesh up before his face like a catcher's mask and they laughed again. Mel Allen, at the public address microphone, was introducing the other old Yankees. You could hear the cheering and the Babe saw Mel Harder, the former Cleveland pitcher, now a coach.

"You remember," he said, after he had poked Harder, "when I got five for five off you and they booed me?"

Harder Didn't Forget

"Yes," Harder said, smiling, "You mean in Cleveland."

The Babe made a series of flat motions with his left hand.

"Like that," the Babe said. "All into left field and they still booed the stuff out of me."

The Babe handed the glove to some one and some one else handed him a bat. He turned it over to see Bob Feller's name on it and he hefted it.

"It's got good balance," he said.

"And now—" Allen's voice said, coming off the field.

They were coming to boo Babe now. In front of him the Indians moved back and when they did the Babe looked up to see a wall of two-dozen photographers focused on him. He stood up and the topcoat slid off his shoulders onto the bench.

"—George Herman," Allen's voice said, "Babe Ruth!"

The Babe took a step and started slowly up the steps. He walked out into the flashing of flash bulbs, into the cauldron of sound he must know better than any other man.

Memories of a
Great Jockey

from the *New York Sun*

In front of an open fire in a pine-paneled room in Aiken, S. C., Ed Christmas was wording the obituary of Georgie Woolf.

Georgie Woolf was killed two years ago at Santa Anita. They used to think something other than blood ran through him and they called him "The Iceman" and he was really one of the best.

"I have never been able to understand that," some one said. "As I read about it he was all alone and there was no one near him so I suppose he must have blacked out."

"No," Ed said. "I can tell you what happened. I can tell you exactly what happened.

"The horse was last," he said. "He had it in behind but you know how he used to ride."

He bent over where he sat on the sofa and he had his hands up close in front of him.

"That boy had a natural seat," he said: "You know what I mean when you see these other boys, but when Georgie rode 'em—hell, he didn't, he didn't lay on 'em and he was over like this—"

He hunched over even more and he tapped his chest.

"There wasn't more than this," he said, indicating with his thumb and his forefinger, "between him and the horse's withers and when he brought the horse up—like this—the head come up and it caught him right here."

He straightened up and placed his hand under his chest and looked around.

"When it hit him," he said, "he went right up in the air—like this—and when he come down his head hit the pole right here on the left.

Was Misunderstood

"They knew he was a goner," he said, "when they got to him and picked him up. His wife wanted to go to him but they wouldn't let her see him like that and he never regained consciousness."

"I wondered," some one said. "I wondered about that."

"Man, he could ride," Ed Christmas said, and he waited a moment and shook his head. "You know, people didn't like him, a lot of them didn't."

"I know," some one said.

"They didn't understand him," Ed said. "He was a sick boy."

"I know."

"That boy had diabetes," Ed said. "People didn't know that. Why, when we'd drive out to the track in the morning he'd sit there, with his head down like this, and I'd say, 'Georgie, you all right?' 'Yeah,' he'd say, 'I'm all right.' His wife carried insulin and he'd take that and he'd be all.

"They used to say," he said, "that he had a swelled head because he would-n't take this horse or that. Hell, all he wanted to do was ride and he'd take every horse in every race if he could. He was a sick boy.

"He was a peculiar boy in some ways, but I understood him. He used to tell me his troubles and I guess I knew him, better than anybody and I guess I understood him.

"You know," he said, smiling, "he come from Canada, and they ask him the date of the Revolutionary War and he said: "The Revolutionary War? I can't tell you that, but I know the date of the next meeting.'

Talked About Racing

"I remember," he said, "the day he won the Futurity with Occupy. After the race I see him taking his shower and he says he will see me that night, and that night he comes to my room in the hotel and he's all excited and like a kid.

"It seems they had a pony race that afternoon for some of them older jock-eys like Earl Sande and him. He's laughin' and talkin' and tellin' me about this race and I said: 'Hey, what the hell is a pony race and you win $6,500 this afternoon?' 'I'm not talkin' about winnin' money,' he says. 'I'm talkin' about racin'.

"He knew a guy," he said, "back in the woods was a crack rifle shot. He talked about him all the time and he thought he was the greatest guy in the world."

He looked around at those with him.

"Man, he could ride," he said. "He'd lay back there and he'd kill those other horses in the stretch. You remember? He'd drive with those hands open like this and when you'd see those fingers go out, boy, you knew he was starting to go."

He stopped for a moment as if he were seeking something more to say.

"He was a rider," he said.

Football's
Muzzled Masses

from the *New York Times*

Last March, in all their might assembled in Palm Desert, Calif., the National Football League owners made a momentous decision. They voted to impose penalties against home teams for crowd noise that continually disrupts the offenses of their opponents, and if they thought they heard noise, the indications are that they ain't heard nothin' yet. After all, you can't smoke in elevators, spit on the sidewalk or shoot off a machine gun in church. Now this.

The vote was 21–7, and proponents of the rule, which allows referees to deduct time-outs from the team whose fans are doing the dinning, and impose yardage penalties if that doesn't impress them, said it was necessary because the crowds were becoming bigger factors than the players. That came as no surprise to anyone who has been watching these past few seasons as the gladiators stood around while the hometown hooters exercised their freedom of expression, their lungs and their vocal chords, the referee having suspended play because the opposing quarterback couldn't hear himself.

Those red-blooded Americans aren't going to take this sitting down, something they seldom do anyway during the height of their hysteria. Already in preseason we have heard their clamors and seen their banners, an army of freedom fighters in training for the season that starts today and—who knows?—may end with William Kunstler quarterbacking them up the courthouse steps.

To cast light on how this has come about, a little history is called for. Once within living memory the game was played by 22 men—currently the number of some college coaching staffs—and attended by audiences of admirers who came to cheer, providing a sort of operatic chorus to the drama at hand.

Now it is played by an ever-changing cast of characters who commute in and out—sometimes to their own confusion—and attended by crowds who come not to cheer but to jeer and, as noted, hold up the proceedings until the question is not who will win but will they let the game continue before the team trainers and water boys are asked to bring out the mail from home.

A college football game was televised for the first time on Sept. 30, 1939, when Fordham beat Waynesburg, 34–7. Next we settle in on Dec. 22, 1952, when from Balboa Stadium in San Diego NBC prepared to telecast coast to coast something called the Poinsettia Bowl. It pitted the San Diego Naval Training Station against Bolling Field, for the championship of the armed services.

According to Lindsey Nelson, the retired sportscaster, on the morning of the game the rain was hitting the skylight of the hotel coffee shop with such intensity that it was impossible to tell the waitress now you wanted your eggs done. "As kickoff time approached," Nelson wrote of the Poinsettia Affair in his 1985 autobiography, "we became aware of another interesting development. There were no spectators. I do not mean that it was a small crowd. I mean there did not appear to be one single paid admission. We were about to televise from coast to coast on NBC a football game to which nobody had come."

Tom Gallery, the director of NBC sports, convened a quick conference of Navy brass. He explained that you could no more televise a game without an audience than you could christen a battleship in secrecy.

"Gentlemen," he said, "we have to have a crowd of some sort."

Those were the words, the dictum from which all that would follow would derive. Within the hour the Shore Patrol, having made clean sweepdowns fore and aft in every movie house and ale house, paraded in some 200 soggy, sullen and shanghaied sailors—Hayden Fry, now the coach of Iowa, among them. When Bill Bennington, the director, punched in the crowd shot of them sitting in a sodden and unsmiling square, wondering what they were doing there under Niagara Falls, it was established, apparently forevermore, that the crowd shot is an indispensable part of the televised game.

Since then, successive creative directors have embellished and embroidered the basic principle that you can't enjoy anything, whether it be a football game, a painting or a sunset, without company, the more and more raucous the merrier. To the obligatory long shot of partisans cheering a gain or a score—and what else would they be doing?—was added the close-up. The sideline camera, initially installed to capture play at ground level, was swung up toward the stands, inviting every closet clown in the area out into the open, his face and torso often painted in team colors, raising the question at college games of the benefits of higher education and, at pro games, of the wisdom of universal suffrage.

It was in Cleveland's Municipal Stadium on Jan. 11, 1987, when, by my calculations, the Poinsettia Principle, as formulated in San Diego more than three decades before, finally came to full flower. While the Denver Broncos defeated the Cleveland Browns in overtime, 23–20, there were, by official count, 143 plays on the field and, by my count, 69 crowd shots on NBC. This not only entitled the Broncos to meet the New York Giants in the Super Bowl—a dubious honor as it turned out—but crowds anywhere to assume that, if they were that indispensable to the game on the tube, they might now be similarly important to the play on the field.

This was a concept that had not escaped the keen and inventive minds of a number of coaches who had already begun to include it in their game plans. Some weeks before, Don James, the foresighted head man at the University of Washington, had implored Huskie fans to come to the home game with Arizona State and scream their brains, or whatever, out. A record gathering of 73,883 packed the place, and set up such a clamor whenever Arizona State had the ball that, not only were the visitors unable to hear their snap count, but a member of the gendarmerie became concerned that the sportsmanship might get out of hand. He requested of Mike Lude, the Washington athletic director, that Lude make an announcement asking for calm.

"I told him," Lude said, "to go to hell."

More recently—last Dec. 31, in fact—the NBC commentators at the Cincinnati-Seattle contest reported that Sam Wyche, the Bengals' resident conductor, had been leading the home crowd in the manner, I judged, of Arturo Toscanini. You'll recall that the Maestro regularly not only conducted the New York Philharmonic but also the NBC Symphony, so that was keeping the old baton in the house.

"Crowds," Merlin Olsen, the network's leading musicologist, informed us in seeming admiration that day, "have become so much more sophisticated in knowing when they can make so much noise that the other team can't hear."

So the games, repeatedly interrupted by the a capella concerts, dragged on—on Sundays on the East Coast into TV prime time, and on Monday nights into Tuesdays. And the viewers began to drop off or doze off. This left the owners faced with an economic reality. Few things stir these sportsmen like an economic reality, so when they realized that for every TV rating dip there would be a comparable dollar drop, their decree to muffle the huddled masses yearning to be free was as inevitable as it may be vulnerable.

It seems to this observer that, while you can't get away with hollering "Fire!" in a crowded theater, there's a constitutional question here that the American Civil Liberties Union will pounce upon as on a fumble on the 5-yard line. The right peaceably to assemble and of freedom of speech are guaranteed by the First Amendment of the Constitution. Should the National Collegiate Athletic Association follow in step, I can hear now the cheers change from "U.C.L.A.! U.C.L.A.!" to "A.C.L.U.! A.C.L.U.!" and foresee the first N.F.L. draft pick coming, not as this year out of that eminent California institution, but out of Harvard Law.

What Happens at a Bike Race

from the *New York Sun*

There were a few people spread out here and there in the seats that run along the sides of the Twenty-second Engineers Armory, where the six-day bike race is now in its third day. On the track the riders barely moved, and in the infield a woman wearing a gray dress was sitting at the organ and playing softly for her own amusement.

The riders ignored the people in the seats. When occasionally they looked toward them they seemed to be seeing beyond them, and as they made their slow circles they kidded among themselves.

"You see?" a stout man said to the girl sitting next to him. "You're not too old. You could learn to play the organ. You could get a good job out of it."

He motioned toward the woman at the organ, who was sitting back now kidding with a young man in a white coat from the soft drink stand beyond the organ. The girl looked at the woman and said nothing. The girl was wearing blue dungarees, rolled almost to the knees, and a plaid woolen shirt and white saddle shoes, and she looked like some of them in this town look when they start to go to college.

"There's a woman made a good job out of it," the stout man said, still talking about the organist.

Letourner Reads His Mail

On the track Alf Letourner, in a red jersey, was reading a letter written on lavender stationery. It must have been a long letter, because Letourner and

the rest of the field made about eight trips around the track before Letourner finished it.

"Is that the American champ?" the girl sitting with the stout man said.
"He doesn't look like his picture."

The girl had a program in her hand, and she pointed to Bill Anderson,
wearing a red, white and blue jersey. Anderson, steering with one foot on the
handlebar, was pumping with the other. In one hand he held a plate and in
the other a fork, and while he rode he ate a lunch of meat and vegetables.

"Whatever the program says," the stout man said. "How should I know
him?"

"One hundred and forty-six consecutive hours," the girl said, reading
from her program. "That's a long time."

The stout man said nothing and on the track the riders started to warm up
a little. You could hear the whir of their tires and as they started to move the
organist began to play. She played a song called "Underneath the Arches."

"Hey!" the girl said. "They're starting to go faster."

"They can't go slow all the time," the stout man said. "That gets too
monotonous."

As he said this a pistol shot rang out. It startled the girl and she jumped a
little.

"What's that?" she said.

"The pistol shot," the voice on the amplifier said, "denotes the starting of
five two-minute sprints for points."

"What's points?" the girl said.

"Quiet," the stout man said. "Listen to him. I don't pay much attention to
it."

She's a Bit Confused

The riders were whirling now, and at the track side a man held up black
cards with white numerals on them to denote the number of laps remaining
in the sprint. As he held up the card with the number 3 on it the relief riders
started to come out onto the track to get ready for the pickups when the
sprint ended.

"Say," the girl said, "there's two on who have the same colors."

"Just watch," the man said.

"But how do you know who's ahead?" the girl said.

"Just watch," the man said. "I'm not payin' much attention to how they're
runnin'."

"I don't get it," the girl said.

The track was a maze of moving colors now as the sprinters moved between the relief riders on the bell lap. As the sprinters moved across the finish and then touched off their partners the girl seemed to sense that the first sprint was over.

"Who won?" she said.

The stout man just shook his head.

"I don't understand this," the girl said. "I don't get it."

Why Can't TV Encourage Class Instead of Crass?

from *TV Guide*

The reader is hereby forewarned to move back about 10 paces, for the writer is about to throw yet another brick through the biggest plate-glass window in the land. Television, applauded or condemned for precipitating just about every virtue or vice from peace-marching to hostage-taking, is now going to be accused of gradually destroying in this country that quality that used to be known as class.

Television is not—repeat not—responsible for acid rain or the 17-year cicada. Since almost annual studies establish, however, that the mass of young and impressionable take their cues not as much from what they are force-fed at home and in school as from what the tube tells them, television must take the rap for the lessons in loutish behavior it ladles out as entertaining examples, and for the role models it supplies, particularly through sports.

Sports, attracting those multimillions on TV, are not, as some indifferent to the sweat set may believe, merely fun and games, for the entertainments of any time provide a revealing portrait of the people and of that time. It is not what remains of the Appian Way and the Roman aqueducts that for almost two thousand years have indelibly identified the mores of the Roman Empire, but rather the Coliseum and what went on there.

What goes on in the coliseums of our country and on the home screens is, of course, benign by comparison. It reflects, nevertheless, an egregious egomania and an insensitivity to the feelings of the bested opponent and to the code of conduct that used to be known as sportsmanship, as professionalism, as Ernest Hemingway's grace under pressure, as behavior beyond reproach.

College and professional basketball players, amazing athletes that they are, have become aerial exhibitionists, turning the most simple shots into circus performances, during which one of them—Darryl Dawkins—attained instant fame and acclaim when he managed to shatter a backboard. In professional football, a Neanderthal Nureyev named Mark Gastineau, until restrained by official edict, became a household hero doing a dance of derision around the collapsed carcasses of his fallen foes, a courtesy that won for him and his doting mother a TV commercial. In baseball, a home run is followed by a hot-dog high five, a stretching of the musculature that no stretch of the imagination conjures up Joe DiMaggio or Stan Musial sharing.

This one member of a departing generation finds it impossible to picture Red Grange, the most celebrated football player of all time, running through airports in a TV commercial, hurdling barriers erected to confine the common fold and endangering the safety of others while a worshipful crone exhorts him to "Go!" He wonders what social graces Lawrence Taylor, the TV-lionized linebacker, acquired during the course of his college education on the cuff and was exhibiting Super Bowl week when, during a mass interview, to quote one observer, he "grossed out reporters by repeatedly spitting tobacco juice on the carpet of the interview room."

A middleweight boxing champion, Marvin Hagler, perhaps too young to have heard of Joe Louis and unable to find "modest" in the dictionary, legally takes Marvelous as his first name. In this striving for superlatives, however, his choice had been somewhat constricted by the loquacious heavyweight champion Muhammad Ali, who had pre-empted "The Greatest," and who during bouts taunted inferior opponents with humiliating gestures and degraded the art form to which he owed so much by interjecting shuffle steps that are as out of place in boxing as clog steps in classical ballet.

The trouble with modesty, of course, is that it doesn't play on TV. While the soft answer may turn away wrath, it also turns away the viewer. But for many of us so do the rantings and ravings of male tennis demigods who spew vulgarities at officials and spectators and threaten to eradicate from public memory what used to be known simply as good manners and respect and consideration for others.

In Albany, N.Y., before the Super Bowl, a priest prayed for the New York (i.e., New Jersey) Giants, explaining to the TV interviewer that he had merely entreated God to see that they played well enough to win. This brought to mind an illiterate prizefighter called Beau Jack. In his native Georgia, Beau had survived the battles royal, an enlightened form of entertainment that had come in when bearbaiting went out, and in which a half dozen or more blacks were gloved, blindfolded and pushed into a ring where they were forced to flail at one another until only one remained standing.

"I understand," I said to Beau while he reigned in the 1940s as lightweight champion, "that you pray before every fight."

"That's right," he said, grinning and nodding.

"For what do you pray?"

"I pray that nobody get hurt," he said. "Then I pray that it be a good fight."

"Don't you ever pray to win?"

"No," he said, shaking his head. "I would never do that."

"Why not?" I said.

"Suppose I pray to win," he said. "The other boy, he pray to win, too. Then what God gonna do?"

That was class. I must believe it is still out there somewhere, to be seen if somebody will just turn a camera and a commentary on it ere it dies with those of us who may be the last generation to remember it.

One candidate for such attention is another professional footballer, hardly the spitting image of his more celebrated, carpet-staining contemporary, but good enough an offensive tackle to be selected by his peers for the Pro Bowl. On Jan. 28, 1986, Brian Holloway, then of the New England Patriots, was getting ready to practice for that contest in Honolulu when he saw the space shuttle Challenger's explosion on television.

"I sat there and wept," he told Art Spander, the San Francisco sportswriter. "I couldn't move for half an hour. I never felt so completely helpless in my entire life."

He had met Christa McAuliffe, the New Hampshire schoolteacher who perished with the others, when one day in 1985 outside the Patriots' locker room, she had asked for his autograph for her two young children. In return she had written: "To Brian, reach for the stars. I'll be there."

"When the shuttle blew up," Holloway told Spander, "I was devastated. I knew I had to do something."

Working up to 20 hours a day for six months, he organized and promoted two National Football League Celebrity Item Auctions, to which athletes from various sports contributed personal memorabilia. The money raised—approximately $85,000—went to the Challenger Center for Space Science Education in Washington, D.C., a $30-million project to be linked into the Nation's school system.

"Why do I do it?" Holloway said. "For America. The people of this country, in a sense, are my employers—not the Patriots. The people have made the NFL the number one sport in this country. They've given me my chance. This is simply my way of giving back something to the people."

Holloway, who earlier this year was traded to the Los Angeles Raiders, was pondering retirement at the end of this football season. Whenever it occurs, his departure will leave a hole in more than the Raiders' offensive line. It is television's proudest boast that it "tells it like it is." But even as it ignores the rule of grammar it ignores its responsibility not only to depict but to deplore the brash and the boorish. If it doesn't soon start condemning rather than condoning the crass, then Brian Holloway and the few others like him will be the last examples of what used to be known as class.

It Was Like a Light Bulb Busted in Your Brain

from *TV Guide*

It is rather odd, I guess, what I remember first of all about Joe Louis. They are going to do the story of his life on TV, and they won't have the time or perhaps even the taste for this, but I remember the way it was, and the way he was, when he used to train out at Pompton Lakes, N.J., for his title fights in New York.

The way it was at Pompton, the outdoor ring was set up under the trees with bleachers on three sides, and the people who came on Saturdays and Sundays out of Harlem and Newark and Jersey City and Philadelphia made a day of it. They brought their lunches, and they used to sit there on the bleachers, eating and laughing until, finally, Joe would come through the sunlight to the ring, his handlers around him and Joe in a white terry-cloth robe and with a white towel over his head. Then all the talking and the laughing and even the eating would stop.

Joe would climb up into the ring and Mannie Seamon, who trained him after Jack Blackburn died, would take his robe and the towel and Joe would shadowbox. He would be wearing brief, white woolen trunks and a white top, and the bandages and tape on his hands would be a gleaming white. He would move smoothly and silently, except for the scraping of his ring shoes on the canvas, and it would be so quiet there in the open-under the trees that you could hear a breeze stir the leaves on the branches overhead and sometimes, from somewhere, hear a bird call.

Before Joe would go down to the ring, he would meet the newspapermen in his dressing room off the gym. Joe would be sitting on the rubbing table with the clean white sheet on it and his white robe over him. Beside him would be a medicine ball, and resting an arm on the ball, he would be holding that hand out so that Mannie Seamon could bandage it.

"How do you feel, Joe?" one of the newspapermen would say after a while.

They came from all over this country and from outside of it for Joe's big fights, and some of them remembered Dempsey and Willard at Toledo. Many of them had known all the great sports figures of their time, and although there were those among them who never backed off a debate, in print or in person, they never took any liberties with Joe.

"I feel fine," Joe would say, watching Mannie bandage the hand.

There would be another pause. In the silence of the crowded room the newspapermen would be watching the bandaging too, or just looking at Joe.

"Have you heard what the other guy is saying?" someone would say, finally.

"No," Joe would say, still watching the bandaging.

There would be another pause. It was a great tribute, the way they stood in awe of Joe, and when Joe fought Billy Conn the second time there were more than 200 of them in for the fight and they wrote millions of words.

"Up at Conn's camp," one of them said to Joe that day at Pompton, when Joe came up with that big line, "they figure his speed will lick you."

"That so?" Joe said, watching the bandaging again.

"That's right," somebody else said. "They've even got him working with a middleweight."

"That so?" Joe said.

"So don't you think Conn's speed will bother you?"

"Maybe it bothers me," Joe said, "but I don't think so."

"Why not?" one of them said.

"Cause Billy can run," Joe said, "but he can't hide."

Joe not only knocked out Conn in the eighth round, but he beat that pack of professional writers, none of whom came up with as good a line. He had done that before, after we got into World War II and, like all peoples with a religious heritage, we held to the assumption, as the orators kept telling us, that we would win because God was on our side.

"No," Joe said.

"We're gonna win in the end because we're on God's side."

When a man speaks even as he fights so is the man, so you took no liberties with Joe, outside or inside the ropes, without truth on your side. In that ring he was the almost perfect fighting machine, the relentless, expressionless stalker, poised and dispassionate—except against Max Schmeling the second time—who neither humiliated the opponent nor degraded the art form with dance steps or taunts.

When his jab landed, Jim Braddock said, "It's like a light bulb busted in your brain." He could take you out with either hand, and, again as Braddock said, "It's like getting hit with a bag full of nuts and bolts."

With a single right hand he knocked out Al Ettore, and Ettore's cheek looked as if it had been sliced with a knife. For three rounds Paolino Uzcudun moved around him, shielding himself with his forearms. In the fourth round he raised one arm just enough to look through the mail slot at Joe, and Joe shot the right. It drove Uzcudun's teeth through the mouth-piece and through his lower lip, and gold teeth bounced, glittering, on the canvas.

Uzcudun was one of 12 Louis opponents whom Ray Arcel, the great trainer who worked with 20 world champions, helped drag back to their corners. This earned Arcel the dubious distinction of being known on the sports pages as "The Meat Wagon" and "The Pallbearer of Pugilism" before, finally, he trained Ezzard Charles, who outpointed Joe when Joe was 36.

"One night," Arcel was telling me once, "I forget who the fighter was, but when we went to the center of the ring for the referee's instructions, Joe looked at me and he said, 'You here again?' I wanted to laugh.

"The fear he inspired, though," Ray said, "was something. In Johnny Paycheck's dressing room they had a guy in there talking to him, but Johnny never heard a word. In the ring, during the instructions, he just shook, and he never got by the second round. I didn't work with Max Baer, but he told me once, 'Ray, you wouldn't believe what it was like. In camp, when I looked in the mirror, I saw Joe Louis. When I went to the toilet, there was Joe Louis. It was awful'."

As a fighter, Joe had that one flaw that Schmeling saw before their first fight and that Jersey Joe Walcott also exploited 11 years later. After he jabbed, he would bring his left hand back low without then stepping to take himself off the straight line of the right-hand counter. Jack Blackburn, who developed him, had boxed as a lightweight in the early years of the century, and he had built Joe so completely in his own fighting image that, unknowingly, he had even built in the same flaw.

As I last remember Joe, we were flying from New York to Las Vegas for the second Liston-Patterson fight 25 years ago. In the forward section of the plane, Joe was sitting across the aisle and facing the partition. When we were put down for a 20-minute layover in Chicago, Joe got up, took one of those

"Reserved" cards from the pocket on the partition, put it on his seat and turned to start down the aisle. Across from him a rather short, elderly man was standing in apparent confusion. Seeing him, Joe turned back, took out another card, handed it to him, and, without saying anything, turned back down the aisle.

I don't know if the old man knew that was Joe, and I wondered how many others in this time in which we live would so instinctively have done the same thing. Alex Haley has been quoted as saying, when he was introduced to Joe, "I feel like I'm finally meeting with God." I don't propose him for sainthood for, son of Alabama sharecroppers and with a 6th-grade education, he squandered much of his earnings and fell to cocaine before his death in 1981. Jimmy Cannon put it best.

"He's a credit to his race," Jimmy wrote, "the human race."

Quick, Thomas, a Brick!

from *TV Guide*

Let this be about what it was like during television's Paleozoic Era, about 250,000,000 years ago. I am reminded of it now when I hear that it cost the American Broadcasting Company, with their color cameras, their experts and their instant replays, $12,000,000 to bring us the Winter Olympics and $25,000,000 to cover the Summer Games. This was the year 1952, however, and we were spread around the sitting room of a hotel suite in Washington and smoking. The sponsor's product was a cigarette, and at times like this we were ever grateful that it was not a candy bar, a cat food or a cathartic.

The show was called *Meet the Champ*, and at 9:30 P.M. each Thursday it was broadcast live from a different armed-forces base in this country, where, for a half hour, it brought together boxers representing the various military services. It was about to complete its first 13-week network cycle, and it had been diagnosed as suffering from a severe case of Nielsen's anemia. This accounted for the presence in the suite now of the sponsor's director of advertising, a vice president of the ad agency, the account executive and the six of us indentured to the show.

The show was a result of the second cerebral cataclysm of a man named Wally Butterworth. A couple of decades earlier, Butterworth and Parks Johnson had given birth to another brainchild, a radio program called "Vox Pop." With microphones in hands, they went around, as I remember, collaring people on street corners, under theater marquees and in railroad stations, asking for opinions.

The lineal descent from "Vox Pop" to *Meet the Champ* was clear. *Champ* had inherited from "Vox" that singular characteristic that inspires producers to write poetry, walk into doors and send the chauffeur around with flowers.

The talent was free. The armed services provided that, and *Champ* supplied the trunks, robes, gloves and, where one was not available, a rented ring. It also provided the military with network exposure, carloads of free cigarettes, Butterworth at ringside and, in the wings, Tommy Loughran, Billy Cavanaugh and Bow Tie Jimmy Bronson.

Loughran, the former light-heavy-weight champion of the world, had been one of the all-time greats in his division and the first man to discover that Primo Carnera, "The Ambling Alp," couldn't stand on his own two feet. In 1934, while Carnera was heavyweight champion of the world, Loughran boxed him for 15 rounds in Miami, giving away 7 inches in height, 75 pounds and his mobility, as Carnera stood on Loughran's feet. "He beat me with his size–15 brogans," Loughran said.

Cavanaugh was a former professional fighter and referee and, more important, he had been boxing coach at West Point. In the latter capacity, it was reported, he had bloodied a lot of noses, including those of a number of incipient generals, an accomplishment that, it was reasoned, would endear him to any of the tens of millions of enlisted men, past or present, who might tune into the show.

Bronson was a former manager of prize fighters, a rather small, gracefully aging, immaculate man with the manners and command of English of a Groton headmaster and the powers of persuasion of a successful encyclopedia salesman. It was Bronson's claim that it was he who had persuaded the Illinois Athletic Commission, before the second fight between Jack Dempsey and Gene Tunney in Chicago in 1927, to institute the rule requiring the perpetrator of a knockdown to refire to a neutral corner before the start of the 10-count. After Dempsey floored Tunney in the seventh round and hovered in his vicinity, it was this decree that saved the heavyweight title for Tunney, who was seated for 14 seconds. It was also Bronson's story that, at Tunney's training camp some days before the fight, he had inadvertently persuaded Edward P.F. Eagan, Yale graduate, Rhodes scholar, the only man in the world to win a gold medal in both the Summer and Winter Olympics—the first as a light-heavyweight boxer and the second as a bobsledder—and a future chairman of the New York State Athletic Commission, to fall down the same flight of stairs twice.

"It was in the dark of a pleasant evening," Bronson told me years later, "and I was out for a stroll. As I was passing one of the buildings, I saw, at the foot of this precipitous outside stairway, what appeared to me to be a bundle of laundry. As I approached closer to examine it, I saw it move. It wasn't a bundle of laundry at all, but Eddie Eagan, clad in white flannels and a white tennis sweater. 'Edward,' I said, 'what are you doing lying here?' He said: 'I just fell down those stairs.' I said: 'Edward, that's impossible. You'd have broken every bone in you body.' He said: 'You don't believe me?' And, before I could restrain him, he went up and fell down again."

The duties of this triumvirate were several. As the show moved around the country they would precede it by three or four days and ballyhoo it by implanting their reminiscenses in the local papers. On the day of the show they would move backstage to supervise the setting up of the ring, to sort out the fighters into weight classes, to get them into their togs and then into the ring on time, and to take care of such last-minute emergencies as arose one night in Quantico, Va.

"It was about a half hour before we went on the air," Loughran reported later. "I stepped outside for a breath of fresh air, and there was Jimmy Bronson stumbling around in the dark and pawing through some rubble between a couple of buildings. When he saw me he said: 'Quick, Thomas, a brick. Help me find a brick.' I said: 'What do you want with a brick?' He said: 'I haven't the time to explain now'."

During the show, as the camera closed in on Butterworth at his ringside table, it was to reveal, resting there as if it had just descended as manna from heaven, a carton of the sponsor's cigarettes. The previous week Butterworth's elbow, or perhaps the flick of a passing stranger's coattail, had displaced the carton so that the camera had been unable to show the sponsor's brand. Once Bronson and Loughran had found a brick, it was inserted into the carton as ballast, and Bronson then had the added responsibility of lugging it in his suitcase from coast to coast.

It was Bronson who, on another night and again just before air time, saved the show once more. Although it was professed that *Champ* was designed to develop boxing talent in the services, the only real fighter to emerge on it was a ready-made welterweight out of Toledo. Ohio, named Pat Lowry, who represented, as one might suspect, the Marines. Lowry was one of those walkin left hookers who held his hands low and who, when he punched to the body, left the impression, if the look on the faces of his opponents was any indication, that he had just run them through with a red-hot crowbar. Then he would rise out of his semicrouch and, with a grenade in either hand, let go at the chin, leaving his erstwhile antagonists, when they came to, convinced that they never should have listened to that con man in the recruiting office back home.

"Let us cross our fingers," Bronson said to me one night outside the dressing rooms, "and offer up a prayer, too."

"You lose your brick?" I asked.

"No." Bronson said, "but we are now confronted by a far more serious crisis. I am not sure that we still have an opponent for Lowry."

As Bronson recounted it, the Marines, apparently not convinced that Lowry, with his crowbar and his grenades, was sufficiently armed, had taken to introducing psychological warfare. An hour or so earlier they had marched him into the arena like Old Glory, surrounded by an informal honor guard, and after depositing him in his dressing room, they had paid a courtesy call on his Air Force opponent.

"By the time I was called in," Bronson explained, "they had already departed, and apparently they had convinced the young man he should be measured for a pine box. I was summoned because he announced he was not going to fight."

"And?" I said.

"Well," Bronson said, "I invoked every loyalty I could imagine—to his family, to his friends and, most important, to the Air Force. Of course, I also disparaged Lowry's ability and praised his own."

The truth was, the airman pro tem did have a chance. He was a Golden Gloves champion, a stand-up boxer with a fine left jab and the combinations and footwork to fend off Lowry and, perhaps, even outpoint him.

"I don't know," Bronson said. "I think I have convinced him to climb into the ring."

It was a good fight for as long as it lasted—the classic contest of the boxer versus the puncher, with the former earning admiration and piling up points until Lowry unloaded inside and the crowbar effect took over. Thanks to Bronson, the young man's honor, that of the Air Force and that of the show, as well as Lowry's unblemished record, had all been preserved.

"Our primary problem," one of the agency men was saying in that hotel suite now, "is that, in recent weeks. Wally here has had to fill seven or eight minutes at the end of the show with interviews. Every show should end with a fight."

It was a dilemma around the horns of which Butterworth and the rest of us had been trying to jab and move since the inception of the program. As Butterworth explained now, each fight, except those such as Lowry's that ended abruptly in knockouts, consisted of three two-minute rounds, with a minute's rest between. When you added a minute to introduce the fighters and another to announce a decision, you were left with the realization that you could not start a final fight with the assurance that you could present it in its entirety unless there were 10 minutes plus time for the end commercial and the sign off remaining.

"Ah, but we have the answer to that," the agency man said. "We'll simply start a fight one week, and if we have to go off the air before it's over, we'll just put the fighters back in again the next week and let them finish it then."

They say you can measure the distance from you that lightning has struck by counting, during the ensuing silence, the seconds that pass before you hear the thunder clap. In such a stillness I waited now, counting, my eyes moving from Loughran to Cavanaugh to Bronson, the Old Persuader. My money was on Bronson, but after six seconds it was Loughran who spoke.

"We can't do that," he said. "The AAU won't permit it."

"What's the AAU?" the agency man said.

"The Amateur Athletic Union," Loughran said.

"The Amateur Athletic Union?" the other agency man said. "Don't worry about that. We'll take care of them."

I looked again at Bronson. This time I recognized what I saw on his face. It was the old crowbar effect, and it must have been that that moved me.

"A great ideal" I said, rising in my enthusiasm. "And let me give you the perfect situation. We're 10 seconds before going off the air and one fighter is bit on the chin and down he goes, flat on his back. The referee starts his count: 'One! Two! Three! Four! Five! Six! . . .' And Butterworth says: 'So tune in next week, folks, to see whether he gets up or not.'

"Now don't stop me." I said, "because here's the beauty part. I jump into the ring, and with a heavy pencil I mark the outline of his body. Then, the next week, we put him back where he lay, and as we go on the air the referee picks up the count where he left off the week before: 'Seven! Eight! Nine! . . .'"

"Oh, come on now," the agency man said. "You're carrying this to a ridiculous extreme."

That was the last we heard of that, and we limped into our second 13-week cycle, during which we were crowbarred into submission by James Melton and grenaded into obscurity by something called *Big Town*. As is obvious, however, I still wear the badge of honor bestowed upon me, as we walked out of that meeting, by Bow Tie Jimmy Bronson.

"Well done," the Old Persuader whispered. "Splendid."

Excerpt from *Transition*

from *Once They Heard the Cheers*
(Autumn 1945)

On this morning it was cold, but the air was clear and the sun was shining. The Giants were running through passing plays in deep right field near the outfield wall with the signs, painted on the dark green, advertising razor blades and hot dogs and ice cream. Steve Owen was standing with his hands in his hip pockets talking to several of us and watching Arnie Herber throw the ball.

Herber threw a pass to an end named Hubert Barker. It was deep and Barker ran for it, but when he was about to run into the wall where the sign advertised Gem blades, he slowed and the pass went over his outstretched hands.

"What are you scared of Barker?" Owen said, shouting at him. "What are you scared of?"

"He's scared of the five o'clock shadow," Bert Gumpert, who wrote sports for The *Bronx Home News*, said.

Owen turned to Bill Abbott. Abbott was the publicity man for the Giants, and Owen asked him for a copy of the team roster. When Abbott gave it to him Owen ran a finger down the list of players.

"Take this McNamara off the list," Owen said to Abbott, and he was talking about Edmund McNamara, a tackle from Holy Cross. "I just sold him to Pittsburgh."

"In other words," Gumpert said, "McNamara's banned."

"He's a pretty nice kid," Owen said, "He has the Silver Star, and they needed tackles more than we do, and I like to give those war kids jobs."

That was how Abbott got to explaining about Marion Pugh. Marion Pugh was one of Owen's good backs, and before that he had been a star at Texas A. & M. I could remember hearing another broadcast of another game, and

Ted Husing was doing the game and he talked a lot about Pugh. He kept calling him Dukey Pugh, and Husing had a resonant voice and afterwards the name kept running around in my mind . . . Dukey Pugh . . . Dukey Pugh . . . Dukey Pugh.

"A year ago he was fighting in Europe," Abbott said. "He had a company of tank destroyers. He was wounded twice and got the Bronze Star."

"You should talk to him," Owen said to me. "You might get a story."

After the players had finished running through their plays he had them run up and down the field a couple of times, and then he sent them to the showers. When Pugh came down the old, worn wooden steps from the shower room he was still drying himself, and he walked across the room to his locker. As he started to dress I walked over and introduced myself and stood talking with him.

"They tell me you were in Europe?" I said.

"That's right," he said.

"Where were you?" I said.

"Oh, from France all the way into Germany."

"What outfit were you attached to?"

"The Second Division and the Fourth."

"Is that right? I was with both of them."

"Also the Twenty-eighth."

"Were you with the Twenty-eighth when they were in the Huertgen Forest?" I said. "I mean that time they were chewed up at Schmidt and Kommerscheidt?"

Marion Pugh was not large for a professional football player. He was rather slim, but nicely muscled. He had started to pull on a pair of slacks, but he stopped and straightened up.

"You know something?" he said, looking at me. "You're the first guy I've met who has even heard of those places."

We stood in the locker room of the Polo Grounds and talked about one of the bad beatings the Americans took in the war. Schmidt and Kommerscheidt were two small towns in a break in the Huertgen, and the German attack there was a prelude, a first step by which they positioned themselves for their breakthrough later in The Bulge.

"I lost eleven of my twelve T.D.'s in that," Pugh said, and it is what tank destroyers are called. "We were cut off for six days."

"I remember one thing about it in particular," I said. "There were some wounded Americans cut off in a forester's cabin in the woods, and we were trying to get to them. I wrote a story about it, and I also remember that that was the day we had our first snow."

"I was in that cabin," Pugh said, looking at me again. "That's an odd thing. I was in that cabin."

We had been, with Germans between us, not much more than the length of a football field apart, and now he stuck out a finger. He showed me the scar on it.

"They ambushed my jeep," he said, "and we jumped out and hid in some bushes in the dark. A German was probing through the bushes with his bayonet, and it went right through my finger."

"I'd say you're lucky," I said.

"You're telling me?" he said.

"That was just about a year ago, too," I said. "I think it was right about now."

"No," Pugh said. "It was November fifth. I'll never forget that."

Around us the other players had finished dressing and Steve Owen was calling them together. They were preparing to play Boston on the following Sunday, and Owen was going to show them the movies of the Boston game of the previous year.

The players pulled the wooden folding chairs up in front of a small movie screen set up in the middle of the old locker room. Somebody turned out the lights, and when the film started and the titles came on the screen, there was the date. Marion Pugh and I sat side by side in the darkness in the locker room in the Polo Grounds, and we read on the screen that the game had been played the previous year on November 5.

"I'll be damned," Marion Pugh said.

Five weeks later the Giants played the Eagles in the mist and rain in Philadelphia. The Eagles won easily, 38–17, and after the game the Giants, burting and sullen and silent, had crowded into the bus. Now the bus was moving, halting and then moving again through the honking traffic of a Sunday evening and over the wet streets between Shibe Park and the North Philadelphia station.

"Kilroy," somebody said. "Kilroy is the guy who did it."

"How bad is it?" somebody else said. "Is it broken?"

"They don't know," one of the players who had been the last to crowd into the bus said. "They're trying to get a cast on it so they can carry him home."

They were talking about Marion Pugh. Near the end of the game he had just completed a pass and Frank Kilroy, the 240-pound Eagle tackle, had hit him. When they had gone down, Pugh had folded forward in a peculiar position so that he was half on top of Kilroy.

Four players had had to carry Pugh off the muddy field. He had been half lying and half sitting in their arms, and from the press box and through my field glasses I had been able to see his face and he had been grimacing with the pain.

When they had brought Pugh into the dressing room they had placed him on one of the rubbing tables, and then they had looked at his leg and had tried to take off his uniform. Every time they had moved him the muscles of his face had tightened and he had shut his eyes, but finally they had got him out of his uniform and dressed him in his street clothes. He had been sitting there with his leg stretched out on the rubbing table when he had looked up and seen me.

"Hey!" he said, "How are you?"

"That's not the question," I had said. "How are you?"

"The way they were coming at me out there," he had said, "I thought I was back at Kommerscheidt."

Behind me now in the crowded bus George Franck was talking. He had been an All-American halfback at Minnesota and he had flown for the Marines in the Pacific, and he was talking to Mel Hein, the All-Pro center.

"When I was shot down over Wotje," Franck was saying, "I was going to kill myself."

"You were going to *kill* yourself?" Hein said.

"Rather than let those bastards get their hands on me," Franck said, "I was going to put a slug through my own head."

"Good God!" Hein said.

I wasn't seeking them, but when I found them I could not ignore them. They were a part of America and of a world in transition, and one Friday night about three weeks later I was walking down the hallway under the main arena seats on the Fiftieth Street side of Madison Square Garden. It was about eight o'clock, with the crowd starting to come in, and Bob Mele, a fight manager from New Haven, was standing outside one of the dressing rooms they used for preliminary fighters. He was smoking a cigarette and he said he had two fighters in the four-round bouts that night, two brothers named Joe and Jimmy Rogers.

"They were on the *Juneau* when she was sunk," he said.

The *Juneau* was a light cruiser, and when it had gone down in the Pacific it had taken the five Sullivan brothers with it, and that had become a part of the history of the war. Mele was saying now that there had been four Rogers brothers on it, too, and that Pat and Louie had been lost and Joe and Jimmy had had to swim for it, and now they were waiting to fight in the Garden.

"It's a good thing for them," he said. "All the time after they came back they kept talking about Pat and Louie. Pat and Louie were better fighters than these two, and they thought about them all the time. Now they've got their minds on this, and it's a good thing."

"Do you mind if I go in and talk to them?" I said.

"No," he said. "They're a little nervous, you know, about being in the Garden, and it'll probably help them relax a little."

There were several other fighters and their handlers in the room. The Rogers brothers, in their ring trunks and blue satin robes, were sitting together on one of the benches and Mele introduced me. I did not want to ask them about the *Juneau*, but if I were going to write about them I would have to, and so I told them I was sorry about their loss and I asked them how the four brothers happened to be on the same ship.

"We enlisted together right after Pearl Harbor," the one named Joe said. "When the war started we said let's get into it together and take care of one another. We didn't know a damn thing about war. How are you gonna take care of one another on a ship like that?"

I was hoping very much that they would turn out to be good fighters, at least good enough to win their bouts. Joe went on first, just before the main event, and when they called him, Jimmy walked out with him and then stood at the top of the aisle, trying to see over the heads. It was a slow fight, with the crowd, impatient for the main event to come on, booing, and when Joe lost the decision and came back up the aisle, Jimmy threw an arm around Joe's shoulders.

"You did all right," he said. "You did okay."

"You do it," Joe said. "I couldn't get my hands up in there, but you do it."

Jimmy went on in the walk-out bout after the main event, with the Garden emptying now. For whatever reason, the few who stayed got to rooting for Jimmy's opponent, and when Jimmy lost the decision and came up the aisle where Joe was waiting, there was a loudmouth hollering at him.

"Go back to New Haven," he was hollering. "You're a bum!"

I walked back to the dressing room with them and said I was sorry that they hadn't won, and I wished them luck. They thanked me and we shook hands and I walked out of the dressing room and out of the war again.

Printed in the United States
107340LV00005B/103/A

9 780306 810435